New Perspectives on Israeli History

NEW PERSPECTIVES ON JEWISH STUDIES

*A Series of the
Philip and Muriel Berman Center for Jewish Studies
Lehigh University, Bethlehem, Pennsylvania*

General Editor: Laurence J. Silberstein

*New Perspectives on Israeli History:
The Early Years of the State*
Edited by Laurence J. Silberstein

NEW PERSPECTIVES ON ISRAELI HISTORY

The Early Years of the State

Edited by
Laurence J. Silberstein

NEW YORK UNIVERSITY PRESS
New York & London

Copyright © 1991 by New York University
All rights reserved
Manufactured in the United States

Library of Congress Cataloging-in-Publication Data

New perspectives on Israeli history : the early years of the state / edited by Laurence J. Silberstein.
   p.   cm. — (New perspectives on Jewish studies)
Includes index.
ISBN 0-8147-7928-X (alk. paper) — ISBN 0-8147-7929-8 (pbk. : alk. paper)
1. Israel—History—1948–1949. 2. Jewish-Arab relations—1949–1967.
I. Silberstein, Laurence J. (Laurence Jay), 1936– . II. Series.
DS126.5.N48   1991
956.9405'2—dc20   91-22242
                                                                     CIP

New York University Press books are printed on acid-free paper, and their binding materials are chosen for strength and durability.
10 9 8 7 6 5 4 3 2

This volume and the series of which it is a part are dedicated to Philip and Muriel Berman, devoted patrons of the Arts and Humanities.

Contents

Foreword ix

Acknowledgments xi

I. Frameworks and Perspectives

1. Reading Perspectives/Perspectives on Reading:
   An Introduction 3
   Laurence J. Silberstein

II. The Transition to Statehood: Jews and Arabs in Conflict

2. The Transition from Yishuv to State:
   Social and Ideological Changes 27
   Jehuda Reinharz

3. The Origins of the Palestinian Refugee Problem 42
   Benny Morris

4. One Hundred Years of Social Change:
   The Creation of the Palestinian Refugee Problem 57
   Kenneth W. Stein

5. Early State Policy towards the Arab Population,
   1948–1955 82
   Don Peretz

6. Initial Israeli Policy Guidelines towards
   the Arab Minority, 1948–1949 103
   Elie Rekhess

7. Arab Historiography of the 1948 War:
   The Quest for Legitimacy 124
   Avraham Sela

III. Myths, Symbols, Values: The Struggle for National Identity

8. Attitudes of the Young State of Israel toward the Holocaust and Its Survivors: A Debate over Identity and Values — *Dina Porat* ... 157

9. Myths, Symbols, and Rituals of the Emerging State — *Myron J. Aronoff* ... 175

10. New Beginning, Old Past: The Collective Memory of Pioneering in Israeli Culture — *Yael Zerubavel* ... 193

11. At Half-Mast—Myths, Symbols, and Rituals of the Emerging State: A Personal Testimony of an "Israeli Arab" — *Anton Shammas* ... 216

IV. Conflicts Within and Conflicts Without: Diplomacy and Foreign Policy

12. Israel's Global Foreign Policy, 1948–1956 — *Uri Bialer* ... 227

13. Zionist-Arab Diplomacy: Patterns and Ambiguities on the Eve of Statehood — *Neil Caplan* ... 242

14. Israel-Diaspora Relations in the Early Years of the State — *Ronald W. Zweig* ... 258

About the Editor ... 271

About the Contributors ... 273

Index ... 277

Foreword

This volume is the first in the series, New Perspectives on Jewish Studies, published by the Berman Center for Jewish Studies and New York University Press. Drawing upon recent Israeli and North American historiography, the present volume seeks to shed new light on fundamental social, political, and cultural issues surrounding the emergence of the State of Israel. Juxtaposing the perspectives of folklore and political anthropology to that of history, it offers insights into the basic myths and symbols of Israeli culture that are missing from conventional historical studies. Finally, by including a voice from the Arab minority, it introduces a critical perspective on Israeli culture as well as the network of social institutions through which it is disseminated and reinforced.

In recent decades, discussions in such fields as literary theory, philosophy, and social theory have challenged the prevailing philosophical premises and methodological assumptions of the humanities and social sciences. Selected volumes in this series will explore the usefulness of these discussions for the study of Jewish history, society, and culture. Such exploration will, we hope, stimulate critical reflection on the theoretical premises and methodological presuppositions that currently prevail in the field of Jewish studies. Volumes will also be devoted to interdisciplinary inquiries into issues such as religious fundamentalism and the "other" in Jewish thought and history that significantly broaden the parameters of the conventional Jewish studies conversation.

Acknowledgments

Earlier versions of the chapters in this volume were first presented as papers at a conference on "New Perspectives on Israeli History: The Early Years of the State," held at Lehigh University in May 1990. I want to express my appreciation to Itamar Rabinovich, Asher Susser, and Elie Rekhess of the Moshe Dayan Center for Near Eastern and African Studies at Tel Aviv University, and Ron Zweig of the Institute for Research in the History of Zionism at Tel Aviv University for their significant role in organizing the conference. I am particularly indebted to Elie Rekhess, Philip and Muriel Berman Visiting Scholar at Lehigh from 1988 to 1990, who suggested the theme of the conference, enlisted the participation of many of the speakers, and actively joined in the planning process at every stage. Myra Rosenhaus was responsible for the administrative tasks relating to the conference. Grants from the Belfer Foundation and the Philip and Muriel Berman Foundation provided support for the conference.

Shirley Ratushny of the Berman Center assumed major responsibilities for both the editing and the technical preparation of the manuscript. It is no exaggeration to say that without her participation this volume would never have seen publication. The Berman Center is particularly fortunate to have her services as Assistant to the Director. She and I are both indebted to Erica Nastasi, the most recent member of the Center's staff, who upon arriving at the Center was greeted with responsibility for typing the manuscript and performing other administrative tasks associated with its preparation.

Colin Jones of New York University Press first suggested the series which this volume initiates and played a major role in bringing it to fruition. Despina Papazoglou Gimbel supervised the copyediting at NYU Press and provided ongoing counsel during the editing process.

Finally, I wish to express my appreciation to Philip and Muriel Berman, to whom this volume is appropriately dedicated, whose ongoing support has made it possible for us to enter this new phase in the Berman Center's development. This volume and the conference on which it is based are a fulfillment of their vision of a significant academic center for Jewish studies based at Lehigh University.

I. FRAMEWORKS AND PERSPECTIVES

CHAPTER 1

Reading Perspectives/Perspectives on Reading: An Introduction

LAURENCE J. SILBERSTEIN

The chapters in this volume are revised versions of papers presented at a conference on "New Perspectives on Israeli History: The Early Years of the State" held at Lehigh University in May 1990.[1] The conference was organized against the background of recent debates among scholars relating to the beginnings and early years of the State of Israel. Spurred by the release of new archival material, books by such scholars as Avi Shlaim, Ilan Pappe, and Benny Morris have helped to precipitate a rethinking of basic issues surrounding the birth of Israel.[2]

Morris, a contributor to this volume, has identified works by these and other authors as examples of a "new historiography."[3] In Morris's view, the emergence of this "new historiography" can be attributed to two basic events. As a result of Israel's Archives Law, hundreds of thousands of state papers became available to researchers, beginning in the early 1980s. These papers include correspondence, memoranda, and minutes of official government agencies, both civilian and military, as well as the papers of private individuals and political parties. As interpreted by Morris, Shlaim, and others, these documents shed new light on the creation and early years of the state.

A second but no less important factor contributing to the new historians' revision of Israeli history was the emergence of a new generation of Israeli historians.[4] Unlike the earlier generation of Israeli historians, whose perspective was shaped by the idealism of both pre-state and early-state Zionist ideology and by the memories of the 1948 War, the new generation was born around the time of the war.

Growing to adulthood amidst the uncertainties, doubts, and self-criticism generated by the occupation of the West Bank and Gaza, the Yom Kippur War, the War in Lebanon, and currently, the Intifada, the younger generation assumed a skeptical attitude toward the dominant myths of Israeli culture and the accepted truths of Israeli historiography.[5]

According to Morris, the new historiography has challenged four basic assumptions that govern the older, established version of Israeli history: (1) While the Jewish state was open to the United Nations partition plan in 1947, the Arab states rejected it. (2) The 1948 War "was waged between a relatively defenseless and weak (Jewish) David and a relatively strong (Arab) Goliath." (3) The Arab refugee problem is primarily the result of the mass flight of Arabs from their homes and villages either voluntarily or at the behest/order of the Arab leaders. (4) At the war's end, Israel was interested in making peace, but the recalcitrant Arabs displayed no such interest, opting for a perpetual—if sporadic—"war to the finish."[6]

Morris's claims for the new historiography have been aggressively challenged by the noted Israeli historian Shabtai Teveth.[7] In a series of articles, Teveth lashed out at both Morris and Avi Shlaim, whose book, *Collusion across the Jordan*, focusing on the relations between Israel and Jordan during the 1940s, challenges long-held assumptions concerning the 1948 War.[8] Besides casting doubt on their scholarly qualifications, Teveth accuses them of politicizing the study of history, of being sympathetic to the Palestinians, and seeking "to delegitimize Zionism."[9]

The Morris-Teveth debate clearly indicates the significant impact that the opening of the archives has had on recent scholarly writing. Moreover, as many of the articles in the present volume make clear, the younger generation of historians, such as Morris, Porat, Bialer, Sela, and Zweig, raise new, often painful questions for the present generation of Israelis. While one could question Morris's claim that this generation of new historians has assumed a more impartial stance, they have undoubtedly opened avenues of investigation that earlier generations preferred to leave closed.

Thus, scholarly debate surrounding the new interpretations of Israeli history provides one framework through which the chapters in this volume may be read. Consistent with the revisionist historiography described by Morris, many of the chapters in this volume, written by young scholars utilizing the newly released documents, take issue with the prevailing version of how the new state responded to the challenges that confronted it.

A lucid overview of many of these challenges is found in Jehuda Reinharz's opening chapter. Reinharz focuses on the challenges posed by statehood to the social structure that had emerged in the Jewish community in Palestine during the Mandate period. On the one hand, Reinharz argues that many of the challenges facing the new State of Israel were similar to the problems facing other new "underdeveloped" nations. Like other such nations, Israel's social structure was shaped in the highly fluid, tentative, provisional conditions of a rapidly developing nation. As with other new nations, the abrupt transition to statehood posed challenges and strains for existing pre-state institutions.

On the other hand, as Reinharz points out, there were many unique aspects to the birth of Israel. Among these was a conflict between the pre-state ideals of group autonomy and social, economic, and cultural experimentation and the new leadership's felt need for central authority, obedience, and discipline. Another unique dimension of the early state derived from the conception of Israel as the homeland of the entire worldwide Jewish people.

From the beginning, the new state was confronted by an enormous influx of immigrants, each bringing habits and attitudes shaped by life in the Diaspora. In the absence of rigid local traditions, the state had to adapt its institutions to the new immigrants no less than the immigrants had to adapt to the established institutions. Such a situation exacerbated the tentativeness and provisionality that characterize the institutions and values of a developing social structure.

Israel's abrupt split with Britain also had far-reaching economic effects on the new state. In addition, cut off from her immediate neighbors with whom she existed in a perpetual state of war, Israel was deprived of needed markets and resources. Finally, as a result of the mass exodus of Palestinian Arabs, the government was cut off from a significant portion of its own Arab populace.

The ongoing state of war with her neighbors and the continued presence of a population of Palestinian refugees demanding return to their homeland forced Israel into a continual state of military preparedness, thereby placing an excessive burden on both human and material resources. Moreover, as Reinharz points out, this situation led to an inordinate emphasis on the militant dimension of Zionism. At the same time, the conditions of Israel's birth made the actualization of other Zionist principles highly problematic.

While Reinharz describes the challenges facing the new State of Israel with the broad sweeping strokes of social history, other contributors focus on specific problems and issues. These include the internal and external Arab-Jewish conflict, the plight of the Palestinian refugees, the struggle to create a national identity and shape a cohesive set of values, and the need to formulate a foreign policy.

The chapters by Stein, Morris, Caplan, Rekhess, Peretz, and Sela all address issues relating to the Israeli-Arab conflict. Stein and Morris, albeit from differing perspectives, attempt to unravel the complex factors leading to the flight of the Palestinian refugees. Focusing on the diplomatic front, Caplan analyzes the ongoing, futile efforts of Jews and Arabs to arrive at a peaceful diplomatic solution to their conflict. Exploring the efforts of the new state to formulate policies relating to the Arab population that remained after the war, Peretz and Rekhess offer different views on attitudes and concerns that infused that policy.

As mentioned above, Morris's study of the origins of the Palestinian refugee problem comprises one of the basic texts of the new historiography. Morris's chapter in this volume, like the book on which it is based, directly challenges prevailing scholarly explanations of the flight of 750,000 Palestinian Arabs in 1948. According to Morris, existing historiography attributes the flight of the Arabs primarily to broadcasts by Arab governments and leaders urging the Palestinian Arabs to flee and to return in the wake of the conquering Arab armies. Popular assumptions notwithstanding, Morris found no evidence of a blanket call for Palestinian Arabs to leave or of an Arab radio or press campaign to that end.

Morris rejects the claims that either an all-out Arab propaganda campaign or an overall Israeli policy of expulsions was the cause of the exodus. Painstakingly investigating the conditions surrounding the flight of Arabs from hundreds of villages, Morris argues that multiple factors contributed to the Arab flight, including threats and intimidation by the Jewish military, military attacks, expulsion orders by Israeli and/or political leaders, atrocities committed by Jewish soldiers and terrorist groups, orders from local Arab commanders and politicians, and decisions by local Arab leaders. On a village-by-village basis, Morris analyzes the complex circumstances that precipitated what turned out to be a mass exodus.[10]

While not disagreeing with Morris's explanation of the immediate factors leading to the Arab flight, Kenneth Stein argues that the causes explored by Morris should be set against the broader background of political disunity and impotence, social fragmentation, and economic ruin that infested the Palestinian Arab community by the early 1940s. Whereas Morris's account focuses on the political, military, and psychological factors that combined to create the Arab refugee problem, Stein focuses on the impact of social and economic policies, some of which can be traced back to the nineteenth century. Laws and practices surrounding land purchase and usage during the Ottoman and Mandate periods that discriminated against the peasants, the greed of wealthy landowners, the desire of peasants to avoid taxation and conscription, and the policies of Jewish land settlement organizations to evacuate and resettle the Arab population from newly purchased land—all wreaked havoc on the Palestinian Arab society and economy.[11]

During the 1920s and 1930s, large numbers of Arabs left their villages either to distance themselves from pending Jewish settlements or to comply with eviction notices from Arab vendors obeying the wishes of Jewish purchasers. The shift of many former rural peasants to the urban labor force led to a fraying of their social ties with their former villages and to growing estrangement from the urban Arab landowners. This process, according to Stein, resulted in both personal disillusionment and the dissolution of villages.

A further consequence was the growing social and economic isolation of Palestinian Arab villages from one another, together with a general fragmentation of Palestinian society. This was paralleled by a growing disintegration of local Palestinian Arab leadership, a process which was exacerbated by the Arab revolt in 1939. Moreover, with the departure of the British, the Arab population lost whatever protection they had been provided by the British Mandate authorities.

Thus, complementing Morris's analysis of the political and military conditions of 1947–48, Stein argues that, by the time the 1948 War began, the Palestinian Arab community was socially fragmented and economically decimated. Moreover, suffering from exploitation, dispossession, and dislocation, and lacking effective leadership, they were psychologically demoralized. These conditions, argues Stein, paved the way for panic in the face of war and created the conditions for the community's social collapse and flight.

Yet another example of alternative perspectives on a common historical problem is provided in the chapters by Don Peretz and Elie Rekhess. Taking up where Morris and Stein leave off, Peretz and Rekhess analyze state policies and practices regarding the Israeli Arab population in the early years of the state. Although a significant portion of the Arab population fled from the new state in 1948, over a quarter of a million Arabs remained. Consequently, the Israeli leaders were confronted with the problem of how to deal with a sizable minority population that, in the eyes of many members of the Jewish majority, was a security threat.

Peretz's analysis focuses on the policies of the government and the actions carried out in support of these policies. These included maintaining a military government over a significant portion of the Arab population until 1966, forced evacuations of Arabs from their homes and villages, the destruction of numerous Arab villages, and the expropriation of Arab-owned land through the Absentee Property Law and the office of the Custodian of Absentee Property. To Peretz, these practices and institutions provide ample evidence that the early state policy toward the Arabs was rife with oppression and injustice.

While acknowledging, for the most part, the existence of policies and actions described by Peretz, Rekhess argues that alongside the security-motivated actions and policies, one finds evidence of a definite democratic-humanitarian approach. Rekhess's evidence includes statements by a number of Israeli leaders, and actions by various government bodies that sought to provide for the needs of the Arab population in such areas as education, health, and agriculture. According to Rekhess, this evidence calls for a more balanced conclusion than that reached by Peretz and other scholars. Their disagreements notwithstanding, both Rekhess and Peretz acknowledge a conflict between a hard line, security-oriented policy toward the minority Arab population in Israel and a humane, democratic policy that continues to inform Israeli society to this day.

In light of the growing body of literature on the 1948 War by Israeli scholars, it is reasonable to seek out similar studies by Arab scholars. However, Avraham Sela's seminal investigation of the treatment of the 1948 War in Arab historical writings reveals a paucity of such scholarly works. Instead, argues Sela, the overwhelming proportion of Arab writings on the 1948 War takes the form of ideological controversies or efforts to legitimate or delegitimate nations and/or political leaders.

While official archives in Arab countries are still closed to scholars, Arab scholars, with few exceptions, make little use of available British, American, and Israeli archival material. Similarly, most of the studies fail to take advantage of the information provided in such important sources as political and military memoirs. To Sela, Arab writings on the war are "based more on collective memory than critical historiography."

Nevertheless, judiciously probing the available material and juxtaposing these historical studies with available official reports and existing scholarly studies emanating from other countries, Sela succeeds in piecing together recurring motifs in Arab policy and behavior prior to and during the war. Repeatedly, the sources tell of inter-Arab rivalry and conflict, internal conflict between military and political authorities, and the gap between the interests of the Arab states and those of the Palestinian Arabs. Moreover, the documents reveal that military unpreparedness, inadequate supplies, and the lack of military coordination among the participating armies played a key role in the Arab defeat.

As problematic as the documents are to historians seeking to attain a balanced view of the war, they do provide useful material to augment the scholarly discussions. Thus, the picture that they paint supports the claims of Stein and Morris concerning the deterioration of the Palestinian infrastructure, and supports Morris's claim concerning the military superiority of the Israelis. Finally, although Arab sources continually reiterate the claim that the Zionists deliberately expelled the Palestinians, they also provide useful insights concerning the multiplicity of factors that contributed to the Palestinian Arab exodus.

In addition, these sources offer fertile ground for those wishing to understand the role of myth and popular memory in shaping the perspective of Arab political leaders, intellectuals, and common people. Moreover, as Sela demonstrates, these sources provide significant insights into struggles, both internal and inter-Arab, since 1948. Finally, while not offering a balanced, critical perspective on the war, these Arab accounts are clearly valuable sources for those wishing to understand contemporary Arab thinking on the war, on inter-Arab relations, and on Arab-Jewish relations.

It is clear from Dina Porat's chapter that she fits into the category of new historians. Drawing upon newly released material, Porat, like Morris, addresses issues that are painful for the Israeli psyche. Specifically, she poses difficult, provocative questions concerning the attitudes and behavior of Zionist and Israeli leaders toward both the victims and the survivors of the Holocaust. Her conclusions shed light on the complexities, problems, and implications of the Zionist effort to create a new Israeli identity grounded in a radical break with the ethos and values of Diaspora Jewry.[12]

In spite of the classical Zionist view that the movement entailed a revolt against Diaspora Jewish history and culture, the State of Israel, from the outset, declared a clear, almost causal link between the Holocaust and the establishment of the state. As articulated in the Israeli Declaration of Independence, the Holocaust, its victims, and its survivors constituted a central component in Israeli civil religion and exercised a powerful and decisive influence on Israeli political and cultural discourse.[13]

However, as Porat shows, statements by Zionist and Israeli leaders from the period of the Holocaust and after reveal both ambivalence and conflict concerning the behavior of the victims, the moral character of the survivors, and their value to the Israeli enterprise of state building. Moreover, Porat's study raises serious questions concerning the priorities of some Zionist leaders who seemed to view the establishment of a state as a greater priority than the rescue of victims. Such questions, as she indicates, still provoke volatile reactions in Israeli culture and political life.

The chapters by Caplan, Bialer, and Zweig focus on the efforts of the pre-state *yishuv* (Palestinian Jewish community) and the new state to formulate diplomatic policies. While Caplan focuses on the negotiations between Zionist and Arab leaders in the pre-state period, Bialer analyzes the formulation of Israel's international foreign policy. Zweig, addressing a diplomatic issue unique to Israel, explores the challenge posed by the need to develop effective working relationships with Diaspora Jewish communal organizations, a need deriving primarily from Israel's self-perception as a state representing world Jewry.

Caplan, drawing on his earlier research on Arab-Jewish efforts at negotiation from the immediate post–World War I period up until the 1948 War, relates the pre-state Arab-Jewish negotiating experiences to the attitudes and expectations of Israeli leaders in the post-state period. Between 1918 and 1948, a series of forty high-level or mid-level negotiations between Zionists and the Arabs all ended in failure. By the 1940s, a combination of suspicion, cynicism, and a hardening of negotiating positions spawned the conclusion among both Zionist and Arab leaders that such direct negotiations could not yield a successful outcome.

The Zionist preference to bypass direct negotiations with the Palestinian Arabs in favor of negotiations with non-Palestinian Arab leaders emerged as a clear pattern during the Mandate period. For their part, Palestinian leaders were highly suspicious of such negotiations. Nevertheless, the Zionist's repeated failure to elicit Palestinian sympathy for their aims led them to prefer this approach. As Caplan observes, this preference for negotiating only with non-Palestinian Arab leaders remains a key factor in Israeli diplomacy to the present.

The failure of early efforts at multilateral negotiations notwithstanding, Zionist leaders concluded by 1939 that the only hope of a favorable settlement lay in negotiations involving outside powers such as the United States. Moreover, such negotiations gave both Jews and Arabs an opportunity to lobby for their own positions and exert other kinds of pressure on government officials and public opinion.

While Caplan focuses on Arab-Jewish diplomacy, Uri Bialer explores the formation of early Israeli foreign policy toward the great powers. Drawing extensively upon newly released archival material, Bialer elucidates the factors, internal and external, that led Israel to adopt a policy of nonalignment in the period immediately following the establishment of the state. These documents, argues Bialer, indicate that Israeli foreign policy was shaped to a significant degree by domestic political debates both within and between the major political parties. While the archives reveal resistance within Mapai against alignment with the West, Bialer argues that it is Mapai's ongoing struggle against the leftist Mapam party that best explains Israel's early policy of nonalignment with the West as well as her shift toward such an alignment in the mid-1950s.

According to Bialer, in addition to concern for *aliyah* from Eastern Europe and the need for arms and fuel, emotional factors linking Israel's largely Eastern European population with the Eastern bloc countries also militated against alignment with the West. Moreover, Bialer finds evidence of greater Soviet support for Israel until the late 1950s, presumably in response to Israel's nonalignment stance, than had previously been assumed. Besides yielding a far more complicated picture concerning the formation of Israel's early foreign policy than previously existed, Bialer believes the documents challenge the popular image that Israel was created by the West as part of an effort to further its imperialistic goals in the Middle East.

Whereas Caplan and Bialer analyze Israel's foreign policy toward other nations, Ron Zweig focuses on Israel's policy toward Diaspora Jewish communities. Zweig's chapter exemplifies the impact of passing generations on historiography. Under the influence of Zionist ideology, previous generations focused on the ideological issues surrounding

Israel-Diaspora relations. To Zweig, the present generation of Israelis find classical Zionism's negative ideological perspective on Diaspora Jewry to be obsolete. Consequently, the time is ripe for reevaluating the prevailing understanding of Israel-Diaspora relations.

Zweig believes that such relations are best understood in the context of the practical problems confronting world Jewry in the pre-state and early state period. These practical problems included the restitution of Jewish assets stolen by the Nazis, the payment of reparations to the survivors and the heirs of the murdered victims, and the overall needs of the Jewish Displaced Persons. It was, he argues, the organizational and institutional processes developed in response to these problems that most decisively influenced Israel-Diaspora relations during that period. In an effort to address these issues, new cooperative ventures were undertaken by Israel with Diaspora Jewish organizations. While ideological concerns never completely disappeared, the ongoing cooperation and interaction that resulted from these endeavors were significant in shaping the relationship between Israel and the Diaspora Jewish communities.

Beyond Historiography

As the previous discussion indicates, one may understand the term "new perspectives" in the title of this volume as the new perspectives provided by a younger generation of historians engaged in the revising of previously held perspectives. However, although these revisionist historians challenge "official history" through their use of new texts and their employment of new perspectives, they, nevertheless, identify with the community of scholars engaged in the enterprise of historical inquiry and submit to the rules of investigation, argumentation, and evidence that prevail in that community. Accordingly, concepts such as continuity, development, cause and effect, and influence still form a basic part of their vocabulary. As historians, they are essentially concerned with telling us "what really happened."

However, another way to understand "new perspectives" is in terms of the alternative perspectives offered by different academic disciplines and fields. As contemporary critics have argued, academic disciplines may be viewed as alternative ways of organizing, conceptualizing, analyzing, producing, and disseminating knowledge and defining truth.[14] Challenging the assumptions that historical documents provide us with a clear reflection of events or reality, those who emphasize the constitutive role of discourse and rhetoric seek to shift our attention away from the contents of specific bodies of knowledge and toward the linguistic, discursive, and interpretive processes that produce such knowledge.[15]

> Evidence—texts, documents, artifacts—is by definition a sign, and it signifies within a system of signs. The historian's narrative is constructed not upon reality itself or upon transparent images of it, but on signifiers which the historian's own actions transform into signs. It is not historical reality itself but the present signs of the historian that limit and order the historical narrative.[16]

Moreover, as contemporary critics have argued, academic disciplines, rather than utilizing natural, pre-existing conceptual frameworks to objectively formulate and transmit knowledge of reality, are engaged in power struggles to privilege one intellectual perspective over others.[17] In keeping with this orientation to academic disciplines, several critics have challenged the claim that privileges the historical perspective over other perspectives. Like any disciplinary community, historians can offer us no more than, but certainly no less than, an alternative perspective on society and culture. Thus, by juxtaposing the perspectives of other disciplines to that of history, we can significantly enhance our understanding of the topic at hand.

Accordingly, the perspectives of social scientists like Aronoff and Zerubavel, and a novelist and social critic like Shammas, broaden our understanding of the formation of Israeli society and culture. Aronoff and Zerubavel, each in his or her own way, explore the basic myths, symbols, and rituals that shape the worldview and the identity of the citizens of the new state, what sociologists have called civil religion.[18] Whereas historians often ignore the mythic and symbolic dimensions of communal life, or accept myths and symbols as givens, writers like Aronoff and Zerubavel focus on the processes by means of which myths and symbols are generated, preserved, disseminated, and transmitted. Accordingly, their chapters significantly contribute to our understanding of the ways in which meaning and identity have been shaped and formed in Israeli society.

Aronoff explores the sources of the political culture of the emerging State of Israel. According to Aronoff, Israel had to transform a new historical construct, the Jewish state, into what would be accepted as a natural phenomenon. Zionist ideology served as the basic vehicle in this process. However, insofar as Zionism embodies conflicting, even contradictory principles and visions, the meaning of the symbols and myths of Israeli society was continually contested. Moreover, insofar as Zionism formed the root cultural paradigm of Israeli political culture, both Arabs and non-Zionist orthodox Jews were politically marginalized. Challenging the evolutionary approach that informs the work of such students of Israeli civil religion as Charles Liebman and Eliezer Don-Yehiya, Aronoff focuses on the role of power, conflict, and struggle in the formation of Israeli political culture.[19]

Yael Zerubavel's in-depth case study of the ongoing controversies surrounding the myth of Tel Hai and Yosef Trumpeldor provides an excellent complement to Aronoff's more general discussion. Zerubavel, a folklorist, analyzes the ways in which one of the basic legitimating myths of Israeli civil religion, the story of Yosef Trumpeldor and the battle of Tel Hai, has been shaped, transformed, and eventually undermined as a result of decades of political and cultural conflict. Utilizing a concept drawn from the history of religion, Zerubavel describes the Tel Hai story as a "myth of beginning."

Focusing, like Aronoff, on the contested nature of myths, she describes the development of the Tel Hai myth from a position of cultural dominance to that of a source of sick humor. Zerubavel shows how Trumpeldor, although born and raised in Russia, was transformed into a counter-model to the traditional Diaspora Jew. Tracing the evolution of the Tel Hai myth through school textbooks, popular biography, poems, popular rituals, humorous literature, and jokes, she offers an insightful portrayal of the way in which a key legitimating Zionist myth became transformed into an object of cynicism and the butt of sick jokes.

Zerubavel's examination of official guidelines for teachers, educational texts of the Israel Defense Forces, plays, and monuments provides a concrete example of the process by which official Zionist ideology was disseminated. At the same time, her study reveals the problems inherent in preserving the power of national myths, symbols, and rituals over a period of several generations. Like Aronoff, she depicts the inherently precarious, contested character of legitimating myths and symbols of the new state.

Dina Porat's chapter discussed above, while ostensibly a historical analysis, also contributes to our understanding of Israeli civil religion. As Liebman, Don-Yehiya, and Aronoff have shown, a whole complex of myths, symbols, and rituals in Israeli society relates to the Holocaust. As Porat notes, the references to the Holocaust in the Israeli Declaration of Independence function to historically legitimate the new state. Accordingly, insofar as her discussion reveals conflicts and ambivalences regarding the victims and survivors of the Holocaust, it is clearly relevant to an understanding of Israeli civil religion and the value system to which it relates.

From Academic Disciplines to Cultural Critique

At first glance, a chapter by Anton Shammas, a highly respected novelist and social critic, appears to be out of place in a volume of studies by academic scholars. On one level, Shammas's article could certainly be read as an alternative perspective on the civil religion of the newly emerging state. Like the chapters by Aronoff and Zerubavel, Shammas explores and analyzes basic myths, symbols, and rituals in Israeli civil religion. However, insofar as Shammas's chapter shifts the site of discourse from the majority Jewish community to the minority Arab community, it has the effect of reformulating the questions being addressed in this volume in the language of cultural criticism.[20] Shammas is not interested in tracing the emergence and development of Israeli myths and symbols. Instead, his concern is to reveal the hegemonizing effect of these myths and symbols in the Jewish state.[21] Poignantly describing the marginalizing and exclusionary effects of the myths, symbols, and rituals on the Arab minority, Shammas brings to the surface ideological issues inherent in the social and cultural processes which are passed over by most scholarly discussions. In the spirit of Roland Barthes, Shammas calls into question the "naturalness" of the dominant cultural discourse within Israeli society.[22] Moreover, his critique reveals the exclusions or silences that inhere in conventional historical and social scientific discourse.

Shammas's chapter also provides a different perspective on the issues discussed by Rekhess and Peretz. Whereas their chapters focus on efforts to formulate and carry out state policy toward the Arab minority, Shammas provides the perspective of a member of the group that was the subject/object of this policy. He thus offers a "consumer's" view of the way in which the government's actions were received/perceived by the audience/group for which they were intended.

Moving beyond the discourse of legal enfranchisement, Shammas, while not using the technical terms, frames the discussion in terms of cultural hegemony, exclusion, and marginalization. Thus, Shammas's essay adds yet another perspective to our discussion of the early years of the state. To the perspectives of historical and social scientific inquiry, Shammas, focusing on the process by means of which the dominant ideology of a society is formed and disseminated, adds the perspective of social and cultural criticism.

To many, including an article rooted in ideological and cultural criticism in a scholarly volume may seem inappropriate. However, it is the editor's view, not necessarily shared by the contributors, that the study of ideology, meaning the "frameworks of thinking and calculation about the world, schemas of interpretation, codes of intelligibility that people use to figure out how the social world works, what their place is in it, and what they ought to do," forms an essential part of any effort to make sense out of Israeli society, or any society.[23] Ideologies call us into being as subjects by teaching us, relating us to, and making us recognize what is real and true; what is good, right, just, beautiful, and their opposites; and what is possible and impossible.[24] Ideologies, which include myths, symbols, concepts, ideas, and images, operate not through single units, but in discursive chains and clusters, "through discursive practices inscribed in matrices of non-discursive practices."[25]

Insofar as Shammas's chapter reveals the power of what can be known or said by the majority to affect the lives of the minority, it raises the issue of the relationship between discourse and power, an issue with which I shall bring this introductory essay to a close. The questions raised by contemporary students of ideology and discourse have, as indicated earlier, posed a powerful challenge to any discipline's claim to privileged status. These thinkers have emphasized, albeit in different ways, the power of language to actively shape the ways in which we conceptualize and think about reality, the ways in which individuals and groups conceive of and relate to one another, the frameworks within which social and cultural activities are carried on, and the processes through which society is hierarchized and power distributed.

The focus on language, discourse, and ideology directs our attention to a variety of socio-cultural factors often ignored or underplayed in scholarly writing. Thus, for example, by focusing on discourse, here understood as the social and linguistic processes by means of which we make, disseminate, legitimate, and preserve meaning, our attention is drawn to the conditions, social and linguistic, in which texts, meanings, and cultural forms are produced, interpreted, and disseminated; the ways in which language functions as a medium of control and power;

and the ways in which discourse, ideology, and culture in general all emerge out of power conflicts and relations, and subsequently serve as sites of ongoing conflicts and struggles.[26]

Moreover, these theorists have helped us to understand the ways in which discourse functions to constitute, organize, and hierarchize entire fields of knowledge. Thus, as Bove has argued: (a) discourse produces and regulates the generation and dissemination of knowledge; and (b) discourse constitutes and hierarchizes identity and difference, authority and subservience, taste and vulgarity, and continuity and discontinuity.[27]

Accordingly, discourses and the ideologies formed from them generate, legitimate, support, and empower certain kinds of questions and conversations while suppressing, delegitimating, and disempowering others. Therefore, the focus on discourse leads students of culture and society to ask: What are the conditions that enable particular discourses and ideologies to emerge and survive? How do particular discourses constitute objects, and classes of objects for study? How do discourses constitute objects as subjects of statements which are held to be true/false according to the logic, semantics, and syntax of the empowered discourse? How do discourses legitimate/delegitimate certain kinds of questions and answers? Whose interests do particular discourses serve? What configurations of power sustain particular discourses and are in turn sustained by them? Who is included/excluded by particular discursive frameworks?

A few brief examples of the relationship of discourse and ideology to political power may be useful here. As the chapters by Morris and Sela indicate, Jews and Arabs drew upon different narratives in order to emplot the story of the 1948 War. For the Israelis, the Zionist ideology, built around such concepts as Diaspora/homeland, exile/return, and election (whether Ahad Haam's version or the traditional rabbinic one), situated the Jews in a particular relationship to the land and privileged this relationship over that of other groups, particularly the Palestinian Arabs. This discourse also provided the basic ideological framework through which the Israelis were able to legitimate the creation of the Palestinian refugee problem, discussed by Morris.

The Arabs, on the other hand, view the 1948 War and the creation of the State of Israel from a totally different perspective. Thus, whereas the Israelis, consistent with Zionist assumptions, refer to the 1948 War as the War of Liberation, Arab historical accounts, as Sela shows, speak of it as *Nakba* (catastrophe), *Karitha* (disaster), or *Mihna* (misfortune). Drawing upon different discursive frameworks, Jewish and Arab historians emplot history in ways that legitimate their own political claims while delegitimating those of the other nation.

The discourse used to speak of the Arabs living in the West Bank and Gaza is yet another example of the relationship of discourse, ideology, and power.[28] Until fairly recently, the term "Palestinian" was not a part of Israeli discourse, either political or scholarly. Today, Israelis, including the authors in this volume, freely employ the term. Moreover, the Palestinian Arabs have succeeded in making the term a part of international political discourse. It is not that ten years ago there was no Palestinian people and now there is. Only since 1967, however, when the term Palestinian became part of the prevailing discourse, has it been possible for Israelis to frame the conflict, as many Israelis are now prepared to do, as one between two national movements.

Another example of the relationship between discourse and power is the language that one employs when referring to the territories conquered by Israel in the June 1967 War. Those who speak of Judea and Samaria or the Greater Land of Israel frame the political realities in a significantly different way than those who speak of the West Bank or the occupied territories.

Further examples of the political significance of language are implied in other chapters in this volume. Does one speak of Jews who live outside of Israel as living in the Diaspora or in *galut*/exile (Zweig)? Does one refer to the period 1933–45 as the Shoah, the Holocaust, the Nazi era, or the period of the attempted destruction of European Jewry?[29] Similarly, does one refer to the Jews who died during that period as those who were murdered, those who were slaughtered, or those who died *Al Kiddush HaShem* (for the sanctification of God's name)(Porat)?

The discussion of discourse and power suggests yet another framework for reading the chapters in this volume to which I shall only briefly refer. In the studies by Reinharz, Morris, Rekhess, Peretz, Caplan, and Stein, issues of political, social, and economic power and control abound. Similarly, while Bialer reveals ways in which the struggle for domestic political power influences foreign policy, Zweig describes the struggle for power between Israeli leaders and those of Diaspora Jewish communities. In Sela's discussion, the power of available knowledge to shape political perspectives and the power of governments to limit what may be known historically is a central concern. Finally, Aronoff, Zerubavel, and Porat provide valuable insights into the role of power in those socio-cultural processes by means of which meaning and identity are formed. Each, in his or her own way, treats culture as a site of ongoing conflict.

As I have sought to show, there are a number of ways in which the reader can frame the essays in this volume and a variety of perspectives through which he or she can view the creation and early years of the State of Israel. These include the following: (a) the perspectives of different historians; (b) the perspectives of different generations of historians; (c) the perspectives provided by different academic fields or disciplines; and (d) the perspective of cultural and social critique that focuses our attention on such issues as ideology, majority/minority discourse, power/knowledge, and the conflicts inherent to any society and culture.

While new generations of historians, utilizing new archival material, may revise our previous understanding of history in a way that affects our understanding of contemporary realities, the nature of historical discourse necessarily limits the kind of insights one can gain regarding a society or culture. Juxtaposing other disciplinary approaches to that of history broadens the parameters of our inquiry by bringing new interpretive frameworks to bear on the discussion. However, by reaching beyond the disciplinary frameworks to incorporate the issues of ideology and discourse, we leave the way open to radically different ways of thinking about historical issues.

NOTES

I wish to thank my daughter Rachel and my son-in-law, Ken Daley, for reading and commenting on an earlier draft of this chapter. Their suggestions, which I have incorporated, are greatly appreciated.

1. The conference was sponsored by Lehigh's Philip and Muriel Berman Center for Jewish Studies, together with the Moshe Dayan Center for Middle Eastern and African Studies and the Institute for Research in the History of Zionism, both of Tel Aviv University.
2. Ilan Pappe, *Britain and the Arab-Israeli Conflict* (London and Oxford: Macmillan/St. Anthony's, 1988); Avi Shlaim, *Collusion across the Jordan* (New York: Columbia University Press, 1988); and Benny Morris, *The Birth of the Palestinian Refugee Problem* (Cambridge: Cambridge University Press, 1988).
3. Benny Morris, "The New Historiography: Israel Confronts Its Past," *Tikkun* 3, 6 (November/December 1988): 19–23, 99–102.
4. An interesting study of the stages in the revision of Israeli history is Mordecai Bar On, "A Second Look at the Past—Revisions of Historiography of the 1948 Arab-Israeli War" (Hebrew), in *Contemporary Jewry: A Research Annual* 6 (Jerusalem: Hebrew University, 1990): 89–115. Bar On analyzes the forms such revisions take, the different functions they are meant to fulfill, and the variety of factors motivating such writings.
5. Nonacademic studies that first raised many of the issues addressed by the younger historians include Amos Elon, *The Israelis: Founders and Sons* (New York: Holt, Rinehart & Winston, 1971); and Tom Segev, *1949—The First Israelis* (New York: The Free Press, 1986). Segev, an investigative journalist, was one of the first to make widespread use of the newly opened archives. A highly politicized effort to debunk the basic myths of early Israeli historiography is Simcha Flapam, *The Birth of Israel* (New York: Pantheon, 1987).
6. Morris, "The New Historiography," 21.
7. Teveth originally published his critique in a three-part series in the Hebrew newspaper *Ha-aretz*. A revised English version is "Charging Israel with Original Sin," *Commentary* (September 1989): 24–33. Morris responded to Teveth's criticisms in "The Eel and Zionist History: A Reply to Shabtai Teveth," *Tikkun* 5, 1 (March/April 1990): 19–22, 79–86.
8. An invitation to present a paper at the conference was extended to Teveth who, after initially accepting, reconsidered and withdrew, thereby depriving us of the opportunity to include his perspective in this volume.
9. See Teveth, "Charging Israel with Original Sin," 24–25. It is significant that the English-language version of the Morris-Teveth debate was

published in two nonacademic, intellectual Jewish journals, representing the conservative and left wings of American Jewish intellectuals. In the first issue, *Tikkun* openly defined itself as a left-wing alternative to *Commentary*.

10. While Morris's chapter does not address this issue, during the discussion period at the conference he reiterated a claim made in his book that challenges the widespread view that Israel's victory over the Arab forces in 1948 was the victory of a besieged David over a larger, more powerful Goliath. According to Morris, with the exception of a brief period early in the war, Israel enjoyed a distinct advantage over the Arab forces in numbers, arms, organization, efficiency, and technological know-how. As Sela reports in his chapter, the available Arab sources provide a picture of widespread disorganization, unpreparedness, and internal conflicts among the Arab armies.

11. On the problems engendered by such concepts as birth, beginning, or origin, see Edward Said, *Beginnings: Intention and Method* (Baltimore: Johns Hopkins University Press, 1975); and Michel Foucault, ed., "Nietzsche, Genealogy, History," in Foucault, *Language, Counter-Memory, Practice*, with introduction by Donald F. Bouchard (Ithaca: Cornell University Press, 1977), 139–64.

12. For a discussion of the efforts of Zionist thinkers to negate the history and culture of the Diaspora, see Amnon Rubinstein, *From Herzl to Gush Emunim: The Zionist Dream Revisited* (New York: Schocken Books, 1984), chs. 1 and 2; and Arnold Eisen, *Galut: Modern Jewish Reflections on Homelessness and Homecoming* (Bloomington: Indiana University Press, 1986), especially chs. 4–7.

13. On the role of the Holocaust in Israeli culture and civil religion, see Charles Liebman and Eliezer Don-Yehiya, *Civil Religion in Israel* (Berkeley: University of California Press, 1983), chs. 4–5. On the Holocaust in Israeli popular discourse, see Amos Oz, *In the Land of Israel* (New York: Vintage Books, 1983).

14. For recent discussions of the social nature of academic disciplines, see Gary Gutting, ed., *Paradigms and Revolutions: Applications and Appraisals of Thomas Kuhn's Philosophy of Science* (Notre Dame: University of Notre Dame Press, 1980); and Linda Brodkey, *Academic Writing as Social Practice* (Philadelphia: Temple University Press, 1987).

15. Concerning the impact of language and discourse on historical inquiry, see Hayden White, *Metahistory: The Historical Imagination in Nineteenth-Century Europe* (Baltimore: Johns Hopkins University Press, 1973); idem, *Tropics of Discourse: Essays in Cultural Criticism* (Baltimore: Johns Hopkins University Press, 1978); and idem, *The Content of the Form: Narrative Discourse and Historical Representation* (Baltimore: Johns Hopkins University Press, 1987); Lionel Gossman, *Between History and Literature* (Cambridge: Harvard University Press, 1990), chs. 7–9; John S. Nelson, Allan Megill,

and Donald N. McCloskey, eds., *The Rhetoric of the Human Sciences* (Madison: University of Wisconsin Press, 1987), especially chs. 1 and 13. See also the seminal essay by Roland Barthes, "Historical Discourse," in Barthes, *The Rustle of Language*, trans. Richard Howard (New York: Hill & Wang, 1986), 127–40; and Sande Cohen, *Historical Culture: On the Recoding of an Academic Discipline* (Berkeley and Los Angeles: University of California Press, 1986).

16. Gossman, *History and Literature*, 247–48.
17. See Paul Bove, "The Rationality of Disciplines," in Jonathan Arac, ed., *After Foucault: Humanistic Knowledge, Postmodern Challenges* (New Brunswick: Rutgers University Press, 1988); *Intellectuals in Power: A Genealogy of Critical Humanism* (New York: Columbia University Press, 1986), 299–310; and "Discourse," in Frank Lentricchia and Thomas McLaughlin, eds., *Critical Terms for Literary Study* (Chicago: University of Chicago Press, 1990). See also Michel Foucault, *Power/Knowledge: Selected Interviews and Other Writings, 1972–1977*, ed. Colin Gordon (New York: Pantheon, 1980). Stanley Fish provides a moderate alternative to Bove and Foucault. See Fish, *Is There a Text in This Class?* (Cambridge: Harvard University Press, 1980), 1–17; and idem, *Doing What Comes Naturally* (Durham: Duke University Press, 1989), chs. 1, 6, and 7.
18. On the concept of civil religion, see the seminal essay by Robert Bellah, "Civil Religion in America," in Bellah, *Beyond Belief: Essays on Religion in a Post-Traditional World* (New York: Harper and Row, 1970), 168–89; and Liebman and Don-Yehiya, *Civil Religion*.
19. See Liebman and Don-Yehiya, *Civil Religion*. Aronoff has discussed these issues further in *Israeli Visions and Divisions* (New Brunswick and Oxford: Transaction Publishers, 1989), ch. 6.
20. For a discussion of the social and cultural significance of minority discourse in Israeli society with particular attention to Shammas, see Hannan Hever's "Hebrew in an Israeli Arab Hand: Six Miniatures on Anton Shammas's *Arabesques*," in *The Nature and Context of Minority Discourse*, ed. Abdul R. JanMohamed and David Lloyd (New York: Oxford University Press, 1990), 264–93. See also Hannan Hever, "Israeli Literature's Achilles' Heel," *Tikkun* 4, 5 (September/October 1989): 30–33; and idem, "Minority Discourse of a National Majority: Israeli Fiction of the Early Sixties," *Prooftexts: A Journal of Jewish Literary History* 10, 1 (January 1990): 129–47. The articles in the JanMohamed and Lloyd volume provide broad-ranging discussions of the issues relating to minority discourse in general.
21. See Anton Shammas, "Diary," in *Every Sixth Israeli: Relations between the Jewish Majority and the Arab Minority in Israel*, ed. Alouph Hareven (Jerusalem: The Van Leer Foundation, 1983): 29–44; idem, "Kitsch 22: On the Problems of the Relations between Majority and Minority Cultures in Israel," *Tikkun* 2 (September/October 1987): 22–26; and idem, "A Stone's Throw," *New York Review of Books*, 31 March 1988, 9–10.

22. Roland Barthes, *Mythologies*, selected by and trans. Annette Lavers (New York: Hill & Wang, 1972). For other interpretations of ideology as a discursive system through which meaning is created and disseminated, see Louis Althusser, "Ideology and Ideological State Apparatuses," in Althusser, *Lenin and Philosophy* (New York: Monthly Review Press, 1971), 127–86; Stuart Hall, "Signification, Representation, Ideology: Althusser and the Post-Structuralist Debates," *Critical Studies in Mass Communication* 2, 2 (June 1985): 91–114; J. B. Thompson, *Studies in the Theory of Ideology* (Berkeley: University of California Press, 1984); and John Frow, *Marxism and Literary History* (Cambridge: Harvard University Press, 1986).
23. Hall, "Signification, Representation, Ideology," 99. According to the conception of ideology being discussed, to understand the conditions that allowed the problem of Arab refugees to come into being, one has to explore the ideology, including the discursive processes that shaped peoples' views of reality, in such a way as to legitimate one group's claims at the expense of the other's. This ideology, including such concepts as homeland, exile/redemption, and chosenness, also entails ways of emplotting history that result in the exclusion or delegitimation of particular groups.
24. Goran Therborn, *The Ideology of Power and the Power of Ideology* (London and New York: Verso, 1980), 18.
25. Therborn, *Ideology of Power*, 81.
26. "Discourses and their related disciplines and institutions are functions of power: they distribute the effects of power. They are power's relays throughout the modern social system." (Bove, "Discourse," 58.) Bove's article presents a very useful summary of the ways in which the concept of discourse operates in the writings of contemporary critics. See also Diane Macdonell, *Theories of Discourse* (Oxford: Basil Blackwell, 1986); Michel Foucault, *Discipline and Punish: The Birth of the Prison*, trans. Alan Sheridan (New York: Vintage Books, 1979); Richard Terdiman, *Discourse/Counter Discourse* (Ithaca: Cornell University Press, 1985). See also n. 23.
27. See Bove, "Discourse."
28. For discussions of the relationship of discourse and political power, see Stuart Hall, "The Toad in the Garden: Thatcherism among the Theorists," in *Marxism and the Interpretation of Culture*, ed. Cary Nelson and Lawrence Grossberg (Urbana and Chicago: University of Illinois Press, 1988), 35–73; Therborn, *Ideology of Power*; and Bove, "Discourse." Foucault, *Power/Knowledge*, and the works referred to in n. 26.
29. On the problems relating to this terminology, see Uriel Tal, "On the Study of the Holocaust and Genocide," *Yad vaShem Studies* 13 (Jerusalem, 1979): 7–52; and Richard Rubenstein and John Roth, *Approaches to Auschwitz: The Holocaust and Its Legacy* (Atlanta: John Knox Press, 1987), 4–7.

II. THE TRANSITION TO STATEHOOD: JEWS AND ARABS IN CONFLICT

CHAPTER 2

The Transition from Yishuv to State: Social and Ideological Changes

JEHUDA REINHARZ

The new State of Israel, born to independence on 14 May 1948, arose upon the foundation of a society that was itself young and incomplete. In the first years of its existence, Israel absorbed a mass of immigrants equal in number to its original population but sharply different in many significant social, economic, and cultural traits. What does it mean, then, if, under these circumstances, one speaks of the social structure of the new Jewish state?

Obviously, an analysis of the structure of a society implies a description of its stable elements, but only the future can really tell us how far and in what respects Israel today exhibits the elements of stability characteristic of older, better established societies. Thus, a description of Israel's social structure is necessarily a venture in prediction. The best approach may be to analyze Israel's most significant unsolved social problems—those, that is, whose solution is likely to have the most significant historic effect.

In this respect Israel is similar to other states that have emerged in our time. History and social structure are inseparably joined in such states, as they are in all revolutionary—or, as we now call them, rapidly developing—situations. The contemporary social problems of the new "underdeveloped" nations are clearly rooted in their past history, while the shape of their historic future is being decided by the very policies through which they attempt to solve these contemporary social problems. Thus, the extreme poverty and wretched conditions of India's "untouchables" are closely connected with the religious tradition of Hinduism; and, on the other hand, whether India will become a united, stable, and powerful modern nation greatly depends on its raising the level of literacy, the degree of social acceptance, and the economic productivity of the pariahs and other depressed groups.[1]

These relationships are usually well understood by those responsible for determining the policies of new or rejuvenated nations. Even half a century ago, the Young Turks under Kemal Pasha Atatürk held the veiling of women and other Moslem traditions to be responsible for the cultural stagnation and social debility of the Ottoman regime. Consequently, they made "Westernization" a paramount aim of nationalist policy. Thus, measures intended to abolish social ills were also intended to accomplish historic—or even more precisely, political—aims.[2]

The same observations apply to Israel. The Jewish state is one of those modern societies that seeks to make itself more easily understood by proclaiming its fundamental purposes (not only political, but also social, economic, and cultural) as elaborately articulated principles. Israel is both a state and a social structure, conceived before its birth as a means of solving a specific social problem—the modern Jewish Problem—in all its ramifications. Moreover, since its establishment, Israel has continued to regard the solution of the Jewish Problem as a fundamental purpose. Consequently, the institutions and values of Israel, both the state and the society, have been and continue to be structured by the goal of solving the Jewish Problem. This, at least, is an ideological demand that Israel accepts. History alone will decide how far reality will conform to the ideal.

Before the rise of Israel, the Zionist movement proclaimed, in addition to the goal of political sovereignty, the following nationalist objectives: to develop Hebrew as a spoken language and as the foundation of a Jewish national consensus; to transfer to Palestine all Jews who could not or did not wish to live in Diaspora countries; to establish a Jewish community in Palestine free from the peculiar social, economic, and cultural problems that beset the Jews' status as a minority people scattered throughout the world; to carry out the transformations in the Jewish social and economic distribution; and to create the appropriate social institutions and foster the cultural changes that were necessary for attaining the above ends.

The State of Israel has committed itself to elaborately articulated ideological principles no less clearly and comprehensively than did the Zionist movement before it. With the establishment of the state in

1948, the ideal of national independence was institutionalized in its ultimate form, that of political sovereignty. By that date, the Jewish community in Palestine had already developed institutions aimed at realizing the above-mentioned nationalist aims. Hebrew as a spoken language was widely enough disseminated to become the national tongue of the new state. Social and economic institutions had been developed, an occupational distribution achieved, and cultural values established consistent with the ideal of a self-sustaining, balanced community controlling its own destiny in the same way as other free peoples do. However, following 1948, by extending its welcome to all Jews who could not or would not remain in their old homes, Israel received a mass immigration that, for the most part, lacked the specific national attributes already developed in the settled population. As a consequence of this immigration policy, Israel's tasks henceforth included the following: enabling the newcomers to master the language and share in the other elements of social consensus existing in the settled community; and enabling them to participate in the social institutions and cultural life of the settled community. In addition, Israel confronted the task of transforming the social and occupational distribution of the new immigrants so that they would, like the settled population, become self-supporting and at the same time help the state to become economically self-sustaining.

From this survey it is evident, however, that in certain respects, Israel differs sharply from the other new states to which I have compared it. The problem to be solved by acquiring sovereignty in Israel and establishing a free Jewish society there was not the problem of an autochthonous community whose pattern of living had emerged through centuries of adjustment to its own locale. It was, instead, the problem of a people living in exile. The first stage, therefore, was to return the people to a homeland to which they were intimately attached, not only in their dreams but in the minute details of their diverse ways of life.

In the very act of migration, the returning Zionists implicitly committed themselves (as did other emigrants to other overseas lands) to renounce habits that might not be suited to the new country. At the same time, their adjustment to modern requirements in the new country, too, was relatively unencumbered by the handicaps of a rigid local tradition. Thus, the establishment of new patterns of living, rationally suited for adjustment to the social, cultural, and economic, as well as political, requirements of a modern nation in Palestine, was far easier for Israel than it was for the native Asian and African communities that have acquired independence in our time. A more suitable comparison would be those new nations of the Western Hemisphere that were colonized by immigrants from Europe.

Another major difference between Israel and the new Asian and African states (and here, too, the situation may properly be compared with other modern societies built up by colonization) is closely related to the first. Israeli society, as it stood in 1948, represented (in conception, at least, and to a considerable degree in fact) a successful solution of the social problems with which the Zionist movement is concerned. While the mass influx of new immigrants after 1948 undoubtedly produced severe new social problems, I would contend that Israel had already succeeded in developing the social institutions, or at any rate the values and principles, which, appropriately applied, could solve the new problems. If this is a fully satisfactory description of Israel's present situation, Israel from the 1950s on would more closely resemble the United States during the mass immigration of 1880–1920 than countries like contemporary India or Egypt. Its major task, then, would appear to be *merely* social (how to absorb a "formless" mass of newcomers into an already established social milieu) rather than historic (how to devise new institutions or convert traditional social forms into a suitable environment for "modern" living).

Israel's differences from other "underdeveloped" countries in this respect must indeed be recognized from the outset. But it is equally essential to recognize how different in magnitude and in kind was Israel's task of integrating immigrants from that which confronted rapidly developing, nineteenth-century America. If there is a proper comparison to be made, it would more nearly be with the impact of immigration in colonial America[3] or later, just behind the moving Western frontier.

The relative scale of immigration to Israel was so great that the "established" institutions had to adjust to the immigrants no less than the immigrants to the institutions. In addition, the change from a community living under a Mandate government to an independent Jewish state, with all the other political, social, economic, and cultural upheavals that attended it, undoubtedly loosened the underpinnings of the old institutions. It could be said, therefore, that Israel's social institutions and values were and are more in flux than fixed.

In sum, the study of Israel's pressing domestic problems today can and should be more than a study of *merely* social issues. The questions that demand solution, if we may put the issue in technical terms, arise from something more than a merely frictional maladjustment, and the solutions require something more than the restored equilibrium of a stable, "boundary-maintaining" social structure. Moreover, the solutions of Israel's social problems are likely to have historic significance. They may, in fact, determine the forms in which as yet incompletely defined current Israeli social institutions and values eventually become fixed and stable.

Any social structure, to the extent that it is at all involved in historic processes, is tentative, provisional, and continually challenged by alternatives. In a situation as fluid as that of Israel, such alternatives assert themselves with special force. In a rapidly developing country that absorbs large numbers of immigrants, newcomers are not confronted by a monolithic code of values. Instead, they find a range of nuanced alternatives that are recognized as legitimate by the settled community. In rapidly developing countries, the newcomers do not enter into direct social relationships with all or even a representative sample of the settled population. Instead, they enter into complex relationships of reciprocal acceptance and rejection with selected elements among the old settlers, according to the newcomers' particular social functions.

Where the relative weight of the immigrant population is as large as it is in Israel, the support that the newcomers lend to alternative values which may lie latent among the older settlers could well force the revision of the political, economic, cultural, and social patterns. So large an immigration relative to the settled population could also result in new institutions which do not even exist as latent, deviant trends among the older settlers. Moreover, the right of Jewish immigrants to determine the patterns of Israel's future existence is firmly grounded in Zionist principles.

Israel exists, according to its own proclamation, in order to solve the problem of the Jewish people's homelessness and lack of independence.[4] Israel's purpose, therefore, is to provide a rational solution for the problem of Jews in exile by allowing the Jews of the dispersion to return to the homeland and become masters of their own national destiny. This surely means that the new immigrants are no less entitled to advocate their own patterns of living as appropriate for Israeli society as a whole, or for part of it, than were their predecessors who established Israel's original social institutions.

I

In all the new states that have emerged in our day, the conversion from dependency to sovereignty has produced new, complex social problems and raised issues of historic significance. In Israel, as in many other countries, the colonial administration did not hand over to the new state functioning institutions or trained officials fully able to cope with the responsibilities of sovereignty. On this count alone, the transfer of authority in Israel could not have been smooth. It came as an abrupt shock that had to be met by improvised expedients with many attendant difficulties. In the ensuing years, the adjustment to a new governmental structure placed a severe strain on many of the institutions of the *yishuv* (the Hebrew community in Palestine) which had been built up in the absence of a Jewish state. Here, too, difficulties arose similar to those of other new states.

From the very beginning, however, the Jewish state was confronted not only by these common readjustments to independence, taxing enough in all cases, but by quite unusual special difficulties. Israel's independence was won in rebellion and war; and the conditions under which Israel had to plan its future after the hostilities subsided were radically different from all that had existed under the Mandate. Such conditions differed from anything for which the Zionists had planned or even deemed likely.

In some ways, however, Israel was much better equipped for sovereignty as a result of its legacy from the Mandate period than were other ex-colonial areas. Even though the Mandate administration was unable to create a legislative council or an advisory council which would have enabled the population to gain experience in government at the highest level, a fair number of Jews were employed in the higher ranks of various government departments. Also, additional personnel with general administrative experience could be drawn from the many welfare and development agencies with which the *yishuv* was so well supplied. The Jewish Agency, the Histadrut (trade union federation), and the minor party organizations conducted social, economic, cultural, and political activities in many ways parallel to those of a state. There were, nevertheless, many important functions not paralleled or not adequately represented in the experience of the Jewish public institutions.

The Mandate government was bitterly hostile to the United Nations' resolution to partition Palestine and particularly antagonistic to the plan for a Jewish state. Consequently, it did nothing to help, and a great deal to hinder, Jewish preparations for statehood during the brief transition from Mandate to independence in 1947 and 1948. Nevertheless, the United Nations Palestine Commission worked to the best of its ability under difficult conditions to help the Jews cope with this problem, and the Jews applied themselves vigorously to the task. Owing to these efforts and to the well-established infrastructure of a modern state that the *yishuv* bequeathed to Israel, the new Jewish polity was able to avoid the crippling confusion, conflict, and general political instability that have often beset other states during their early years of independence.

Even so, Israel at its birth had to struggle with severe and urgent problems of reorganization in order to convert its existing institutions and improvise supplementary agencies capable of preserving its independence. The extraordinary extent of the activities carried on by the *yishuv*'s partisan organizations separately, as well as jointly through the Jewish Agency and the Palestinian Jewish community council, was a curse as well as a blessing in the first years. The new state was born with relatively well-developed organs of self-maintenance, education, and self-defense. The difficulty was that it had not only one but many well-staffed agencies for absorbing immigrants; not only one but many full-scale school systems; and, worst of all, not only one but many military organizations each seeking to establish and defend the Jewish state according to its own strategic and tactical plans.

Israel was able to overcome its inherited, plural form of military organization very early. The clear and present danger of defeat was enough to make the Israeli government take drastic measures and the Israeli population support them. The state, however, represented a new force intent upon unification not only in military matters but of a wide range of inherited institutional structures; and in these unifications it did not have the same support as it was able to muster for its defense measures. There were strong interests and strong functional demands as well for the continuation of the pluralistic institutional structure Israel had derived from the *yishuv*. This applies even to Israel's political institutions.

The values and habits essential to the efficient functioning of a state were not lacking in Israel to such a dangerous extent as they were in many another new state. Although large numbers of the new immigrants came from countries not familiar with industrial civilization and democratic government, the *yishuv* had long been accustomed to modern ways of administration and was prepared by experience to induct newcomers into its advanced institutions.

Nevertheless, there were certain respects in which the sudden assumption of new governmental functions and the sudden expansion of central bureaucracies sharply altered the conventional attitudes of the *yishuv*. The *yishuv* had valued expansion, growth, dynamism, and initiative as much as any modern code of rational values could wish, and it had generally favored the idea of planning. But from the beginning of the Second Aliyah, it had also strongly stressed the autonomy of small groups and the right to experiment with a variety of approaches to social, economic, and cultural problems. It had grown into a pluralistic society even more diverse, perhaps, than was desired by the protagonists of group autonomy themselves—for each partisan group felt, after all, that the others ought to accept the principles it upheld. But the rise of the state machinery, with its broad-range drive toward unity, endangered the vested interest of established partisan organizations. The value the state machinery placed on central authority, on discipline, and on obedience also ran counter to the established values of grass-roots autonomy, spontaneity, and initiative that were conventional in the *yishuv*. Thus, the sudden rise of the state machinery forecast possible conflicts not only over matters of social organization but over values. Not only were the vested interests of the *yishuv* challenged, but its ideals were questioned and its sensibilities shocked.

The assumption of sovereignty, then, meant the rise of social problems and historic issues for Israel, as for other new states of our time, though not of the same kind or severity. The circumstances in which Israel gained its independence and had to defend it in the early years raised almost unique difficulties. Not to recognize the legitimate existence of new states is an innovation not infrequent in our times; but few new states are so completely encircled as Israel by neighbors that deny its right to exist. Undeclared, cold, and other varieties of unconventional war are also not without precedent in our times; but few states are so harried with blockades, boycotts, and border clashes as Israel has been since its birth. As a result, Israel has been an armed camp and its entire population a citizen army.

The social and cultural consequences of a virtually total conscription policy have been far-reaching and significant. The army has been the meeting place of all Israelis, segregated so sharply in their civilian capacities. The common danger and the common service have inspired a high *esprit de corps* throughout the nation, particularly in response to external threats. For the immigrants, the army has served, by conscious plan, as a primary school of Israeli socialization.

No less significant have been the economic and political effects of Israel's exceptional security situation. Only by a high productive capacity can Israel sustain relatively huge military capabilities. Cut off from its immediate neighbors, Israel has been forced to seek economic ties abroad. It has had to compete in the markets of the advanced industrial countries of the West; and it has had to seek economic as well as political relations with distant, newly emerging states in Asia and Africa. Unable to rely on resistance to Arab blacklisting by foreign transport lines, Israel has been driven to organize its own merchant marine and airline, to develop new ports, and expand its airline terminal facilities.

Even an Israel left at peace by its neighbors would face extraordinary social and economic problems. The new country was half arid, and the mass of entering immigrants unprecedentedly great. The insecurity of Israel immeasurably complicated the situation. As political refugees, most immigrants entered in a state of utter deprivation and many were in poor health. So, too, the supply of capital and the location of industry and agricultural settlements, the methods of absorption, and the aims of acculturation of immigrants were all different in the encircled Israel that arose out of the Arab-Israeli conflict than would otherwise have been the case.

Like other new countries, independent Israel faced social and economic readjustments that developed from its having severed the ties that bound it to another people during its colonial period. The new Israel not only broke its bonds with Britain, the far-off colonial power, it also found itself, after the war of independence, separated from a major part of the local population of prewar Palestine, the Arabs. Both changes involved drastic revisions in the social and economic relationships that had been contemplated for the new state.

It was, of course, the fundamental purpose of Zionism to make the Jews autonomous, not only in their political institutions but also in their social and economic institutions. Nevertheless, success in achieving sovereignty brought with it unexpected problems arising from the sudden erection of a state apparatus. So, too, even as Zionism achieved an intrinsic aim by freeing Israel from the subordination of its judiciary to British legal practices and legal authorities, it encountered the unexplored difficulties of living according to Jewish law.

British control of Palestine's economic policy had been a major obstacle to Zionism, most serious after the adoption of the 1939 White Paper. The advantages of Britain's departure were clear. Israel now had a free hand to explore the mineral resources of Palestine and to plan the intensive development of land and water without restriction. A particular economic grievance had been the tariff policy of the Mandatory government. Zionists charged that it was unduly rigid in granting equal access to the Palestine market to all League of Nations members, unduly responsive to the commercial interests of neighboring countries, and inconsistent with the rapid development of a modern, industrial economy in Palestine. With independence, Israel obtained the freedom to adopt such foreign trade policies as would best serve its ends.

But the economic consultants of the Zionist Organization, in criticizing British economic policy in Palestine, had naturally proposed alternatives that assumed the continuance of the Mandate—that is, the persistence of an economic connection with Great Britain. They proposed, for example, the inclusion of Palestine within Britain's imperial preference scheme. The immediate effect of Israel's independence, even before the formal proclamation, was the severance of all economic ties with Britain. Palestine was removed from the sterling bloc. The new Jewish state was now obliged to devise such policies that could support a more or less stable currency upon the sole basis of its own economy, instead of sharing, as previously, in a balance comprising total economic activities of the sterling bloc.

Whether or not the severance of economic ties with Britain had critical economic significance, it gave new prominence to a task that Zionism had not clearly considered earlier and required emphasizing somewhat different economic criteria. In the many plans that Zionists had made for the economic development of Palestine, the stress had been strongly technological: how to derive maximum yields from the land and to achieve the most efficient employment of all available men and women and capital. The criterion of a profitable balance at a given level of productivity was given less prominence, having been regarded as an economic goal that could be deferred until the prior aim of raising the level of productivity to a maximum had been achieved. The questions the Zionists asked were how they could best use *any* piece of land in Palestine and in what way they could best provide employment for any immigrant who might come. Questions such as which lands should be exploited first, at what point land became submarginal, or how many immigrants should be allowed to enter at a given time were, of course, based upon criteria that a hostile Mandatory had pressed upon them. After Israel was created and cast upon its own resources to achieve a balance of its accounts, the objective situation required it to make solvency, not merely efficiency, a major economic aim.

Much more far-reaching were the effects of separation from the Palestinian Arabs. In their economic planning during the Mandate, Zionists had elaborated proposals for large-scale land acquisition throughout Palestine. This involved gradually, but radically, reducing the overwhelming preponderance of Arab landownership and extending to the maximum the area cultivated by the advanced methods of the Jews. It also involved specific plans for raising Arab agriculture in the available areas of reduced Arab landownership to the highest level. The idea was to begin with the resources and techniques available to the Palestinian *fellaheen* (peasant) and, by a graded progression, supply them with new facilities and accustom them to new methods, thereby arriving by a different route at the same destination as Jewish agriculture.

The fighting of 1947 and 1948 brought in its train the mass flight and some expulsions of Arabs out of the area of Israel. All at once, instead of by gradual stages, virtually the whole land area became available for development by Jews. The problem became not one of slowly purchasing occupied areas, but of rapidly settling vacant areas which would otherwise run to weed and which, unoccupied, might be overrun by the unopposed incursion of border raiders and enemy forces. Plans for agricultural retraining now had to be designed for new Jewish immigrants with virtually no farming tradition, not for the much less pliant Arab *fellaheen* with their set ways and ancient precedents.

The absence of the Arabs also altered the terms in which the agricultural problems facing the Jews had to be understood. In spite of the Zionist aim to build a balanced economy in which Jews would themselves produce all their own necessities, at least to the same extent as other nations in their own land, Jewish farming under the Mandate had developed unevenly. Many characteristic farm products natural to the Palestinian soil were provided to the Jewish economy either entirely or in large part by the Palestinian Arab farmers. Unable to compete with local Arabs in growing native grains and certain fruits and vegetables, Jewish farms produced, like these Arabs, citrus for export and dairy products for the *yishuv*.

Many factors threw the new State of Israel on its own resources: the Arab states' boycott and blockade of all goods, services, and diplomatic ties with Israel; the severance of economic ties with Britain; the disappearance of many Arab farmers from Israel; and—following Israel's independence—the cessation of trade with Arab suppliers across the border. Jewish farming now had to supply many basic commodities previously available from Arab sources. In view of the new importance of national solvency, it now also had to use the whole area at its free disposal in the light of the requirements of Israel's foreign trade balance.

The sudden absence of the Arabs from Israel's countryside and from the cities where they had been neighbors of the Jews obviously had direct social and cultural effects. Among these was the significant impact on the Israeli system of values. Living next door to a hostile neighbor nurtured the militancy inherent in the Zionist ethos. This was as true when the Arabs lived in close proximity with Jews throughout a common land under the Mandate as when they were separated by political boundaries after independence.

In the Mandate period, however, the fact that Jews and Arabs would someday have to reach a *modus vivendi* was brought home to the Zionists in every sphere of their daily activity: at work, in the marketplace, at home, and on the roads. After independence and the flight of much of the Arab population, the need for an understanding with Arabs decreased and was relegated mainly to the field of external politics. As a result, the need to relate to Arabs seemed to concern the average Israeli only when he or she was mobilized for military service.

Another value of the Zionist ethos was also affected, albeit in a more tenuous way. This was the principle that Jews, in order to liberate themselves from economic dependency (or "parasitism"), must become workers. This principle was especially relevant and significant when Arab farmers and workers were readily available. Jewish labor and Jewish self-supply, the slogans of the socialist Zionist parties, although evoking considerable opposition from the middle-class Zionists, were, nonetheless, ideals generally recognized within the *yishuv*. Yet these ideals constantly clashed with Palestinian realities— the employment of cheaper and readily available Arab laborers— thereby making Jewish labor a particularly live issue in the community. Those who dedicated themselves to realizing the Zionist ideals of Jewish labor and Jewish self-supply enjoyed an undisputed elite position.

However, with the flight of most of the Arab population, the significance of the whole question sharply declined. Now the Jewish community had no choice but to supply itself to the fullest extent possible—quite apart from any ideals involved. Insofar as many of the new immigrants had to become workers and farmers, it was a bureaucracy, not an idealistic youth movement, that proved best suited to the task.

II

For the new State of Israel, independence generated sharp changes in the conditions under which it would thenceforth have to pursue its national purpose. In some respects, the transition was smoother for Israel than for other new states of our era. Before becoming independent, the community had already created a social infrastructure quite capable of supporting a modern polity. There would undoubtedly be strains to overcome but, in the long as well as the short run, the fundamental political stability of Israel was beyond question.

In other respects, Israel's situation was unusually difficult. The land was small and poor. The Israeli policy of open doors for all displaced or unsettled Jews presented unprecedented problems of economic absorption and social adjustment. These difficulties had been foreseen and were more or less intrinsic to the essential purpose of Zionism. However, other problems, the result of extraneous circumstances, had not been expected. The sudden collapse of the Mandate, the sharp conflict with and persisting hostility of the Arab states, and particularly the vacuum created by the absence of the Palestinian Arabs abruptly and totally altered the conditions under which Israeli policy would thenceforth have to be formulated.

The changes were no less significant for Israel's domestic problems than for its foreign policy. To some of the new demands of the times, Israel was able to adjust its institutional structure rapidly and effectively. To others, the adjustment is still to be made. The problems involved not only comprise the major social questions that concern the people of Israel today, but constitute the historic issues that will shape the institutions of Israel in the future.

NOTES

1. See, for example, the following: Dilip Hero, *Untouchables of India* (London: Minority Rights Groups, 1982); Veena Das, *Structure and Cognition: Aspects of Hindu Caste and Ritual*, 2d ed. (Delhi: Oxford University Press, 1982); Mark Juergensmeyer, *Religion as Social Vision: The Movement against Untouchability in 20th Century Punjab* (Berkeley: University of California Press, 1981); Milton Israel, *National Unity: The South Asian Experience* (New Delhi: Promilla, 1983).
2. See the following: Bernard Lewis, *The Emergence of Modern Turkey* (London and New York: Oxford University Press, 1961); Seif Mardin, *The Genesis of Young Ottoman Thought: A Study in the Modernization of Turkish Political Ideas* (Princeton: Princeton University Press, 1962); Richard D. Robinson, *The First Turkish Republic: A Case Study in National Development* (Cambridge: Harvard University Press, 1983).
3. See Bernard Bailyn, *Peopling of British North America: An Introduction* (New York: Knopf, 1986); Daniel Boorstein, *The Americas: The Colonial Experience* (New York: Random House, 1958); Richard D. Brown, *Modernization: The Transformation of American Life 1600–1865* (New York: Hill & Wang, 1976).
4. Itamar Rabinovich and Jehuda Reinharz, eds., *Israel in the Middle East* (New York: Oxford University Press, 1984), 14.

Notes on the Bibliography

The literature dealing with Zionism and the State of Israel is voluminous. Recent articles on Zionism and the State of Israel can be found in the yearly bibliographies in the journal *Studies in Zionism*, with older works listed in Israel Klausner's *Toldot ha-zionut* (Jerusalem: Merkaz Zalman Shazar ve-ha-hevrah ha-historit ha-israelit, 1975). David Vital in the back of each of his three volumes on the history of Zionism surveys the literature dealing with the period until 1922. Ben Halpern's *The Idea of the Jewish State*, 2d revised edition (Cambridge: Harvard University Press, 1969), is still the best treatment of the evolution of the concept of Jewish nationality.

The literature dealing with nationality and state-building is too vast to try to summarize here. A good place to start would be the bibliography *Nationalism and National Development: An Interdisciplinary Bibliography*, edited by Karl W. Deutsch and Richard L. Merit (Cambridge, Mass.: MIT Press, 1970). More recent work can be traced through *International Political Science Abstracts* published in Paris by the International Political Science Association. A good general survey of nationalism is Elie Kedourie, *Nationalism* (London: Hutchinson University Library, 1971).

There are any number of surveys dealing with the development and transformation of Israeli society. The following is a brief selection: Mitchell Cohen, *Zion and State: Nation, Class and the Shaping of Modern Israel* (London: Basil Blackwell, 1987); Michael Curtis and Mordechai Chertoff, eds., *Israel: Social Structure and Change* (New Brunswick, N.J.: Transaction Books, 1973); S. N. Eisenstadt, Rivkah Bar Yosef, and Chaim Adler, eds., *Integration and Development in Israel* (New Brunswick, N.J.: Transaction Books, 1970); S. N. Eisenstadt, *The Transformation of Israeli Society* (London: Weidenfeld and Nicolson, 1985); Dan Horowitz and Moshe Lissak, *The Origins of the Israeli Polity* (Chicago: University of Chicago Press, 1979); V. D. Segre, *Israel: A Society in Transition* (London and New York: Oxford University Press, 1971).

The problem of absorption of immigrants is dealt with by Eisenstadt in his *Absorption of Immigrants: A Complete Study* (London: Routledge & Kegan Paul, 1954). See also Moshe Lissak, "Image of Immigrants: Stereotypes and Stigmatization in the Period of Mass Immigration to Israel in the 1950's" (Hebrew), *Cathedra* 43 (March 1987): 125–44; and Judy Shuval, *Immigrants on the Threshold* (New York: Atherton Press, 1963).

For a history of the Israeli army, see Zeev Schiff, *History of the Israeli Army 1874 to the Present* (New York: Macmillan, 1986); and Edward Luttwak and Dan Horowitz, *The Israeli Army* (New York: Harper and Row, 1984).

The following works trace the development of Zionist ideology: Reinhard Weimar, "The Theories of Nationalism and Zionism in the First Decade of the State of Israel," *Middle Eastern Studies* 23 (1987): 172–87; Aharon Kellerman, "To Become a Free Nation in Our Land," *Transitions in the Priorities of Zionist Objectives and Their Geographical Implementation* (Hebrew) (Haifa: University of Haifa, Dept. of Geography, 1987); Yosef Gorny, "The Zionist Movement: From National Liberation to National Self-Preservation," *Zionist Ideas* 11 (1985): 81–88.

For a discussion of Israeli politics and the Arabs, see Gershon Kieval, *Political Politics in Israel and the Occupied Territories* (Westport, Conn.: Greenwood Press, 1983). See also Meron Benvenisti, *West Bank Data Project: A Survey of Israel's Politics* (Washington, D.C.: American Enterprise Institute for Public Policy Research, 1984).

Religious conflict is dealt with among others by Norman Zucker, *The Coming Crisis in Israel: Private Faith and Public Policy* (Cambridge, Mass.: MIT Press, 1973); Eliezer Don-Yehiya and Charles S. Liebman, "The Dilemma of Reconciling Traditional Culture and Political Needs: Civil Religion in Israel" (Hebrew), *Megamot* 38 (1984): 461–85.

CHAPTER 3

The Origins of the Palestinian Refugee Problem

BENNY MORRIS

The Palestinian refugee problem was born of war, not by design, Jewish or Arab. It was largely a by-product of Arab and Jewish fears and of the protracted, bitter fighting that characterized the first Israeli-Arab war. In part, it was the creation of deliberate actions by Jewish military commanders and politicians; in smaller part, it was the result of actions by Arab military commanders and politicians.

The emergence of the problem was almost inevitable, given the geographical intermixing of the Arab and Jewish populations; the history of Arab-Jewish hostility during 1917–47; the resistance on both sides to a binational state and Arab rejection of partition; the outbreak and prolongation of the war for Israel's birth and survival; the depth of Arab animosity towards the *yishuv* and Arab fears of falling under Jewish rule; and the *yishuv*'s fears of what would happen should the Arabs win and, alternately, what would happen to a Jewish state born with a very large, potentially or actively hostile Arab minority in its midst.

Moreover, Palestinian Arab society suffered from a complex of interlocking structural weaknesses that, during 1948's trial of combat, facilitated the rapid socio-political disintegration that underlay the exodus. Among those weaknesses were a largely apolitical or politically primitive populace; enervating regionalism and village-centeredness; a mind-set of reliance on outsiders for succor; widespread illiteracy; a lack of representative norms and self-governing institutions; almost no internal communal taxation; a relatively small, selfish, and disunited elite and middle class, lacking in a national service orientation or tradition; the absence of a large, unified military organization; a lack of weaponry and of a weapons-making capability; and the absence of physical preparations for war (trenches, shelters, and fortifications).

Since 1948, two mutually exclusive, all-embracing explanations have dominated discussion of the Palestinian exodus. The traditional Arab explanation has been that the *yishuv* in 1948 carried out a preplanned, systematic expulsion of the country's Arab inhabitants. The official Jewish explanation, somewhat more complex, has been that the exodus occurred "voluntarily"—that is, not under Jewish compulsion—and on the orders or at the behest of Palestinian and external Arab leaders, in order to tarnish emergent Israel's image and to clear the way, as it were, for the invading Arab armies. However, the massive documentation now available in recently opened Israeli and British archives definitively demonstrates that both these single-cause explanations are fallacious or at least grossly insufficient and that the process by which some 700,000 Arabs departed Jewish/Israeli territory over 1947–49 was multi-staged, varied, and complex.

The exodus occurred in four clearly identifiable stages, with an obvious chronology: December 1947–March 1948; April–June 1948; 9–18 July 1948; and October–November 1948. These stages were inextricably linked to the "stages" and development of the 1948 war. To them one may add the series of population transfers and expulsions that occurred along Israel's borders during the immediate postwar period, November 1948–July 1949.[1]

The Palestinian Arab exodus began in December 1947–March 1948 with the departure of many of the country's upper- and middle-class families, especially from Haifa and Jaffa, towns destined to be in, or at the mercy of, the Jewish state-to-be and from Jewish-dominated districts of western Jerusalem. Flight proved infectious. Household followed household; neighbor followed neighbor; street, street; and neighborhood, neighborhood (as, later, village was to follow neighboring village). The prosperous and educated feared death or injury in the ever-spreading hostilities, the anarchy that attended the gradual withdrawal of the British administration and security forces, the brigandage and intimidation of the Arab militias and irregulars, and more vaguely but generally, the unknown, probably dark future that awaited them under Jewish or, indeed, Husayni rule (the Husayni family and its supporters). Some of these considerations, as well as a variety of direct and indirect military pressures, also during these months, caused the almost complete evacuation of the Arab rural communities of the coastal plain, which was predominantly Jewish and which was to be the core of the Jewish state.

Most of the upper- and middle-class families who moved from Jaffa, Haifa, Jerusalem, Ramle, Acre, and Tiberias to Nablus, Amman, Beirut, Gaza, and Cairo probably thought their exile would be temporary. These families had the financial wherewithal to tide them over; many had wealthy relatives and accommodations outside the country. The urban masses and the *fellahin* (peasants), however, had nowhere to go, certainly not in comfort. For them, flight meant instant destitution; it was not a course readily adopted. But the daily spectacle of abandonment by their "betters," the middle and upper classes, with the concomitant progressive closure of businesses, schools, law offices, and medical clinics and the abandonment of civil service and municipal posts led to a steady attrition of morale and a cumulative sapping of faith and trust in the world around them: their leaders were going or had gone; the British were packing. They had been left "alone" to face the Zionist enemy. Palestinian urban society began to disintegrate.

Daily, week-in, week-out, over December 1947, January, February, and March 1948, there were clashes along the "seams" between the two communities in the mixed towns, ambushes in the fields and on the roads, sniping, machine-gun fire, bomb attacks, and occasional mortaring. Problems of movement and communication, unemployment, and food distribution intensified, especially in the towns, as the hostilities continued.

There is probably no accounting for the mass exodus that followed without understanding the prevalence and depth of the general sense of collapse, of "falling apart," that permeated Arab Palestine, especially the towns, by April 1948. In many places, it would take very little to induce the inhabitants to pack up and flee.

With the Haganah and IZL-LHI (Irgun Zvai Leumi—Lohamei Herut Yisrael) offensives of April–May, the cumulative effect of the fears, deprivations, abandonment, and depredations of the previous months, in both towns and villages, overcame the natural, basic reluctance to abandon home and property and go into exile. The second and principal stage of the exodus unfolded. As Palestinian military power was swiftly and dramatically crushed and the Haganah demonstrated almost unchallenged superiority in successive conquests, Arab morale cracked, giving way to general, blind panic, to a "psychosis of flight," as one Israel Defense Forces (IDF) intelligence report put it.

Towns fell first—Tiberias, Haifa, Jaffa, Beisan, Safad—and their populations fled. The panic then affected the surrounding rural hinterlands: after Haifa came the flight from Balad ash Sheikh and Hawassa; after Jaffa, Salama, Al Kheiriya, and Yazur; after Safad, Dhahiriya Tahta, Sammu'i, and Meirun. For decades the villagers had looked to the towns for leadership; now they followed the townspeople into exile.

If Jewish attacks directly and indirectly triggered most of the Arab exodus up to June 1948, a small but significant proportion of that flight was due to direct Jewish expulsion orders issued after the conquest of a site and to Jewish psychological warfare ploys (*ta'amulat lahash* or whispering propaganda, as it was called by the Haganah) designed to intimidate inhabitants into leaving. The Haganah ordered more than a dozen villages to evacuate during April–June. The expulsions were usually from areas considered strategically vital and in conformity with Plan D, which called for clear main lines of communications and border areas.

Given Palestinian topography, the geographic intermingling of the two communities, and the nature of the partition plan and Palestine's frontiers, there were few Arab villages that did not, arguably, fall into either (or both) of these headings: most villages could be seen as either "strategically vital" or as lying within "border areas." Also, it was standard Haganah and IDF practice to round up and expel the remaining villagers (usually old people, widows, and cripples) from each site already evacuated by most of its inhabitants, mainly because the occupying force wanted to avoid having to leave behind a garrison. An undermanned Haganah/IDF understandably preferred empty to populated Arab villages behind its front lines.

Moreover, for military and political reasons, during the spring and early summer of 1948, Arab local commanders and the Arab Higher Committee (AHC) issued orders to evacuate close to two dozen villages. This included the Arab Legion order of 13 May for the temporary evacuation of villages north and east of Jerusalem for strategic reasons—to clear the prospective battle area. Military reasons also underlay orders to some local National Committees and villages to remove women and children to safer areas. Later in May, Arab irregulars' commanders intimidated villagers into leaving seven sites in the lower Galilee, apparently because they feared the villagers would acquiesce in Israeli rule.

In April–May and indeed again in October, the "atrocity factor" played a major role in precipitating flight from certain areas of the country. Arab villagers and townspeople took to their heels, prompted by the fear that the Jews, if victorious, would do unto them what, in the reverse circumstances, victorious Arab fighters would have done to defeated Jews (and did, occasionally, as in May in the Etzion Bloc, a bloc of four *kibbutzim* between Jerusalem and Hebron). The actual atrocities committed by the Jewish forces (primarily at Deir Yassin) reinforced such fears considerably, especially when amplified and magnified loudly and persistently in the Arab media, particularly by AHC spokesmen, for weeks thereafter.

To what extent was the Arab exodus up to July a product of *yishuv* or Arab policy? The answer is as complex as was the situation on the ground. Up to the beginning of April 1948, there was no *yishuv* plan or policy to expel the Arab inhabitants of Palestine, either from the area destined for Jewish statehood or from those areas lying outside it. The Haganah adopted a forceful retaliatory strategy against suspected bases of Arab irregular bands which triggered a certain amount of flight. But it was not a strategy designed to precipitate civilian flight.

The prospect and need to prepare for the invasion gave birth to the Haganah's Plan D, prepared in early March. It was not a grand plan of expulsion (as Arab propagandists, such as Walid Khalidi, have depicted it). However, it gave the Haganah brigade and battalion-level commanders carte blanche to completely clear vital areas; it allowed the expulsion of hostile or potentially hostile Arab villages (and "potentially hostile" was, indeed, open to a very liberal interpretation). Many villages were bases for bands of irregulars; most villages had armed militias and could serve as bases for hostile bands.

During April–May, the local Haganah commanders, sometimes with specific instruction from the Haganah General Staff, carried out elements of Plan D, each interpreting and implementing the plan in his area as he saw fit and in relation to the prevailing local circumstances. In general, the commanders saw fit to completely clear the vital roads and border areas of Arab communities—Allon in eastern Galilee, Carmel around Haifa and western Galilee, Avidan in the south. Most of the villagers fled before or during the fighting. Those who initially stayed put were almost invariably expelled.

There was never, during April–June, any national-political or General Staff decision to expel "the Arabs" from the Jewish state's areas. There was no "plan" or policy decision. The matter was never discussed in the supreme, political, decision-making bodies; but it was understood by all concerned that, militarily, in the struggle to survive, the fewer Arabs remaining behind and along the front lines, the better and, politically, the fewer Arabs remaining in the Jewish state, the better. At each level of command and execution, Haganah officers in those April–June days when the fate of the state hung in the balance, simply "understood" what the military and political exigencies of survival required. Even most Mapam (generally Ahdut Ha'avodah) officers—ideologically committed to coexistence with the Arabs—failed to "adhere" to the party line: conditions in the field, tactically and strategically, gave precedence to a mentality of immediate survival over the long-term desirability of coexistence.

The Arab leadership inside and outside Palestine probably helped precipitate the exodus in the sense that it was disunited, had decided on no fixed uniform policy vis-à-vis the civilian evacuation, and gave the Palestinians no consistent, hard-and-fast guidelines and instructions about how to act and what to do, especially during the crucial month of April. The records are incomplete, but they show overwhelming confusion and disparate purpose, with "policy" changing from week to week and area to area. No guiding hand or central control is evident.

During the first months, the flight of the middle and upper classes from the towns provoked little Arab interest, except at the immediate local level affected. The rich families arrived in Nablus, Amman, and Beirut in a trickle and were not needy. It seemed to be merely a repeat of the similar exodus of 1936–39. The Husaynis were probably happy that many of the wealthy, opposition-linked families were leaving.

No Arab government closed its borders or otherwise tried to stem the exodus. The AHC, its members already dispersed around the Arab world, issued no blanket condemnation of the flight though, according to IDF intelligence, it tried during these early months to halt the flow out of Palestine, especially of army-age males. At the local level, some of the National Committees (in Haifa and Jerusalem, for example) and local irregulars' commanders tried to fight the exodus, even setting up people's courts to try offenders and threatening to confiscate the property of the departees. However, enforcement seems to have been weak and haphazard; the measures proved largely ineffective. The irregulars often had an interest in encouraging flight as money was to be made out of it (in the form of "departure taxes" or lootable abandoned dwellings).

As to April and the start of the main stage of the exodus, I have found no evidence to show that the AHC issued blanket instructions, by radio or otherwise, to Palestine's Arabs to flee. However, AHC and Husayni supporters in certain areas may have ordered or encouraged flight for various reasons and may have done so, on occasion, in the belief that they were doing what the AHC wanted or would have wanted them to do. Haifa affords an illustration of this.

While it is unlikely that Husayni or the AHC from outside Palestine on 22 April instructed the Haifa Arab leadership to opt for evacuation rather than surrender, Husayni's local supporters, led by Sheikh Murad, did so. The lack of AHC and Husayni orders, appeals, or broadcasts *against* the departure during the following week-long Haifa exodus indicates that Husayni and the AHC did not dissent from their supporters' decision. Silence was consent. The absence of clear, public instructions and broadcasts for or against the Haifa exodus over 23–30 April is extremely instructive concerning the ambivalence of Husayni and the AHC at this stage towards the exodus.

The Arab states, apart from appealing to the British to halt the Haganah offensives and charging that the Haganah was expelling Palestine's Arabs, seem to have taken weeks to digest and understand what was happening. They did not appeal to the Palestinian masses to leave, but neither, in April, did they demand that the Palestinians stay put. Perhaps the politicians in Damascus, Cairo, and Amman, like Husayni, understood that they would need a good reason to justify armed intervention in Palestine on the morrow of the British departure—and the mass exodus, presented as a planned Zionist expulsion, afforded such a reason.

But the dimensions and burden of the problem created by the exodus, falling necessarily and initially upon the shoulders of the host countries, quickly persuaded the Arab states—primarily Transjordan—that it was best to halt the flood tide. The AHC, too, was apparently shocked by the ease and completeness of the uprooting of the Arabs from Palestine. Hence the spate of appeals in early May by Transjordan, the AHC, and various Arab leaders to the Arabs of Palestine to stay put or, if already in exile, to return to their homes.

But the appeals, given the war conditions along the fronts, had little effect: the refugees, who had just left an active or potential combat zone, were hardly inclined to return to it, and especially not on the eve of the expected pan-Arab invasion. Besides, in most areas the Haganah physically barred a return. Later, the Arab invasion of 15 May made any thought of a refugee return impracticable. And it substantially increased the readiness of Haganah commanders to clear border areas of Arab communities.

Already in April–May, on the local and national levels, the *yishuv*'s military and political leaders began to contemplate the problem of a refugee return: should they be allowed back? The approach of the First Truce in early June raised the problem as one of the major political and strategic issues to be faced by the new state. The Arab states, on the local level on each front and in international forums, had begun pressing for Israel to allow the refugees back. And the United Nations' Mediator for Palestine, Folke Bernadotte, had vigorously taken up the cause.

However, politically and militarily, it was clear from the start to most Israelis that a return would be disastrous. Militarily—and the war, all understood, was far from over—it would mean the introduction of a large, potential Fifth Column; politically, it would mean the reintroduction of a large, disruptive Arab minority into the Jewish state. The military commanders argued against a return; so did political common sense. Both were reinforced by strident anti-return lobbying by Jewish settlements around the country.

The mainstream national leaders, led by Ben Gurion, had to confront the issue within two problematic political contexts—the international context of future Israeli-Arab relations, Israeli-United Nations relations, and Israeli-United States relations; and the local political context of a coalition government, in which the Mapam ministers advocated future Jewish-Arab coexistence and a return of "peace-minded" refugees after the war. Hence the cabinet consensus of 16 June was that there would be no return *during the war* and that the matter could be reconsidered after the hostilities. This left Israel's diplomats with room for maneuvering and was sufficiently flexible to allow Mapam to stay in the government, thereby leaving national unity intact.

On the practical level, from the spring of 1948, a series of developments on the ground increasingly precluded any possibility of a future refugee return. The developments were an admixture of incidental, "natural" processes and steps specifically designed to assure the impossibility of a return. These developments and steps included the gradual destruction of the abandoned Arab villages, the destruction or cultivation and long-term takeover of Arab fields, the establishment of new settlements on Arab lands, and the settlement of Jewish immigrants in abandoned Arab villages and urban neighborhoods.

The second half of the war, between the end of the First Truce (8 July 1948) and the signing of the Israeli-Arab armistice agreements in the spring and summer of 1949, was characterized by short, sharp Israeli offensives interspersed with long stretches of cease-fire. In these offensives, the IDF defeated the Transjordanian and Egyptian armies and the Arab Liberation Army, and conquered large tracts of territory earmarked in 1947 by the United Nations for a Palestine Arab state. These offensives—primarily those in July 1948 in the north (Operation Dekel in the Nazareth area) and the center (Operation Dani in the Lydda-Ramle area); and those in October–November in the north (Operation Hiram in the Upper Galilee) and the south (Operation Yoav in the southern coastal plain and the northern Negev)—precipitated, respectively, the third and fourth waves of the exodus. These accounted for the flight of an additional 300,000 refugees from the Israeli-controlled parts of the country.

Again, during these offensives, there was no cabinet or IDF General Staff-level decision to expel. Indeed, the July fighting (the "Ten Days") was preceded by an explicit IDF General Staff directive to all units and corps to avoid destruction of Arab villages and expulsion of Arab communities without prior authorization by the Defense Minister. That order was issued as a result of the cumulative political pressure on Ben Gurion during the summer by the Mapam ministers and Bekhor Shalom Shitrit, the Minister of Minority Affairs.

But from July onwards, there was a growing readiness in the IDF units to expel. This was at least partly due to the political feeling, encouraged by the mass exodus from Jewish-held areas to date, that an almost completely Jewish state was a realistic possibility. There were also powerful vengeful urges at play—revenge for Jewish losses and punishment for having forced upon the *yishuv* and its able-bodied young men the protracted, bitter battle. Generally, all that was needed in each successive newly conquered area was a little nudging.

The tendency of IDF units to expel Arab civilians increased just as the pressures on the remaining Arabs by leaders inside and outside Palestine to stay put grew, and just as their motivation to stay put increased. During the summer, the Arab governments intermittently tried to bar the entry of new refugees into their territory. The Palestinians were encouraged to remain in Palestine or to return to their homes.

At the same time, those Palestinians still in their villages, hearing of the misery that was the lot of their exiled brethren and despairing of the salvation and reconquest of Palestine by the Arab armies, generally preferred to stay put, even though facing the prospect of Israeli rule. Staying put was to be preferred to flight. Arab resistance to flight in the second half of 1948 was far greater than in the pre-July days. Hence, there was much less "spontaneous" flight: villagers tended either to stay put or to leave under duress.

Ben Gurion clearly wanted as few Arabs as possible to remain in the Jewish state. He hoped to see them flee. He said as much to his colleagues and aides in meetings in August, September, and October. But no expulsion policy was ever enunciated and Ben Gurion always refrained from issuing clear or written expulsion orders; he preferred that his generals "understand" what he wanted done. He wished to avoid going down in history as the "great expeller" and he did not want the Israeli government to be implicated in a morally questionable policy. In addition, he sought to preserve national unity in wartime.

Although there was no "expulsion policy," the July and October–November offensives were characterized by more expulsions and, indeed, brutality towards Arab civilians than in the first half of the war. Yet events varied from place to place. In July, Ben Gurion approved the largest expulsion of the war from Lydda and Ramle; but at the same time the IDF Northern Front, with Ben Gurion's agreement if not at his behest, left Nazareth's population, which was mostly Christian, in place. The "Christian factor" was allowed to determine policy, and in the center of the country, three Arab villages—Al Fureidis and Khirbet Jisr az Zarka (along the Haifa-Tel Aviv road), and Abu Ghosh (near Jerusalem)—were allowed to stay, the politicians overriding the clear wishes of the military.[2]

Again, the IDF offensives of October in the Galilee and the south were marked by ambivalence concerning the troops' attitude towards the overrun civilian population. In the south, where Yigal Allon was in command, almost no Arab civilians remained, anywhere. Allon tended to expel and let his subordinates know what he wanted. In the north, where Moshe Carmel was in charge, the picture was varied. Many Upper Galilee Arabs, overrun in Operation Hiram, did not flee, contrary to Ben Gurion's expectations. This was probably due in part to the fact that before October the villagers had hardly been touched by the war or its privations.

The varied religious makeup of the population contributed to the mixed picture. The IDF generally related far more benignly to Christians and Druse than to Muslims. Most Christian and Druse villagers stayed put and were allowed to do so. Many of the Muslim villagers fled; others were expelled. But many other Muslim villagers—for example, in Deir Hanna, Arraba, Sakhnin, and Majd al Kurum—stayed put, and were allowed to stay. Much depended on specific local factors.

During the following months, with the cabinet in Tel Aviv increasingly persuaded that Israeli-Arab enmity would remain a central feature of the Middle East for many years, the IDF was authorized to clear Arab communities from Israel's long, winding, and highly penetrable borders to a depth of five to fifteen kilometers. One of the aims was to prevent infiltration of refugees back to their homes. The IDF was also afraid of sabotage and spying. Early November saw a wave of IDF expulsions or transfers of villagers inland along the northern border. Some villagers, ordered out, were "saved" by last-minute intervention by "soft-hearted" Israeli politicians. The following months and years saw other border areas cleared or partially cleared of Arab inhabitants.

In examining the causes of the Arab exodus from Palestine over 1947–49, accurate quantification is impossible. I have tried to show that the exodus occurred in stages and that causation was multi-layered: a Haifa merchant who fled to Beirut in March 1948 did not leave only because of the weeks or months of sniping and bombings; or because business was getting bad; or because of intimidation and extortion by irregulars; or because he feared the collapse of law and order when the British left; or because he feared for his prospects and livelihood under Jewish rule. He left because of the accumulation of all these factors. A Haifa laborer, who fled with his family at the end of April 1948, left because he had endured months of strife, unemployment, a breakdown of administration and law and order, and intermittent material privations; had seen his "betters"—the rich and privileged, doctors, lawyers, teachers, civil servants—leave in a steady stream during the preceding months; had noted Arab incompetence and weakness and relative Jewish prowess; had seen the Haganah's swift demolition of Arab military power on 21–22 April; had been traumatized by the Jewish mortar barrages during the conquest; had noted the swift Arab collapse and his leaders' decision to quit the city; had witnessed the panic flight of his neighbors, friends, and relatives; and feared for his future under Jewish rule and feared, as well, for what would happen to him should the Arab armies invade Palestine and bomb and assault Haifa.

The decision of rural Arabs to quit their homes and land was often more clear-cut and simple. Usually, the villagers fled as a Haganah/IDF column approached or laid down a preliminary mortar barrage. But here, too, multiple causation often applied, as in Qaluniya, near Jerusalem. There were months of hostilities in the area, intermittent shortages of supplies, severance of communications with Jerusalem, lack of leadership or clear instruction about what to do or expect, rumors or reports of Jewish atrocities, and, finally, a Jewish attack on Qaluniya itself (by which time most of the inhabitants had left). Again, evacuation was the end product of a cumulative process.

Even in the case of a Haganah or IDF expulsion order, the actual departure was often the result of a process rather than of that one act. In Lydda, largely untouched by battle before July 1948, there were unemployment and skyrocketing prices during the first months of the war and the burden caused by the presence of armed irregulars. In April, thousands of refugees from Jaffa and its hinterland arrived in the town, camping out in courtyards and on the town's periphery. They brought demoralization and sickness. Some wealthy families left. There was uncertainty about Abdullah's commitment to the town's defense, and by June there was a feeling that Lydda's "turn" was imminent. Then came the attack, with bombings and shelling, Arab Legion pull-out, collapse of resistance, sniping, massacre—and the expulsion orders of 12–13 July.

What happened in Palestine/Israel over 1947–49 was so complex and varied, the situation radically changing from date to date and place to place, that a single-cause explanation of the exodus from most sites is untenable. At most, one can say that certain causes were important in certain areas at certain times, with a general shift in the spring of 1948 from a prevalence of cumulative internal Arab factors—lack of leadership, economic problems, breakdown of law and order—to a predominance of external, compulsive causes. These included Haganah/IDF attacks and expulsions, fear of Jewish attacks and atrocities, lack of help from the Arab world and AHC, a feeling of impotence and abandonment, and orders from Arab institutions and commanders to leave. In general, in most places, the final and decisive precipitant to flight was a Haganah, IZL, LHI, or IDF attack or the inhabitants' fear of imminent attack.

During the second half of 1948, international concern mounted over the refugee problem. Concern translated into pressures. These pressures, launched by Bernadotte and the Arab states in the summer of 1948, increased as the months passed, as the number of refugees swelled, and as their plight became physically more acute. The refugee problem moved to the forefront of every discussion of the Middle East conflict and the Arabs made their agreement to a settlement with Israel contingent on a solution of the refugee problem by repatriation.

From the summer of 1948, Bernadotte, and from the autumn, the United States pressed Israel to agree to a substantial measure of repatriation as part of a comprehensive solution to the refugee problem and to the general conflict. In December 1948, the United Nations General Assembly upheld the refugees' "right of return." But, as the abandoned villages fell into ruin or were bulldozed or settled, and as more Jewish immigrants poured into the country and were accommodated in abandoned Arab houses, the physical possibility of substantial repatriation grew more remote. Allowing back Arab refugees, Israel argued, would commensurately reduce Israel's ability to absorb Jewish refugees from Europe and the Middle East.

Time worked against a repatriation of the Arab refugees. Bernadotte and the United States wanted Israel to make a "gesture" in the coin of repatriation, to get the efforts for a comprehensive settlement off the ground. In the spring of 1949, the thinking about a "gesture" matured into the United States' demand that Israel agree to take back 250,000, with the remaining refugees to be resettled in the neighboring Arab countries. America threatened and cajoled, but never with sufficient force or conviction to persuade Tel Aviv to relent.

In the spring, in a final major effort, the United Nations and United States engineered the Lausanne Peace Conference. Weeks and months of haggling over agenda and secondary problems led nowhere. The Arabs made all progress contingent on Israeli agreement to mass repatriation. Under American pressure, Tel Aviv reluctantly agreed in July to take back 65,000–70,000 refugees (the "100,000 offer," so called because it would have included an additional 25,000 refugees who had already returned to the country illegally, and 10,000 more who would return under a family reunification scheme) as part of a comprehensive peace settlement. But by the summer of 1949, public and party political opinion in Israel—in part, due to government propaganda—had so hardened against a return that even this minimal offer was greeted by a storm of public protest and howls within Mapai. In any case, the sincerity of the Israeli offer was never tested: the Arabs rejected it out of hand. The United States, too, regarded it as decidedly insufficient, as too little, too late.

The insufficiency of the "100,000 offer," the Arab states' growing rejectionism, their unwillingness to accept and concede defeat, and their inability to publicly agree to absorb and resettle most of the refugees if Israel agreed to repatriation of the rest, the expiry of the "Gaza Plan" (which would have placed the Gaza Strip, with its sizable population of Arab local and refugee populations, under Israeli sovereignty), and America's unwillingness or inability to apply persuasive pressures on Israel and the Arab states to compromise—all meant that the Arab-Israeli impasse would endure and that Palestine's exiled Arabs would remain refugees, to be utilized during the following years by the Arab states as a powerful political and propaganda pawn against Israel. The memory or vicarious memory of 1948 and the subsequent decades of humiliation and deprivation in the refugee camps would ultimately turn generations of Palestinians into potential or active guerrillas and terrorists and the "Palestinian problem" into one of the world's most intractable.

NOTES

This chapter is drawn from the conclusion of my book, *The Birth of the Palestinian Refugee Problem, 1947–1949* (Cambridge: Cambridge University Press, 1988). The reader is referred to that work for documentation.

1. This series of transfers and expulsions, indeed, can be said to have stretched to 1956, when the last Arab inhabitants of the Demilitarized Zone on the Israel-Syria border, from Kirad al Baqqara and Kirad al Ghanama, were pushed across the border into Syria.
2. An analysis of why Abu Ghosh, Al Fureidis, and Khirbet Jisr az Zarka were not uprooted is to be found in Benny Morris, *1948 and After* (Oxford: Oxford University Press, 1990).

CHAPTER 4

One Hundred Years of Social Change: The Creation of the Palestinian Refugee Problem

KENNETH W. STEIN

On 29 November 1947, the United Nations General Assembly passed Resolution 181. It called for the partition of Palestine into independent Arab and Jewish states, the termination of the Mandate no later than August 1948, and the establishment of a special international regime for Jerusalem. Shortly after the United Nations vote, the final and most dramatic phases of the Palestinian Arab refugee problem began. A small migration turned into a steady exodus.

From November 1947 until April 1948, an estimated 200,000 to 300,000 Arabs left Palestine, representing more than a quarter of the ultimate number of Palestinian Arab refugees. Their departure was apparently not due to a generally predetermined and explicitly stated Jewish policy of forced expulsion from the areas which were to become the Jewish state.[1] Arabs who fled Palestine before April 1948 left for a combination of reasons, best summarized as a sense of individual fear and collective impotence in the face of events beyond their control and influence. The first wave of refugees came from urban middle and upper classes (particularly from Haifa, Jerusalem, and Jaffa) as well as from the rural Arab peasant population (from the coastal plain and from the Jezreel and Jordan valleys).[2] After April 1948, a massive proportion of the Palestinian Arab population followed.

There were multiple and varied reasons for the increased numbers of Palestinian Arab refugees.[3] Among them were the physical ravages of war, breakdown of law and order, elimination of employment opportunities, growing panic fed by real and perceived tales of Zionist atrocities, a definite intent by Israeli leaders to minimize the number of Arabs who would ultimately be present in a Jewish state, and a Palestinian desire to protect self and family. Homes were evacuated, businesses closed, and lands abandoned. By the time Israel signed the last armistice agreement with Syria in July 1949, approximately 700,000 Arabs had become refugees from Palestine. More than 40 percent (370) of the more than 850 Arab villages had been abandoned. Less than 15 percent of the total Palestinian Arab population remained in the area that became Israel.[4]

By November 1947, Palestinian Arabs had no international ally, no regional patron, and virtually no national leadership capable of arresting Arab flight from Palestine. Palestinian urban and rural masses were left hopelessly abandoned, without sincere, articulate, or forceful advocates. A defenseless and simple populace faced an aggressive, dynamic, and already established Jewish national movement which had ploddingly developed since the 1880s. The November 1917 Balfour Declaration not only gave the Zionists international recognition of their right to create a Jewish national home, but it also provided for a mere defense of the civil and religious rights of the existing "non-Jewish" population in Palestine.

The successes of Jewish settlement in the late Ottoman period influenced positively His Majesty's Government's (HMG) attitude toward Zionist political aspirations.[5] During the Palestine Mandate, HMG nurtured Zionist demographic and physical presence, while Palestinian Arabs remained defensive, unorganized, and increasingly despondent about their future. In a *volte face* in May 1939, partly because Palestine had been racked by three years of civil rebellion and general strike, HMG issued its 1939 White Paper aimed at mollifying a discontented Arab population. Growth of the Jewish national home was to be conditionally limited with the imposition of immigration and land acquisition restrictions.

At the end of World War II, Palestinians dejectedly faced the decision advocated by the United States President to compensate the Jews for the suffering endured as a consequence of the Holocaust. The decision to admit 100,000 European Jewish refugees into Palestine emotionally drained a politically floundering Palestinian Arab community. In 1882 there were a mere 24,000 Jews in Palestine. By early 1946, Palestine's Jewish population had grown to 500,000; then, more Jewish immigrants were permitted to enter Palestine.

In April 1947, HMG announced its intent to terminate its responsibility for the Mandate, and Palestine's political future was turned over to the newly created United Nations. After being Palestine's umpire and unchallenged executive authority for three decades, HMG retired, leaving Palestine's future to be determined by international politics, the collective strengths and weaknesses of the Jewish and Arab communities in Palestine, and their respective supporters abroad.

From their Arab brethren in surrounding states, the Palestinian Arabs received little more than verbal support. In the late 1940s, the inter-Arab system was rife with personal and national jealousies.[6] No Arab country stepped forward to promote exclusively the Palestinian Arab cause, and the newly born Arab League was relatively ineffective. Each Arab state was fixated on its own national development and on refining diplomatic relations with European powers. Arab nation-state rivalries negated all efforts to confront successfully the Zionist challenge. None of the Arab states made a serious effort to stem the massive Arab flight from Palestine.

From 1947 to 1949 the Arab refugee problem emerged. The preponderance of historical evidence suggests that all the above factors contributed to the emergence of the Palestinian refugee problem in the months and years between 1947 and 1949. Socially and politically, the Palestinian Arab community was inverted and introverted. Feeling wronged and forsaken, Palestinians endured shock and exodus.

A shared national trauma enveloped the Palestinian community. The establishment of Israel was inextricably linked to the creation of a Palestinian diaspora. Either singularly or collectively, Palestinians and their supporters blamed Israel, the British, the international community, the United States, the Arab world, and the aftermath of the Holocaust for conspiring to deny Palestinian national rights.

It would be historically inaccurate to claim that these reasons were less than significant in creating the refugee problem. Yet, these causative factors notwithstanding, the apparent ease with which the Palestinian Arab community collapsed socially is particularly noticeable. Without detracting from the importance of the main causes of the refugee problem, the argument of this chapter is that more than one hundred years of social change tangibly facilitated Palestinian Arab bewilderment and expedited the community's social collapse.

Although some excellent research has focused on Palestinian social history as it developed from late Ottoman times to the establishment of Israel,[7] little scholarly inquiry has concentrated on defining the structural cleavages within Palestinian Arab society which contributed to its vulnerability. To what degree the character and composition of Palestinian Arab society made it susceptible to political disintegration and flight remains to be proven. Yet, it cannot be denied that Palestinian Arab society did not forcefully unite nor successfully withstand the formidable array of external pressures and forces which confronted it.

What caused the society's collapse? What created its internal fragmentation and disunity? What prevented it from being a collective authority? What effected the social divisiveness and animosities that precluded a firmer response to Zionism and British rule? What were the multiple administrative and communal changes which forcefully augmented social dissolution?

There is notable historical evidence from a variety of Arabic, German, Hebrew, and English sources to suggest that the Palestinian Arab community had been significantly prone to dispossession and dislocation before the mass exodus from Palestine began. Before the United Nations partition resolution was passed and before facing the direct causes for displaced refugee status, Palestinian Arab society was in an advanced stage of unraveling.

The Nature of Palestinian Arab Society: The Ottoman Legacy

Foundations for the Palestinian Arab refugee problem commenced in late Ottoman times. It began with the economic pauperization of the peasantry in Palestine[8] and the simultaneous development of large landed estates. For centuries, the overwhelmingly illiterate rural Palestinian peasantry was engaged in primitive agriculture. It was defenseless against rapacious tax collectors and landowning interests. In addition, the peasantry was constantly eligible for military conscription, while suffering prolonged periods of insecurity due to foreign and Bedouin incursions.

The peasantry was skeptical of both its traditional leaders and government officials, who over centuries had handled them maliciously, using extortion and maladministration. In general, the Palestinian Arab peasant was in a chronic state of poverty and indebtedness for a number of reasons: poor soil, lack of water, bad means of communication with the towns, unsuitable marketing arrangements, frequent crop season failures, an antiquated land system, insecurity of tenure, usurious debt commitments, and unscrupulous methods of levying and collecting taxes.[9] Gradually the peasant became inexorably dependent upon those who would provide him with temporary relief from economic hardship, including moneylenders, land brokers, grain merchants, and people with landowning interests. Well before the Ottoman reform movement aimed at establishing bureaucratic efficiency for the purpose of increasing governmental revenue collection and stability in land tenure, the Palestinian Arab peasant began by necessity and preference to forfeit individual control of his life and livelihood to others.

Imposed by the Ottoman authorities after 1839, administrative changes reinforced rather than changed pre-existing traditional social relationships within the Palestinian Arab community.[10] If anything, the Ottoman reform movement strengthened and benefitted a relatively small, urban, landowning elite of no more than several thousand out of a population of more than half a million. Through the dependency of the patron-client relationships that evolved, landowning interests accrued local political prestige and influence, ensured themselves access to the accumulation and disposal of land, and used land as a commodity to obtain capital for maintaining their comfortable life-style.

Landowning interests in Palestine became the collective patrons over their peasant-client population.[11] Ottoman reforms formally put the peasantry into economically and socially addictive relationships with urban landowning interests which were formed in earlier decades and centuries; in later years, the introduction of Ottoman reforms would significantly benefit Jewish settlement and especially the Jewish land acquisition process. The earliest of these administrative reforms began two decades *before* modern Zionism was even formulated in European capitals. Before the first modern Jewish settlement was established in 1855, Palestinian Arab society was already socially fragmented between the peasantry and landowning interests.[12]

It has been authoritatively argued that the introduction of the 1858 Ottoman Land Law into Palestine, instead of fulfilling its intent of checking the growth of large private land ownership, had just the opposite effect.[13] For centuries prior to the introduction of the Land Law and the subsequent introduction of land registration in Palestine and in other parts of the Levant after 1871, peasants farmed land periodically without having proof of ownership. But with the introduction of *kushans*, or title deeds, peasants were compelled to pay fees and additional tax valuations if they wanted land registered in their names.

As a common alternative, most peasants preferred to have an urban notable, merchant, rural *shaykh*, or *mukhtar* register the land in his name, with the original "owning" peasant remaining on the land as a tenant. By resorting to this commonly used proxy system, peasants avoided the registration fees and, more importantly, eluded the conscription rolls, since land records were used to identify those eligible for military service.[14] Furthermore, Ottoman law stated that land not cultivated for three years without a legally acceptable cause would be offered by government for public auction. Hence, peasants who were recruited into the Ottoman army and who were away from their lands for more than three years often found that their land was now "owned" by another.

When these and other peasants suffered successively poor harvests, they habitually turned to moneylenders or mortgaged their lands for cash to obtain agricultural implements, seeds, or perhaps a new plow animal. Loans were computed in money, but given and paid in kind; they were calculated for annual repayment, but the peasant was usually required to repay the interest on the loan, not the capital, within a six- to seven-month period. Interest rates on such varied between 30 to 60 percent per year.[15] When agricultural yields could not meet accrued tax, rent, living, and arrears payments, the peasant relinquished ownership by providing title deed of his land to the moneylender or to a land agent in lieu of debt payment.

Inhabitants particularly of Palestine's coastal plain, who were reckoned as small proprietors in the country, strenuously denied to governmental authorities that they had landed properties in an effort to save the cost of title deeds.[16] Even by 1925, fully three-quarters of all the cultivable land in Palestine was held by unregistered title.[17] In addition, mortgaging land meant selling the property to a creditor with the stipulated right to purchase it back. It seems that, just prior to World War I, peasants in Palestine mortgaged lands in order to pay their way out of military service. When the British military administration took control of Palestine in 1918, it recognized this widespread practice and forbad all land sales in satisfaction of a mortgage debt.

Since the British military authorities did not know how long they would remain in the Holy Land, they sought to prevent portions of the peasantry from becoming displaced and therefore potential financial wards of the occupying administration.[18] Portions of the Palestinian peasantry gave up their right to "legal" ownership because they either sought anonymity from government or found themselves in great debt to moneylenders partly because of the vicissitudes of nature. Thus, over a long interval and because of multiple causes, large landed estates were created in Palestine.[19] Conversely, Palestinian Arab peasants (in)voluntarily disenfranchised themselves by avoiding land registration or by having land registered in another person's name.

By the time the Balfour Declaration was issued in November 1917, Palestinian village peasants had become feeble wards of notable urban and landowning classes. Most Palestinian landowners who had acquired their property over a period of time saw it as a commercial object available for potential revenue, a means to obtain cash, and an irresistible way to turn a fine profit from a previous investment. On the other hand, those who had become tenants on land they or their ancestors had once owned and habitually worked were increasingly susceptible to the planned caprice of land managers, the guile of many urban notables, the greed of moneylenders, and the trade plied by land brokers. Palestine village leaders, such as *mukhtars* or heads of family clans, sometimes enhanced themselves materially in land transactions between Arabs and in transactions involving sales to Jewish buyers.[20]

In addition, it was a regular practice of the urban landowning agent, who often functioned as the intermediary between the landowner and the peasantry, to move tenants or other agricultural laborers from plot to plot within a larger area of land so they could not develop any legal claim to permanence or tenancy on particular parcels of land. Having begun in late Ottoman times, this practice continued with regularity during the Mandate and was refined so that sub-tenants (the land agent in some cases) would not legally be able to receive land as compensation if forced to leave the lands they worked.[21] Not surprisingly, moving a peasant from one plot to another after every growing season disadvantaged him: it did little to engender a sense of economic security; it created harsh local jealousies over who received the most of often meager amounts of good and mediocre land; it caused the peasant to extract what he could from his land and, antithetically, dissuaded him from upgrading a land area with physical (weeding, terracing, manuring) investment because the land would become someone else's during the next growing season.

The extreme insecurity associated with Palestine's agricultural economy was inherent in the routine of the *musha'* system of land tenure practiced in 45 to 60 percent of the cultivated land area of Palestine during the Mandate. At its core, the *musha'* system embraced a land use method which habitually redistributed a number of shares in a village or specific parcels of land every two to five years.[22] Although this widely practiced scheme greatly encouraged village independence, it also contributed to village disharmony. Already strained by *hamula* or clan conflicts, a village regularly withstood periods of uneasiness each time unequal village lands were redistributed. Land disputes, encroachment on another's land, and uprooting of trees were not uncommon where cultivable lands were sparse and the local village population increased over time.[23]

Ultimately, the combination of periodic indebtedness and uncertainties in agricultural yields led to the sale of *musha'* shares to urban interests. Peasants participating in the *musha'* village redistribution process gradually exchanged their parcels or shares for debt relief or for additional loans. It was common for Arab landowning interests, particularly after 1929, to sell previously collected *musha'* shares or parcels to Jewish companies and individuals for considerable profits.[24]

Impact of Jewish Land Settlement upon Palestinian Arab Society

Economic, social, and political circumstances compelled many Palestinians to dislodge or uproot themselves.[25] Over decades, "landlessness" was caused mainly by the peasants' overwhelming indebted condition. It was enhanced by a perilous agricultural economy and augmented by an inhospitable bureaucracy which endorsed a "politics of notables."[26]

Eventually, the peasantry found itself almost totally subservient to urban landowning interests. Bonds that did exist between the urban elite and rural peasantry were forged almost exclusively through economic and financial arrangements which were dominated by crass profit motives and the peasant's inherent fears of government taxation and conscription. As a proletarianization process unfolded, former landowning peasants became agricultural tenants, then per diem urban laborers, and perhaps, ultimately, displaced or "landless."

However, "landlessness" was not due primarily to Jewish land purchase or Arab land sales. A large plurality of Palestinians who were engaged in rural occupations were in fact not landowners, though many may have been in previous decades. According to the *Census for Palestine, 1931*, Palestine's total population numbered 1,035,821, of whom 759,712 were Moslems, 174,610 Jews, 91,398 Christians, and the remainder, Druze, Bahais, Samaritans, and others. Some 465,000 earners and their dependents, or 60 percent of the Muslim Arab population of Palestine, were primarily reliant for their livelihood upon ordinary cultivation and pasturing of flocks. Of the 115,913 earners or heads of households, 50,552 were owner-occupiers; 29,077 were agricultural laborers; 12,638 were agricultural tenants; 7,889 raised, bred, and herded flocks; 7,530 were growers and pickers of fruits, flowers, and vegetables; 2,000 were citrus growers; 43 were agent-managers of estates and rent collectors; and the remainder hunted, fished, or raised small animals.[27] Already by 1931, at least 40 percent of the Muslim Arab population, which was dependent upon land for its primary income, worked on land that was being held, controlled, or owned by someone else. There was an intrinsically precarious essence to the livelihood of the Palestinian Arab peasant.

The influence of urban Palestinian landowning interests was strengthened by the acquisition of land. Later, from the 1880s onward, when they or scions from their families chose to sell lands to Jewish immigrants, profound changes occurred within the Palestinian Arab community. Some former rural workers were attracted by more stable wages in Palestine's burgeoning urban areas. Agricultural tenants who were displaced by Jewish land purchase found additional work in agriculture. The importation of Jewish capital and HMG's focus on infrastructure development in the 1920s and 1930s provided elective work opportunities and stimulated an Arab urban labor force. The transformation of the agricultural peasant into urban workman was prompted by HMG's expenditures on railways, roads, Haifa harbor development, other government employment, and, in the 1940s, wartime expenditures.[28]

Palestinian peasants who totally abandoned occupations in agriculture from the 1880s onwards were not yet "political refugees," because they had not yet left their patrimony to take up residence in another country. Nonetheless, in the decades before the partition resolution, many Palestinians were disenfranchised and then displaced from villages and from lands which they, their fathers, or their grandfathers had either regularly or periodically worked. Well before November 1947 there were significant shifts in Palestine's Arab population.

Villages were not evacuated for the first time immediately prior to the partition resolution. Prior to that time, they had been slowly depopulated or vacated from areas where Jewish land acquisition and settlement had focused. Jewish land buyers preferred that the intended land be handed over free of Arab tenant encumbrances. Generally, it was the Arab vendors (not the Jews) who were responsible for obtaining eviction orders to give vacant possession.[29] Whenever Arab tenants had to abandon land because of Jewish purchase, they were indemnified from Jewish funds, a practice not undertaken when Arabs sold to Arabs.

In the 1920s and 1930s, there were hundreds of examples of Palestinian Arabs voluntarily emigrating away from new or imminent Jewish settlements and enclaves because of economic reasons, Arab sales, and Jewish purchases. For example, when the Palestine Land Development Company purchased land for the Jewish National Fund (JNF) in the Acre area and Jezreel Valley in the 1920s, more than 688 Arab tenants and their families from more than twenty Arab villages comprising more than 250,000 dunams (one dunam equals a quarter acre) vacated their lands after each tenant received financial compensation from Zionist buyers. Most of these former tenants remained in northern Palestine; some were given the option of purchasing other lands with money they had received as compensation; others remained as tenants on the same land for a period of six years.[30] In testifying before the Shaw Commission, which investigated the disturbances in Palestine in 1929, the Palestine Director of Lands noted:

> A[n Arab] vendor would come along and make a contract for sale and purchase with the Jews. We would know nothing of this until four, five, or six months later when the transaction would come to the office. We then instructed the District Officer to report to the tenants. He would go to the village and in some cases he would find that the whole population had already evacuated the village. They [the tenants] had taken certain sums of money and had gone, and we could not afford them any protection whatever.[31]

Arab sales to Jews of land where Arabs were in residence began to change landowner-peasant relationships. When rural peasants became urban laborers, their social ties with their "home" village and with predominantly urban landowning interests were frayed and sometimes irrevocably broken. Moreover, these changes almost always led to peasant disillusion and ultimately village dissolution.

In a prolonged gestation period, well before the "official" birth of the Palestinian Arab refugee issue in late 1947, Palestinian Arabs progressively became detached from lands habitually worked. First they were administratively and legally dispossessed. Then some who owned their own land during the Mandate were physically displaced from lands they habitually worked when land was sold to Jewish buyers or Arab land brokers. After selling their lands, some former owner-occupiers migrated to other parts of Palestine for employment in either rural or urban occupations. Others lived in "their villages" but worked in urban areas when village lands, but not the residential portion of a village, were sold. Some left the rural environment altogether for life in the cities. When land was sold, agricultural laborers, tenants, and mere casual laborers on someone's else land lost an opportunity to earn a portion of their income from that land. As tenants left agricultural occupations, the traditionally entangled connections between them and landowning interests changed. In most cases they began to unravel and eventually were severed. Many landowning patron and peasant-client relationships ended, some not amicably.

For decades, security of tenure for the Palestinian Arab peasant had been greatly compromised by landowning interests. General rural disdain for the urban landowning elite originated in Ottoman times and did not abate during the Mandate.[32] Landowning interests showed little or no sense of social obligation to assist in the amelioration of the peasants' economic condition. Minimal guidance or assistance was offered by the landowning classes about how land should be used to achieve better yields or increase the standard of living of the tenants and agricultural workers.

The social and physical distance which developed between the urban landowner and the rural peasant population was unbridgeable. There was real animosity and even outright hostility between them. Not surprisingly, the peasants' antagonistic feelings toward landowning interests increased in vocality and frequency when, with HMG sanction, Jewish immigrants and land acquisition slowly displaced the agricultural classes from their villages, the peasant's bastion and political environment.[33]

Palestinian village autonomy was jealously guarded against the intrusion by outsiders. But once the boundaries of the peasants' village were pierced by urban landowners, land brokers sometimes purchased their shares or parcels at a very low price and sold them at ten and twenty multiples to Jewish buyers. Peasants who were in *musha'* villages were particularly incensed at landlords, land brokers, or agents after learning that they had been swindled.[34]

Commenting in general on the social distance between the notable *effendi* class and the peasantry in Palestine, Herbert Samuel, the first High Commissioner in Palestine, noted in 1920 that there was "a real antagonism between them." In 1923 Sydney Moody, who served in Palestine and in the British Colonial Office, wrote that "the mass of people whose interest is to agree with Government are afraid to speak.

A village is at best a personal union and at worst a personal disunion."[35] In October 1935 a Palestinian intellectual, Afif I. Tannous, commented:

> The *fellah* until recently has been the subject of oppression, neglect, and ill treatment by his own countrymen and the old political regime. The feudal system played havoc in his life, the *effendi* class looked down upon him, and the old Turkish regime was too corrupt to be concerned with such a vital problem.[36]

Thus, social affinities and communal harmony between urban and rural Palestinians were exceptionally strained and never fully integrated.[37] By the early 1930s "the obedience of the *fellaheen* to their *effendis* [was] not as it used to be."[38] Palestinian Arab villages remained isolated economically and socially from one another. The predominance of the *musha'* land system, with its participatory rights in land use, contributed greatly not only to the village community's solidarity, but also to the general atomization of Palestinian society. The dependence of the village community upon urban interests virtually excluded rural voices from political affairs. As a consequence, Palestine-wide Arab responses to Zionism were severely circumscribed by rural land use patterns alone, leaving the political arena to a relatively small cadre of urban notables.

British Response to the Creation of a Landless Arab Population

During the Mandate, therefore, the peasantry looked beyond the landowning/political elite for a shield from Jewish immigration and land settlement. The Palestine Arab peasantry fervently expected HMG to assist them, for, after all, *it* was facilitating the Jewish national home. But expectations were often unrealistic. By the late 1920s, when hopes went unfulfilled, a sense of alienation, disillusionment, and melancholy conditioned the political environment.

Palestine's High Commissioner, Sir John Chancellor, wanted desperately to redirect the Mandate's course in favor of the Arab population's interest and away from the Jewish national home concept.[39] Chancellor's ideological ally was Sir John Hope Simpson. After investigating the issues of land and immigration as links to the 1929 disturbances, Hope Simpson said, "It cannot be argued that Arabs should be dispossessed in order that the land should be made available for Jewish settlement."[40]

When one Arab sold to another in the years prior to Jewish land purchase, the landowner changed but the Arab tenants remained as sharecroppers. But when Jews purchased lands and wanted to eliminate Arab peasant encumbrances for the purpose of creating a new Jewish settlement, the peasants were most often compelled to move.[41] The process by which Arabs were understood to be made "landless" due to Arab land sales and Jewish land purchases became a central focus for British and Zionist policy considerations from the late 1920s onwards. In this period, almost a dozen major investigatory reports were written,[42] and an unprecedented number of Palestinian laws were proposed or enacted which focused exclusively on the burdensome economic difficulties facing the majority rural population. In addition, a "landless" Arab inquiry was completed by the Palestine administration.[43]

While the reports and statistical inquiries which were issued aimed at evaluating and enumerating the economic well-being of the rural population, the ordinances which were either proposed or promulgated focused on every conceivable means to keep the peasant leashed to his land. These Palestine laws included the 1928 Land Settlement Ordinance, the 1929 and 1933 Protection of Cultivators Ordinances and their amendments, the 1931 Law of Execution Amendment Ordinance, the 1932 Land Disputes Possession Ordinance, the proposed but not passed 1933 *Musha'* Lands Ordinance, the 1934 Usurious Loans Ordinance, the proposed but not passed Damages Bill of 1935, and the 1936 Short Term Crops Loan Ordinance. In the face of social, economic, and political pressures that they could not influence or control, the British naively believed that they could resort to legislative solutions to keep an Arab tenant or agricultural laborer on his land or the land of an Arab landowner.

Until the late 1920s, mostly Arab tenant and agricultural laboring classes were displaced because of Jewish settlement; but in the early 1930s, individual Arab small property owners were the dominant source of land sales made directly to Jewish buyers or indirectly to them through intermediary land brokers. There is irrefutable statistical proof which shows that from 1933 through 1942, 90 percent of all Arab land sale transactions to Jewish purchasers were made by owners of areas of less than 100 dunams.[44] In one sub-district in the hill regions of Palestine, an estimated 30 percent of the land was transferred from Arab small property owners to Arab capitalists and then to Jewish buyers.[45]

So widespread was the alienation of land by Arab small property owners that, on the eve of the 1936 Arab disturbances and general strike, the Palestine administration sought to arrest small sales. It contemplated introducing a law to require the peasant to retain a minimum land area or "lot viable" in order to provide for the subsistence of himself and his family. Palestine administration officials believed in January 1936 that, if this legislation were not introduced (and it ultimately was not), "the result would be further disturbances in Palestine and probably a good deal of bloodshed."[46] Certainly, a major motivation for Palestinian Arab participation in the 1936–39 rebellion was despair created by a sense of irrevocable displacement.[47]

Throughout the country, during the revolt, many members of the Palestinian Arab leadership were either killed, or exiled by the British, or fled to neighboring Arab capitals, Europe, Latin America, or the United States in an effort to escape economic and political insecurity. Other Palestinian political leaders were discredited publicly for selling the most cultivable portions of Palestine to immigrating Zionists and Jewish institutions.[48] Before the 1936–39 Arab revolt against British imperialism and Zionist development had ended, traditional Palestinian Arab communal structure and authority splintered, and bonds between social classes fragmented.

Even with support in the Palestine central administration, as personified by Chancellor and Hope Simpson, and among many British officials in the eighteen sub-district offices throughout Palestine in the early 1930s, the Palestine Arab leadership failed to capitalize on Chancellor's advocacy. By 1935 the Palestine Arab Executive divided into separate political parties dominated by individual and local interests.[49] While political fragmentation occurred among the amorphous notable leadership, the peasantry grew impoverished. A majority of the Arab rural population was already at the poverty line, pauperized, drifting between rural and urban proletarianization, and deeply disenchanted with its political leadership.

Rural poverty did not abate through the late 1930s.[50] Already in 1931, 25 percent of the Arab rural population of 108,000 earners indicated that without a secondary income outside of agriculture, they would not have been able to continue providing for their families. The particular relevance of this statistic is that, of these 27,000 earners, almost 25,000 of them found their subsidiary income in some non-agricultural activity such as selling groceries or oils or working in the building industries in the developing urban areas.[51] With neither economic viability nor residential stability and a severely divided political leadership, it is no wonder that the rural population looked to HMG for support.

At the end of the Arab revolt in 1939, local Palestinian Arab political leadership had virtually disintegrated, due in part to flight and exile.[52] With the May 1939 White Paper, HMG wanted to protect the Palestinian Arabs against Zionism. "Palestine has a large Arab population," said H. F. Downie of the British Colonial Office in 1940, "whose right the Mandatory Power is bound to respect and it is just because Zionist policy is what it is that HMG is compelled to introduce abnormally restrictive measures. Zionism in fact, has to be contained."[53]

Another Colonial Office official, Sir John Shuckburgh, said when speaking after the implementation of the 1940 Land Transfer Regulations, "The Arab landowner has to be protected against himself."[54] In 1930 under Chancellor's influence and again in the 1939 White Paper, HMG wanted to protect the Palestinian Arab community against its own indiscretions in land sales to Jews. Notwithstanding the introduction of the Land Transfer Regulations of 1940, some in the Palestinian Arab community could not refrain from selling lands to eager Jewish buyers, thereby continuing to enlarge Arab displacement if not landlessness.[55] British paternalism neither stopped the development of the Jewish national home nor did it inhibit the growth of a displaced class of people through Arab land sales.

Chancellor's staunchly pro-Arab inclinations were effectively blunted by Zionist interests in London. Pledged economic assistance by HMG in the form of a large development loan for Palestine never materialized in the 1930s. In the 1940s, when HMG relinquished its unchecked executive authority and status as communal umpire in running the Mandate in 1946 and 1947, the Palestinian Arab population was left totally disconnected from any paternal authority. It was essentially defenseless against a demographically inferior but institutionally and organizationally superior Jewish community.

Conclusions

What and when did Zionists and Arabs know about the process of dispossession and its consequences? Writing about the Ottoman and Turkish periods in Palestine, a noted Zionist clearly capsulized the financial relationship between Arab landowners, Arab tenants/peasants, and Jewish buyers. In 1922, he wrote:

> The Arab large landowner quickly recognized that he could now do much better business with his land than continuing to have it worked by tenants. The land had been purely a source of revenue for him which provided him with a work-free income, in the crassest sense of the word. Now it became a welcome object for speculation. It was valid to sell it to the newly arrived [Jewish and German] colonist and indeed for the highest possible price. What was to happen to the renter from whom the land was, so to speak, sold from under his feet concerned the effendi very little. The tenant was just tossed out onto the street and had to take to his heels. So the colonization became an uninterrupted source of tenant tragedies. On the other hand, the price of land rose in an unimaginable manner. The pursuits of the effendi became ever more shameless since there was no competition feared.
>
> Despite their noisy patriotism—which they have discovered only within the last years; the danger began to threaten in earnest because orderly conditions would appear in the country which would make further exploitation of the [peasant] inhabitants impossible—they would indeed rather sell the land for a high price to the Jews than for a lesser price to the Arab farmers.[56]

By the early 1930s, Zionist officials decided for the first time to embark upon a concerted land settlement policy aimed at creating territorially contiguous Jewish land areas[57] and to consider seriously the transfer of Palestinian Arabs to Transjordan. As head of the Jewish Agency, Frederick Kisch sent a seminal letter to his Zionist colleagues in February 1931 seeking their advice on where to resettle Arabs displaced as a result of Jewish land purchase.[58] The consensus Zionist response to Kisch's letter came from Zvi Botkovsky of the Jewish Agency's Settlement Department. He said in March 1931 that if HMG did not allow Zionists to use Transjordan to settle Palestinian Arabs, then the Jewish Agency would be compelled to reserve certain defined areas of the hill country in western Palestine for the resettlement of Arab cultivators.

Like most of his colleagues, Botkovsky believed that the valleys and coastal regions were the only parts of the country suitable for Jewish agriculture. "And on no account," said Botkovsky, "should enclaves separated by strips of [Arab] tenant colonies be agreed to."[59] Later, in early 1936, at a joint coordinating meeting of the Jewish Agency, Jewish National Fund, and Palestine Land Development Company, it was reaffirmed that the Jewish land settlement organizations should continue to evacuate Arab peasants in order to save areas for contiguous Jewish settlement.[60] Physically and demographically dividing Palestine into Jewish and Arab areas was also a policy adopted by the Palestine Development Department when it sought to resettle landless Arabs in the early 1930s.[61]

At the same time that the Zionists were contemplating geographic borders for the Jewish national home in the early 1930s, Palestinian Arabs of all classes articulated their gloom in the face of Zionist growth. The Palestinian newspaper *al-Hayat* noted in September 1930 that "an Arab village shall tomorrow be a Jewish one. Where is the [Supreme] Moslem Council? Where is the Arab Executive?"[62] Regardless of political leaning, virtually every newspaper in Palestine throughout the early 1930s acknowledged and repeatedly warned about the fretful fate of the Palestinian Arab peasant in light of Jewish presence and Zionist growth. Intense fears were expressed regularly.

Two particular articles from the Palestinian Arab press exemplify the deep concern felt at that time about the peasant's future presence in Palestine. One newspaper noted in 1931:

> We are selling our lands to Jews without any remorse. Land brokers are busy day and night with their odious trade without feeling any shame. In the meantime the nation is busy sending protests. Where are we going to? One looks at the quantity of Arab lands transferred daily to Jewish hands, [one] realizes that we are bound to go away from this country. But where? Shall we move to Egypt, Hijaz, or Syria? How could we live there, since we would have sold the lands of our fathers and ancestors to our enemies? Nobody could show us mercy or pity, were we to go away from our country, because we would have lost her with our own hands.[63]

Another newspaper at the end of 1934 remarked:

> Those who adopted this profession [land brokers] aim at becoming rich and at collecting money even if they take it from the liver of this country.... Is it human that the covetous should store capital to evict the peasant from his land and to make him homeless or even sometimes a criminal? The frightened Arab who fears for his future today melts from fear when he imagines his off-spring as homeless and criminals who cannot look at the lands of their fathers.[64]

Whether HMG could have instituted any policy to block the fraying of Palestinian Arab social bonds is a moot question. Nevertheless, there were several remedies that HMG could have executed to stabilize or to reduce the size of the formation of an Arab "landless" class. First, implementation of drastic land reform may have provided the peasantry with stability in land tenure on parcels of land which were not constantly divided up due to inheritance or to application of the *musha'* system. This first alternative was avoided because it would have been perceived as a British effort to turn Arab land over to immigrating Zionists.

Another possibility was continuous governmental provision of monetary loans necessary to sever or reduce the enfeebling addiction between the impoverished tenant and the greedy usurer. But this second alternative was only partially enacted because HMG preferred to spend British or Palestinian taxpayer money on bolstering Britain's strategic interests in Palestine and not on ameliorating the rural population's economic condition specifically or social services generally. As a third option, the imposition of land transfer prohibitions throughout the country was not considered seriously because it would have been contrary to the Mandate's purpose of facilitating the development of the Jewish national home and because it was greatly opposed by many of the Arab landowning classes and Zionist officials.

The 1939 White Paper which included land transfer restrictions but not total land transfer prohibitions was another example of HMG's recourse to legislative antidote in order to correct a fundamentally incurable problem. By 1939, many rural Palestinians were distanced from their political leaders, disconnected from their urban patrons, and increasingly wards of British protection. Frustrated and overwhelmed by economic political conditions they could not influence or change, they were seen by Zionists, for the most part, as nuisances. Socially and financially, their rural environment was collapsing around them.

What then are the origins of the Palestinian refugee problem? No attempt has been made here either to exonerate or to assert or prove complicity for what happened after 1947. Nevertheless, there is conclusive evidence that before the outbreak of World War II, Palestinian Arab society was at an advanced stage of disintegration. Before the Ottoman reform movement commenced, systematic administrative and physical disenfranchisement of the Palestinian Arab from his land had occurred. Peasant security and constancy in the use of a specific parcel of land were rare. Peasants were regularly moved from plot to plot by landowners, and *musha'* shares were periodically redistributed. Between planting and harvesting seasons, it was customary for peasants to find work outside of agriculture.

After the 1870s when land registration was introduced, the Palestinian peasant did not know or foresee that the process of having land registered in other peoples' names would deprive him of legal rights when the land was sold decades later to immigrating Zionists and Jewish settlement organizations. Insecurity in land tenure and the development of large estates preceded administrative dispossession. This was the first step toward physical displacement and the extensive strain that ensued between landowning interests and the peasantry.

For their part, the peasantry feared all conventions that involved record keeping. Ottoman and British administrative systems encouraged and protected landowning interests when the owners interacted with local governmental authorities. Landowners had the patience, energy, money, and knowledge to register land.[65] Arab moneylenders, land agents, and land brokers relentlessly pillaged the peasantry prior to modern Zionism's advent in Palestine. Following that arrival, landowning interests were enticed by an insatiable Zionist demand for land to the detriment of the increasingly indigent rural population.

A Zionist preoccupation to hire exclusively Jewish labor eliminated some alternative employment opportunities and inflamed passions among Arabs displaced because of land sales. When Jewish land purchases took place, village harmony was aggravated and relationships between urban and rural Palestinians were eventually broken. When land brokers assembled small parcels of land by buying them inexpensively from the peasant and then sold them to Jewish buyers, Arab peasants felt their lands had been "stolen" while intermediaries benefitted.

Among some Palestinians with landowning interests, personal gain often prevailed over national priorities. Furthermore, a severe rural economy exacerbated life for the peasant. Peasant dejection, frustration, and anger, articulated through numerous and protracted land disputes, culminated ultimately in the 1936–39 Arab rebellion. Civilian unrest also resulted in the 1939 White Paper, which was one more British effort to protect the Palestinian Arab from Jewish national development without ending the Mandate or stopping Zionist growth totally.

From the 1850s through the early 1940s, an unknown number of displaced Arabs was created by all these factors; and dozens of Arab villages were dissipated in the process of creating a Jewish national home. Thus, by 1947, Palestinian Arab society had become highly susceptible to insecurity and flight. Indeed, a combination of reasons caused hundreds of thousands of Arabs to leave Palestine after November 1947, not the least of which was the internal societal changes that led to a slow disintegration of communal bonds. Although Palestinians became refugees in the 1947–49 period, the origins of their social collapse can be partially attributed to the fractious nature of Arab society and its steady dissolution over the previous century.

NOTES

1. Benny Morris, *The Birth of the Palestinian Refugee Problem, 1947–1949* (Cambridge, 1987), 128, 288.
2. Ibid., 59, 286.
3. Morris, *Palestinian Refugee Problem*, 286–98, especially 293–94; and Don Peretz, *Israel and the Palestine Arabs* (Washington, 1958), 5–8.
4. Morris, *Palestinian Refugee Problem*, xiv–xvii; and Abraham Granott, *The Land System of Palestine History and Structure* (London, 1952), 168.
5. See Neville Mandel, *The Arabs and Zionism before World War I* (Berkeley, 1976), especially 223–31.
6. Mary C. Wilson, *King Abdullah, Britain and the Making of Jordan* (Cambridge, 1987), 112; Avi Shlaim, *Collusion across the Jordan: King Abdullah, The Zionist Movement, and the Partition of Palestine* (New York, 1988), 53, 123.
7. Shulamit Carmi and Henry Rosenfeld, "The Origins of the Process of the Proletarianization and Urbanization of Arab Peasants in Palestine," *Annals of the New York Academy of Sciences* 220 (March 1974): 470–85; Joel S. Migdal, "Urbanization and Political Change: The Impact of Foreign Rule," *Comparative Studies in Society and History* 19 (July 1977): 328–49; Ylana N. Miller, *Government and Society in Rural Palestine* (Texas, 1985); Taysir Nashif, *The Palestinian Arab and Jewish Political Leaderships* (New York, 1979); Yehoshua Porath, "Social Aspects of the Emergence of the Palestine Arab National Movement," in Menahem Milson, ed., *Society and Political Structure in the Arab World* (New York, 1973), 93–144; James Reilly, "The Peasantry of Late Ottoman Palestine," *Journal of Palestine Studies* 10 (Summer 1981): 82–97; Kenneth W. Stein, "Palestine's Rural Economy, 1917–1939," *Studies in Zionism* 8 (1987): 25–49; Rachelle Taqqu, "Peasants into Workmen: Internal Labor Migration and the Arab Village under the Mandate," in Joel S. Migdal, ed., *Palestinian Society and Politics* (Princeton, N.J., 1980), 261–85; Elia Zureik, "Reflections on Twentieth Century Palestinian Class Structure," in Khalil Nakhleh and Elia Zureik, eds., *The Sociology of the Palestinians* (New York, 1980), 47–63.
8. See Zureik, "Reflections," 49.
9. Cooperative Societies in Palestine, *Report by the Registrar of Cooperative Societies on Developments during the Years 1921–1937* (Jerusalem, 1938), 10.
10. Kenneth W. Stein, *The Land Question in Palestine 1917–1939* (Chapel Hill, 1984), 217.
11. Migdal, "Urbanization and Political Change," 338–39.
12. Leon Schulman, *Zur türkischen Agrarfrage Palästina und die Fellachenwirtschaft* (Weimar, 1916), 44–45; and Zureik, "Reflections," 49.
13. Bernard Lewis, *The Emergence of Modern Turkey* (Oxford, 1969), 119; Kemal H. Karpat, "Land Regime, Social Structure, and Modernization," in

William Polk and Richard Chambers, eds., *Beginnings of Modernization in the Middle East* (Chicago, 1968), 86; Moshe Ma'oz, *Ottoman Reform in Syria and Palestine 1840-1861* (Oxford, 1968), 162.

14. Amin Rizk (Palestine Department of Lands), remarks on a note of the Governor of Samaria on Werko and Land Registry, 2 February 1923, p. 1, Israel State Archives (hereafter ISA), Box AG755/File L3/Folio 39.
15. S. Kaplansky (Jewish Agency settlement specialist), *The Land Problem in Palestine*, 1930, Central Zionist Archives (hereafter CZA), Record Group Z4/3444/File III. See also Palestine Government, F. G. Horwill, *The Banking System in Palestine* (July 1936), 80.
16. Gad Frumkin, *Derech Shofat BeYerushalaim* (The path of a judge in Jerusalem) (Tel Aviv, 1973), 305.
17. Harry Sachar of the Anglo-Palestine Bank to Norman Bentwich, Attorney General for the Palestine Administration, 17 March 1925, CZA, Z4/771/File II.
18. Stein, *Land Question in Palestine*, 39-43.
19. See Granott, *Land System*, 34-84; Alfred Bonne, "Die sozial-ökonomischen Strukturwandlungen in Palästina," *Archiv für Sozialwissenschaft und Sozialpolitik* 63, Part 1 (1930): 327; and Schulman, *Zur türkischen Agrarfrage*, 43-56.
20. For examples of *mukhtars* seeking personal enrichment in village land matters, see *al-Jami'ah al-'Arabiyyah*, 22 April 1931; Gaza Settlement Officer to Commissioner of Lands, 17 June 1938, ISA, Box LS274/File 4/Folio 33; "Land Speculation," ISA, Box 2637/File G536. See also Miller, *Government and Society*, 56-62; and Gabriel Baer, "The Office and Functions of the Village Mukhtar," in Joel S. Migdal, ed., *Palestinian Society and Politics* (Princeton, N.J., 1980), 103-23.
21. For these practices exercised in Palestine prior to World War I, see George Post, "Essays on Sects and Nationalities of Syria and Palestine-Land Tenure," *Palestine Exploration Fund Quarterly Statement* (April 1891), 106; Alfred Sursock, *Memorandum on Sursock Lands*, 30 September 1921, ISA, Box 3544/File 21; and Arthur Ruppin, *Syrien als Wirtschaftsgebiet* (Berlin, 1917), 64-65.
22. See Stein, *Land Question in Palestine*, 14-16, 142-43; Joanne Dee Held, *The Effects of the Ottoman Land Laws on the Marginal Population and Musha' Village of Palestine, 1858-1914* (Master's thesis, University of Texas at Austin, 1978).
23. Hubert Auhagen, *Beiträge zur Kenntnis der Landesnatur und der Landwirtschaft Syriens* (Berlin, 1907), 49-51.
24. Hilmi Husseini, Inspector of Lands, Northern District, to Director of Lands, 14 July 1923, ISA, Box 3317/File 6; Ernest Dowson, *Progress on Land Reforms, 1923-1930*, 1931, 27-28, Colonial Office (hereafter CO) Series 733/Box 221/File 97169; "Report on the Work of the Ghor Mudawarra Demarcation Commission," 19 March 1932, ISA, Box 3548/File 1; and

Albert Abramson, former Commissioner of Lands in Palestine, "An Aspect of Village Life in Palestine," *The Palestine Post*, 6 July 1937.
25. For a definition of "refugees" where there is a component of indirect compulsion resulting in their status, see Independent Commission on International Humanitarian Issues, *Refugees: The Dynamics of Displacement* (London, 1986).
26. See Albert Hourani, "Ottoman Reform and the Politics of Notables," in William Polk and Richard Chambers, eds., *Beginnings of Modernization in the Middle East* (Chicago, 1968), 41-68.
27. Palestine Government, *Census for Palestine, 1931* I: 291-92; II, Table 14: 282.
28. Taqqu, "Peasants into Workmen," 261-62.
29. League of Nations, *Permanent Mandates Commission Minutes*, remarks by J. H. Hall, Chief Secretary of the Palestine Administration, Twenty-fifth Session, 1 June 1934, vol. 25, p. 28.
30. Arthur Ruppin, "Jewish Land Purchase and Their Reaction upon the Condition of the Former Arab Cultivators," 1929, CZA, S25/4207.
31. Great Britain, *Report of the Commission on the Palestine Disturbances of August 1929*, Cmd. 3530, March 1930, 115; League of Nations, *Permanent Mandates Commission Minutes*, Seventeenth Session, 6 June 1930, p. 61.
32. See Lawrence Oliphant, *Haifa or Life in Modern Palestine* (New York, 1887), 194-95; for a sampling of Palestine Arab press comment on the deteriorating attitude of the rural peasant for the urban landowner, see *Filastin*, 29 January 1931, and *al-Jami'ah al-'Arabiyyah*, 30 July 1934.
33. See Cooperative Societies in Palestine, *Report by the Registrar of Cooperative Societies on Developments during the Years 1921-1937* (Jerusalem, 1938), 10; and Philip E. Schoenberg, *Palestine in the Year 1914* (Ph.D. diss., New York University, vol. 1, 1978, 163-67).
34. Heinrich Margulies, Anglo-Palestine Bank, to the Palestine Jewish Agency entitled, "The Tenant's Question in Palestine-*fellaheen*-landlord Relationships," 9 November 1931, CZA, S25/7619.
35. Herbert Samuel to Lord Curzon, 2 April 1920, Herbert Samuel Archives, ISA; Note by Sydney Moody, Political Report for January 1923, Minute Sheet, 23 February 1923, CO 733/42/8933.
36. Afif I. Tannous, "The Arab Village Community," *Annual Report of the Smithsonian Institute* (1943), 236.
37. Zureik, "Reflections," 49.
38. I. Chizik, "The Political Parties in Palestine," *Royal Central Asian Society Journal* 21 (1934): 94-128.
39. See Sir John Chancellor's famous dispatch of 17 January 1930 in CO 733/183/77050/Part 1.
40. Palestine, *Report on Immigration, Land Settlement and Development* (hereafter Hope Simpson Report), Cmd. 3686, (London, 1930), 59.
41. Letter from High Commissioner Sir Arthur Wauchope to Secretary of

State for the Colonies, Philip Cunliffe-Lister, 22 December 1932, CO 733/219/97072/99.

42. For the published reports, see Great Britain, Palestine, *Commission on the Disturbances of August 1929* (hereafter Shaw Report), Cmd. 3530 (London, 1930); Hope Simpson Report, 1930; Palestine Government, *Report by Mr. C. F. Strickland of the Indian Civil Service on the Possibility of Introducing a System of Agricultural Cooperation in Palestine* (Palestine, 1930); Palestine Government, *Report of a Committee on the Economic Conditions of Agriculturalists in Palestine and Fiscal Measures of Government in Relation Thereto* (Palestine, 1930); Palestine Government, Lewis French, *First Report on Agricultural Development and Land Settlement in Palestine* (hereafter First French Report) (Palestine, 1931); and Palestine Government, Lewis French, *Supplementary Report on Agricultural Development and Land Settlement in Palestine* (Palestine, 1932).

43. The landless inquiry carried out between 1931 and 1939 showed by a very restrictive definition of a "landless" Arab that only 899 Arab families or approximately 5,000 earners and dependents were landless as a direct result of Jewish land purchase and Arab land sales. For a review of the landless Arab inquiry and its procedures, see Stein, *Land Question in Palestine*, 142-72; High Commissioner Wauchope to Cunliffe-Lister, 6 May 1935, CO 733/270/75049/1; Lewis Andrews, District Officer, to J. M. Martin, Secretary to the Peel Commission, 4 March 1937, CO 733/345/75550/33; High Commissioner MacMichael to Colonial Secretary Malcolm MacDonald, 24 May 1939, CO 733/405/75720.

44. See Stein, *Land Question in Palestine*, 178-82.

45. First French Report, paragraphs 70-73; Arthur Ruppin, "Comments on the French Report," p. 13, 30 June 1932, CZA, S25/7600.

46. Memorandum on points likely to be raised with the Secretary of State for the Colonies by the Arab Deputation from Palestine, January 1936, CO 733/297/75156/Part 1.

47. Theodore Swedenburg, *Memories of a Revolt: The 1936-1939 Rebellion and the Struggle for a Palestinian Nationalist Past* (Ph.D. diss., University of Texas at Austin, 1988), 174; Tom Bowden, "The Politics of the Arab Rebellion in Palestine," *Middle Eastern Studies* 11 (May 1975): 149; Porath, "Social Aspects of the Emergence of the Palestine Arab National Movement," 132. My own research of the last fifteen years also supports this conclusion that the effects of Arab displacement from Arab land sales and Jewish land purchases contributed to the Arab peasant participation in the 1936-1939 revolt.

48. See Stein, *Land Question in Palestine*, 65-70, 182-84, 228-39.

49. Yehoshua Porath, "The Political Awakening of the Palestinian Arabs and Their Leadership towards the End of the Ottoman Period," in Moshe Ma'oz, ed., *Studies on Palestine during the Ottoman Period* (Jerusalem, 1975), 351-81; Porath, *The Emergence of the Palestinian-Arab National Movement*

1918–1929 (London: 1974), 208–40; and Porath, *The Palestinian Arab National Movement 1929–1939* (London, 1977), 49–79.
50. See Stein, "Palestine's Rural Economy, 1917–1939."
51. Palestine Government, *Census for Palestine, 1931*, vol. 1 (Alexandria, 1933), 291.
52. Issa Khalaf, *Palestine Factionalist Politics and Social Disintegration, 1939–1948* (Ph.D. diss., Oxford University, 1985).
53. Minutes by H. F. Downie, 29 April 1940, CO 733/418/75072/9.
54. Minutes by J. E. Shuckburgh, 14 June 1940, CO 733/425/75872/12.
55. For examples of Arab circumventions of the 1940 Land Transfer Regulations, see A. F. Giles, Assistant Inspector of the Criminal Investigation Division to Palestine Chief Secretary, 13 April 1943; Ramadan Mohammad al-'Alami to Jaffa District Commissioner, 12 November 1943; and High Commissioner Sir Harold MacMichael to Secretary of State for the Colonies, Sir Oliver Stanley (with enclosures), 24 December 1943, CO 733/453/75072/9/1944.
56. Arjeh Tartakower, "Bodenfrage und Bodenpolitik in Palästina," *Der Jude* 6 (1921–1922): 731, 735.
57. Letter from Mr. Bawley, Head of the Palestine Zionist Executive's Colonization Department, to Mr. Sachar, 10 January 1929, CZA, Z4/3450/-File III.
58. Frederick Kisch to the Executive of the Histadruth, the Palestine Colonization Association, the Jewish National Fund and Messrs. Botkovsky, Smilansky, Wilkansky, and Thon, 11 February 1931, CZA, S25/6525.
59. Zvi Botkovsky to Frederick Kisch, 3 March 1931, CZA, S25/9836.
60. Minutes of a conjoint meeting of the Jewish Agency, the Jewish National Fund, and the Palestine Land Development Company, 19 February 1936, CZA, S25/6538.
61. Lewis Namier of the London Jewish Agency played an instrumental role in fashioning this geographic and demographic division. See Namier to Mrs. Dugdale, 11 January 1931, CZA, S25/7587. See also Great Britain, *Parliamentary Debates*, Commons, 20 July 1931, 5th series, 225.
62. *Al-Hayat* (Jerusalem), 8 September 1930.
63. *Al-Ikdam*, 19 January 1931. For other examples, see *Filastin*, 29 January 1931; *Al-Carmel*, 5 August 1931; *Filastin*, 6 February 1932; *Al-Jami'ah al-'Arabiyyah*, 17 December 1933; *Filastin*, 8 May 1934; *Al-Jami'ah al-Islamiyyah*, 7 September 1934; *Al-Difa'*, 27 November 1934; *Al-Difa'*, 3 February 1935; and *Al-Liwa*, 3 February 1936.
64. *Al-Difa'*, 5 November 1934.
65. Schoenberg, *Palestine in the Year 1914*, 147.

CHAPTER 5

Early State Policy towards the Arab Population, 1948—1955

DON PERETZ

If by early we mean the period from the establishment of Israel in May 1948 until the mid-1950s, that is, the first six or seven years of the new state, early state policy towards the Arab minority was still largely in a formative stage. This was still a period of confusion and contradictions following the War of Independence that transformed the Palestinian *yishuv* (Jewish community) from a minority in a predominantly Arab environment under British colonial rule into an overwhelming majority that seized absolute control of all territory under its jurisdiction. Political and economic relations between Jews and Arabs in those parts of Palestine that became the new State of Israel were totally reversed. Both self-perceptions and perceptions that Jews and Arabs had of each other changed radically. The policies of the new Jewish state towards its "new" Arab minority reflected these fundamental changes in perceptions, attitudes, and outlooks for the future.

Policy towards the Arab minority was intimately linked with policy towards the 600,000 or 700,000 Arab refugees who fled from their homes between November 1947 and January 1949. It was as much a component of foreign and security policy as it was of the domestic scene, and many actions of the government towards the minority reflected these larger issues.

Few Israelis or Arabs had anticipated the drastic change in the balance of power between the two communities that resulted from the United Nations partition resolution, establishment of the Jewish state, and the first Arab-Israeli war. Before 1948 the *yishuv* was apprehensive about the large Arab population, nearly equal to the Jewish, that was to have inhabited the proposed Jewish state. There were no clear-cut plans for dealing with this situation.

Zionist perspectives ranged from those of some Revisionists who called openly for transfer of Arabs out of the Jewish state, to Marxists in the left wing of the Labor movement who truly believed that the loyalty of the Arab masses could be won from their "feudal" masters by good works, improved living standards, and equal political rights. Although the Zionist mainstream in the pre-state era recognized that initially the Jews would be a minority in Palestine, or just barely a majority in a partitioned entity, they envisaged becoming a majority soon after independence as a result of massive Jewish immigration from Europe. It was assumed that assurance of "complete equality of rights for all inhabitants regardless of race or creed, complete eligibility of all for all offices, up to the highest" (Moshe Sharett, Israel's Foreign Minister, before the 1946 Anglo-American Commission) would assuage Arab fears of Jewish domination.[1] All of these attitudes and perceptions—those of Revisionists, of Marxist Zionists, and of the *yishuv* mainstream—were reflected in early policy of the new state towards its Arab minority.

Although Palestinian Arab fears of displacement were real, they coexisted with confidence in what appeared to be the overwhelming numerical power of the country's Arab majority (which outnumbered the Jews by two to one), the perceived strength of the combined neighboring Arab armies, and the residue of contempt for Jewish fighting ability. Thus, the outcome of the first war and the ensuing refugee flight left the Arab population remaining in Israel in deep shock, so deep that it took nearly a generation for them to recover and to achieve a new identity and a new political resonance.

Nearly all Arab political and community leaders had left Israel for a variety of reasons. Instead of 800,000 Palestinian Arabs, just over 150,000 remained in the new state by 1949. Although Christian community structures remained more or less intact, the vast majority of those in the Muslim sector were in disarray and bereft of guidance. The Arab economy was almost totally demolished. Families were fragmented, with only remnants remaining in Israel, while most members were dispersed and inaccessible across the lines in enemy territory. This, then, was the setting in which the new state began to evolve policy for its Arab minority, a process that emerged and took form between May 1948 and the early 1950s.

A number of internal and external factors shaped the formation of early state policy towards the Arab minority. Among the external factors was the fact that, for whatever reasons, a state of war continued with all the surrounding Arab states even after conclusion of the 1949 armistice agreements between Israel and Egypt, Lebanon, Jordan, and Syria, thereby isolating Israel in its Middle East environment. Some of the so-called revisionist (with small *r*) history of that era postulates that there were lost opportunities for a peaceful settlement following the armistice agreements. The fact remains, however, that because no such settlement was achieved, the country's frontiers remained unrecognized by any other nation and were, therefore, insecure politically, even if well defended by the Israel Defense Forces (hereafter IDF).

A major objective of the country's leaders was to transform these provisional frontiers into permanent, internationally recognized borders, a goal that required absolute control by the state of all territory and all population within the armistice lines. Many of the border areas, especially those in the north, the central region bordering Jordan, and the Negev, were heavily populated by Arabs with lands and villages in Arab hands. Thus, it was necessary for the state to establish and assert its authority in these regions, lest questions be raised about Israel's right to sovereignty there.

The armistice agreements did not bestow sovereignty but only temporary custodianship on territory under Israel's control. These temporary armistice frontiers extended the area under Israel's control by some 2,000 square miles beyond the 6,000 square miles allotted to the Jewish state in the United Nations partition plan, and much of this additional territory was heavily populated by Arabs, even after the refugee flight. Nearly all the land in these border areas was also Arab.

Because sovereignty over the border regions was uncertain, it was necessary to establish firm, uncontested, and unquestioned control over them. While denying their Arab inhabitants citizenship would have added to the uncertainty about the legal status of these regions, to leave them under normal local civilian authority appeared to be dangerous because there was no reason for the inhabitants to assert or feel any loyalty to the new Jewish state. They had never been asked their desires about national affiliation, and for that matter, most of them had been assigned to the proposed Arab state according to the partition plan.

If a referendum had been taken in these border areas at any time during Israel's early years, it is doubtful that the population would have chosen to be annexed by Israel. Therefore, to preempt their affiliation with any other political entity, it was essential that the population become Israeli citizens as soon as possible. On the other hand, this was a population that only a few months earlier had either been neutral in the conflict with the surrounding Arab states or outright enemies of the *yishuv* and the new Jewish state. Israel's problem, therefore, was to reconcile these apparently contradictory pressures—the pressure to integrate as citizens this uncertain Arab population, and the pressure to control and supervise it.

In the first weeks after conquering and establishing authority over these areas, when even the Israeli government was uncertain about their future, they were treated as occupied territory, much like the West Bank and Gaza after the 1967 war. Gradually, however, it became clear that the vast majority of Arabs had left the country and that fewer than 20 percent of the original Arab inhabitants remained. Steps were quickly taken to replace the refugees with new Jewish immigrants; to utilize as much as possible of the former Arab property to settle new Jewish immigrants; and to absorb the refugee fields, farms, houses, and other abandoned property into Israel's overburdened economy.

The largest concentration of remaining Arabs was in the western, central, and upper Galilee, from Nazareth northward. A smaller number remained in the frontier area acquired through the armistice agreement with Jordan. East of the narrow coastal strip, a few thousand Arabs remained in Ramle, Acre, Haifa, Jaffa, the Negev, and in several scores of smaller villages. These constituted Israel's new Arab citizenry which, by the end of 1949, numbered some 160,000 or about 12.5 percent of the population.

By the end of 1948, all these Arab populated areas, most of which were beyond the borders of the U.N. partition plan, were placed under military administration and divided into five military government regions—Nazareth, Western Galilee, Ramle-Lod, Jaffa, and the Negev. Throughout 1949, they were still called occupied territories. In 1950, an integrated system of military government was established, with policy directed and coordinated through the Ministry of Defense in Tel Aviv. Thus, a pattern for dealing with the Arab minority had been instituted, precedents established, attitudes shaped, and a momentum generated that was to continue, with minor modifications, until the military government was abolished in 1966.

I will not enter into a detailed discussion of the Defense (Emergency) Regulations under which the military government operated or the various rules, regulations, and modus operandi of the military government. These have been described, discussed, and debated in numerous other studies including my own, *Israel and the Palestine Arabs*, one of the first critical examinations of the military government regime. It is important, however, to examine the mind-set of those who established this early policy towards the Arab population.

From 1948 until 1953, policy was controlled by David Ben Gurion in his dual capacity as Prime Minister and Minister of Defense. He was assisted by the Office of the Advisor to the Prime Minister on Arab Affairs, which ostensibly was responsible for civil affairs in the Arab community. This office replaced the short-lived Ministry of Minorities and Police, although Police remained a ministry. Within a few months, control of minority affairs was concentrated in Ben Gurion's office where, through his Arab Affairs Advisor, he directed civil matters. As Minister of Defense, he was also responsible for security matters and those related to the military government.

What was Ben Gurion's perception of the Arab community and how to deal with it? It must be emphasized that his overriding concern was the security of the Jewish state, with particular emphasis on its Jewishness. He did not perceive Israel as a Jewish-Arab entity, as some form of binational state. Throughout all his writings, there is continued emphasis on Israel's Jewishness and on Israel as the state, not only of its citizens, but of world Jewry.

There is very little, if any reference in Ben Gurion's post-1948 statements to the multi-ethnic or binational character of Israel, and very little reference to the Arab minority or to the role that it was to play. Perhaps Ben Gurion's attitude was best epitomized by his description of Israel in a speech to the Twenty-Fifth World Zionist Congress in Jerusalem during 1960. "In Israel there are not two spheres," he asserted.

> Here everybody is both Jewish and universal: the soil we walk upon, the trees whose fruit we eat, the roads on which we travel, the houses we live in, the factories where we work, the schools where our children are educated, the army in which they are trained, the ships we sail in and the planes in which we fly, the language we speak and the air we breath, the landscape we see and the vegetation that surrounds us—*all* of it is Jewish.[2]

While these remarks may be attributed to poetic license, they do imply a conception of the new state that overlooks its dual nature. Perhaps we can characterize it as "benign neglect," for rather than assigning

Israel's Arab citizens to a particular category, his words convey the image of a new, de-Arabized Israel. In his essay "Israel among the Nations," the Prime Minister's introduction to the 1952 *Israel Government Yearbook*, Ben Gurion, overlooking the fact that 12.5 percent of Israel's population was Arab, writes that the new State of Israel "was set up in a desert land," and that after the Arabs fled the country, "it was virtually emptied of its former owners."[3] Such references to Arabs as there are in these early exhortative writings about the new state refer to the surrounding nations, their deep animosity to Israel, and the urgency for the country to maintain its security against attack.

A key to understanding Ben Gurion's attitudes towards and perception of Palestinian Arabs can be found in his writings and comments about them during the mandatory era. During the 1930s he, like many in the Labor movement, blamed the *effendi* class for Arab opposition to Jewish settlement in Palestine.

> The majority of the Arab population know that the Jewish immigration and colonization are bringing prosperity to the land. Only the narrow circles of the Arab ruling strata have egotistical reasons to fear the Jewish immigration, and the social and economic changes caused by it. The self-interest of the majority of the Arab inhabitants is not in conflict with Jewish immigration and colonization, but on the contrary is in perfect harmony with it.[4]

While, according to Shabtai Teveth, Ben Gurion later adopted a more realistic view of the extent and depth of Arab nationalist sentiment, many in the Labor movement, especially in Hashomer Hatzair, continued to regard Arab hostility and opposition to Zionism as something that could be overcome with "good works" on behalf of the peasant and working classes.

Once Ben Gurion accepted the principle of partition, the logic of the situation led him to increasingly recognize a need for population transfer. Without such a solution, he was convinced, any partitioned Jewish state would contain an unwieldy and dangerous Arab minority. This was especially evident in Galilee. "It *can* be done," he wrote. "We must prepare ourselves to carry out the transfer scheme." In a letter dating from that period to his sixteen-year-old son, Ben Gurion wrote:

> We have never wanted to dispossess the Arabs. . . . But because Britain is giving them part of the country which had been promised to us, it is only fair that the Arabs in our state be transferred to the Arab portion.[5]

By the late 1930s Ben Gurion, according to Teveth, was "led by circumstances to adopt the language of force." Since the Arabs were determined to break the *yishuv* by force, "displays of good will and attempts at dialogue would not mitigate the conflict." Since war between Jews and Arabs was inevitable, it was necessary to acquire great Jewish strength, for only after the Arabs "had despaired of ever destroying the Zionist enemy would they make peace with a force that they could not break."[6]

As the situation of the Jews in Europe rapidly deteriorated and the specter of war loomed larger, Ben Gurion increasingly emphasized that "facts" rather than "abstract moral calculations of Justice" would determine the fate of the Jews. A Jewish state would further the cause of peace and enable the Jews to "become a force, and the Arabs respect force." In order to survive in this world, Ben Gurion observed, "the Jewish people needed cannons more than Justice."[7]

Ben Gurion further observed that, based on his experience in Palestine, "even the best Arabs" did not welcome the Jews in the country. Both Arabs who supported terror and those opposed to it were united in demands for an end to Jewish immigration and full independence for Arab Palestine. "The Arab is a political creature who is unable to withstand the pressures of his environment, or the emotive and collective drives of his people."[8]

Teveth observes that, although he publicly supported the idea between 1919 and 1929, Ben Gurion never really believed that Jews and Arabs could reconcile their differences through class solidarity. This was a tactic "born of pragmatism rather than profundity of conviction." Nor did Ben Gurion believe political compromise, which he professed between 1929 and 1936, to be feasible. The Arabs "would reconcile themselves to the Jewish presence only after they conceded their inability to destroy it," that is, when they recognized the superior strength of the Jewish nation.

Ben Gurion characterized the idea that Zionism should selflessly aid the Arabs as "moral corruption." While the Arab Bureau of the Jewish Agency maintained an informal network of ties with Arabs prior to 1948, it realized that Ben Gurion believed that there was no possibility for a peaceful settlement. Accordingly, the Bureau's activities were confined to intelligence and "maneuvers to split Arab ranks."[9]

Following the establishment of the state in May 1948, with control of the minority concentrated largely in agencies (Ministry of Defense and Prime Minister's Office) under Ben Gurion's domination, his attitudes were frequently reflected in government policy towards the Arabs. On the one hand, the areas where Arabs lived had to be integrated into the Jewish state. On the other hand, insofar as the Arab population of these areas was not yet trusted, they were perceived as a potential, if not actual, security risk.

Consolidation of the Arab-inhabited areas into the state through a variety of measures pertaining to land and property was principally achieved through the Custodian of Absentee Property, to be discussed below. Security was to be maintained through strict enforcement by the military government of the Defense (Emergency) Regulations and concomitant measures. Implementation of this policy was almost totally in the hands of Israeli officials and military officers affiliated with Ben Gurion's Mapai party.

Policy towards the minority often became the focus of inter-party disagreement, with other parties accusing Mapai of using its control of those government ministries responsible for minority policy for its own, that is, for Mapai advantage. Charges were leveled that, through the Custodian of Absentee Property, controlled by Mapai's Ministry of Finance, the party and those affiliated with it were reaping large material benefits such as the acquisition of former Arab lands by Mapai-affiliated *kibbutzim*. Other charges claimed that through its control of the Arab population by means of the Mapai-dominated Ministry of Defense, the military government organized Arab political support for Mapai or for its Arab-affiliated parties during the first three Knesset elections.

Many civil libertarians were apprehensive about the way in which the IDF administered the military government and enforced the Defense (Emergency) Regulations which had been inherited by the new state from the former British mandatory government. Although the *yishuv* had almost unanimously opposed such legislation during the Mandate when British authorities imposed it on the Jewish community, now many complained that the new state was itself imposing the same hated laws on its newly acquired minority.

Some members of Israel's judiciary initially opposed use of the emergency regulations, citing Jewish opposition to them during the Mandate. In a case brought to the Supreme Court in 1948–49, Justice Shalom Kassan maintained that the regulations were illegal and that, if the mandatory courts had not crossed them off the statute book, "this court is honor-bound to do so and to utterly eradicate them" because they "abolish the rights of citizens and, in particular, the control of the competent courts over the actions of the authorities."[10]

In the first five years of the state, the Israeli courts frequently raised questions about what they perceived to be misuse by the military of its authority over the Arab minority. While the IDF believed that complete legal protection and civil liberty for the country's Arabs would jeopardize national defense, the courts, although recognizing the need for emergency measures, periodically called the security authorities to task for disregarding the law and minority rights. Although, according to the judiciary, national security was the predominant consideration, total disregard for civil liberty endangered the nation's future no less than enemy attacks.

According to the judiciary, maintenance of legal guarantees for Arab citizens was not inconsistent with the army's principal task of defending the frontiers. On several occasions, when the military ordered the expulsion of inhabitants in military government areas, the courts intervened to protect Arabs who were legal residents. In a case involving the IDF's failure to recognize a writ of *habeas corpus*, the court found it necessary to remind the Minister of Defense that: "The authorities are subordinate to the law as is any citizen of the state."[11] If the authorities disregard the rule of law and of the limitations placed by the legislature on the use of emergency powers, then both the interests of the public and of the state would be endangered. Preservation of civil rights, stated the court, was no less significant than national security.

One of the most notable confrontations between the military and the judiciary concerned the IDF's removal of the Arab population from the northern border village of Iqrit. After surrendering to the IDF on 31 October 1948, the villagers were asked to leave for fifteen days because of "security reasons." Most left with only enough personal belongings for two weeks, but five years later the army still gave no indication that it would permit them to return. When the case was brought to the High Court of Justice in 1953, the court did not dispute the army's right to evacuate a population in times of emergency. However, questioning the procedures followed to prevent the return of the villagers after termination of the emergency, it ordered the army to permit the inhabitants to go home. The IDF responded by destroying most of the village and refusing to obey the court.[12]

Throughout the early period of confrontation between the High Court of Justice and the Ministry of Defense, the judiciary viewed principles of English law as consistent with the spirit motivating establishment of the state and with its declaration of independence.

Accordingly, they frequently delved into English law in search of precedents. In the court's opinion, the most important aspect of individual rights was not their declaration, but their implementation:

> The difference in the relationship between British courts and administrative bodies and those of Israel [was] one of attitude. In England this relationship has worked itself out through experience over the past three hundred years. Today it is an accepted part of the country's unwritten constitution that no administrative tribunal would deliberately flout a court order. In Israel the relationship between the High Court of Justice and administrative tribunals, such as those of the army, [was] not yet . . . worked out. Although the spirit of English law pervades the courts and their decisions, it [had] not yet been accepted by the military.[13]

Soon after the military regime was established, questions were raised about it by various parties in the Knesset. As early as July 1949, the government itself introduced a bill to repeal the emergency regulations, but it was finally dropped. Mapam's Aharon Zisling introduced a similar bill in May 1950. That bill was referred to the Knesset's Constitution, Law, and Justice Committee, whose findings were inconclusive. A year later, Zisling again raised the issue and this time it was referred to the Committee on Foreign Affairs and Security. After a week, the Knesset declared the regulations "incompatible with the principles of a democratic society" and asked the Constitution Committee to present a new defense bill within two weeks. But the bill was never prepared, and the question was deferred until 1951 when the Foreign Affairs Committee stated that "as long as the present security situation between the state of Israel and its neighbors continues, the military government has to be maintained for the protection of the nation."[14]

Throughout the annual debates over the renewal of the emergency regulations and the powers of the military government, Ben Gurion consistently defended their use. During a Knesset debate on the issue in 1953 he observed:

> We opposed this law of the Mandate government because a foreign government, neither elected by us, nor responsible to us, had given itself the right to detain any one of us without trial. In the present instance the law is being applied by the state of Israel, through a government chosen by the people and responsible to them.[15]

The Ministry of Defense argued that the issue was not really a minority problem, but one of security. Its officials stated that the issue was analogous to the Russo-Turkish border where, even in peacetime,

Ankara maintains the most rigid controls over the Kurdish minority. Similarly, they insisted, was it not necessary to enforce strict controls along Israel's frontiers, where there was continued incitement and hatred of Israel? Even though there was no peace, Israel's Arabs continued to maintain their family and commercial connections with contacts in "enemy" territory. Israeli intelligence was convinced that the neighboring states were exerting pressure on Israel's minority through psychological warfare, through radio broadcasts from the Arab states, through personal pressure on Israeli Arabs by agents from across the borders, and through murder of Israeli Arabs considered "too friendly with the Jews." To the IDF, refusal of many frontier villages to cooperate with the government in absorbing internal refugees or to accept compensation for lands seized by the government was evidence of their questionable loyalty. Also, according to the military, there was continued evidence of influence by the former Mufti of Jerusalem, al-Haj Amin al-Husayni, in the Arab community.

Despite the extensive influence of Ben Gurion and the security arguments of the Ministry of Defense, there were pockets of strong opposition from political parties both within and outside the governing coalition to government policy towards the Arab minority. This opposition persisted despite charges by the Defense Minister that it was "a provocation of the Arab minority against the State of Israel."[16] In May 1951, Mapam, the United Religious Front, the General Zionists, Herut, the Communists, and two members of the Sephardim party supported a Knesset resolution declaring the Defense (Emergency) Regulations of 1945 a danger to the democratic foundations of the state. By a vote of 53 to 1 with 40 abstentions, the Knesset approved a resolution instructing the Constitution Committee to draft a law to replace the emergency regulations. However, the committee failed to present new legislation, thus leaving the emergency laws on the books. In February 1952 the Knesset reversed itself and passed another resolution stating that: "As long as the present security situation continues and the existing relationship between Israel and its Arab neighbors remains unchanged, the Military Government must continue to protect national security."[17]

Questions concerning the property of the Arab minority living in strategic border areas were second in importance only to questions concerning their loyalty to the state. Those responsible for government policy believed it necessary to control not only the Arab population, but the villages and land where this population lived. Initially land and property abandoned by Arabs was placed under control of the Custodian of Absentee Property, a branch of the Ministry of Finance. Although the Absentee Property Law was formulated for the purpose of dealing with property abandoned by the refugees, it was also imposed on several thousand Israeli Arab citizens as well. Although they had never left the country, some 30,000 Arabs had fled from one place to another within Israel. Applying the Absentee Property Law, the government classified any person who may have traveled to Beirut or to Bethlehem (in Jordanian hands) during the latter days of the Mandate, even for a one-day visit, as an absentee. The term used to designate these individuals was "present absentee."

Through the Absentee Property Law, the Custodian of Absentee Property, and subsequent legislation passed by the Knesset dealing with lands seized by the government for security and for development purposes, the state acquired a substantial proportion of the agricultural areas that had belonged to Israeli Arab citizens. Estimates of land acquired by the state from its Arab citizens varied from 300,000 to one million dunams, as much as 40 percent of Israeli Arab land. Transfer of this agricultural land from Arab to Jewish hands was a major factor in the depeasantization of Israel's Arab community and the basic shift in its occupational patterns from farming to other pursuits.

Israel's Arab community obviously opposed these measures, and even Knesset members of the Mapai-affiliated Arab parties spoke out against them. As early as November 1948, Mrs. Beba Idelson, a member of the Provisional State Council, called the problem to the attention of the Prime Minister, who promised an investigation. Jewish Knesset members from across the political spectrum proposed amendments to the Absentee Property Law that would diminish its impact on the country's Arab citizens. Members of Mapam saw no reason why the state should prevent any citizen from returning to his or her property. Ben-Ami of the Sephardim believed that the law endangered the whole community; he feared that it delegated far too much power to the Custodian.

Even members of the nationalist Herut party feared that the law defined "absentee" too stringently; they too were apprehensive about the extensive powers delegated to the Custodian's office. The opposition General Zionist and Herut parties suspected favoritism by the Mapai Finance Minister who appointed the Custodian, a political plum which gave the Finance Ministry control over a quarter of Israel's wealth. One General Zionist Knesset member attacked the Custodian's office as a "secret organization" operating free of parliamentary control. He accused the Custodian of distributing 90 percent of absentee property to Mapai-controlled institutions such as Tnuva, Hamashbir Hamerkazi, and Solel Boneh, while depriving non-Mapai and private institutions of such benefits.[18]

Other objections to the law came from the former Mapam Minister of Agriculture, Aharon Zisling, who maintained that, because it provided for no long-term planning, it would undermine the country's Arab economy. The newspaper *Haaretz*, agreeing that the law jeopardized possibilities of integrating the country's Arab citizens, called for amendments lest "Israel condemns them to a life of perpetual poverty."[19] Growing restiveness among Israel's Arab community led to a campaign of written and public protests. In June 1951 more than 7,000 Arabs from fourteen villages in Galilee met in Acre to form an organization to fight for return of their land.

In the Knesset, a front was organized against these attacks by Finance Minister Eliezer Kaplan. Kaplan argued that the legislation was necessary to prevent illegal acquisition of absentee property and to assure that it would be used for national development. With this in mind, the Ministers of Finance and Agriculture cooperated in distributing some one million dunams of absentee agricultural land. According to Kaplan, the task of saving abandoned citrus groves and preventing deterioration of irrigation facilities required that the Custodian and the government be provided with broad powers.

The question of absentee property belonging to Israeli Arab citizens was a "delicate matter" involving "national security," Kaplan maintained. While defending equal rights for all citizens, he asked, "Can we disregard the fact that we are still surrounded by enemy countries who have repeatedly declared that they intend to open a second round?" In defense of the land legislation, Kaplan argued, "We must take precautions." This was such a sensitive matter in Israel's international relations and in dealings with her neighbors that complete answers concerning the status of absentee property could not always be given.[20]

Israel's judiciary was often highly critical of the manner in which the Custodian of Absentee Property used his powers and carried out his mandate. In several cases, it maintained that the Absentee Property Law was unnecessarily severe and unfair to Arab citizens of Israel. On occasion, the High Court of Justice accused the Custodian's office of

using its powers arbitrarily to deprive Arab claimants of their property for no valid legal reason. In one case, the court observed:
> this case amounts to an abuse of the law. . . . The Custodian thought that these regulations grant him unlimited power to violate or cancel binding agreements. He attempted to lend this action a legal appearance by issuing a verdict favorable to himself . . .[21]

By the early 1950s, several laws were passed to facilitate absorption of land and property acquired through the Custodian of Absentee Property into Israel's economy. This legislation caused great concern among Israeli Arabs, who feared that their "absentee" property would also be disposed of in this way. As a result of this apprehension and of interest in the matter by a number of Jewish Knesset members who believed that the minority was being treated unfairly, the Custodian began to release property to Arab citizens as early as 1949.

By 1954, over 100,000 dunams of land were leased to about 5,000 Arab families in some 100 villages, mostly refugees or absentees who had never left Israel. In 1953, legislation was adopted offering compensation for some 300,000 dunams of land which had formerly belonged to the country's Arab citizens. However, this Compensation Law was opposed by the Knesset's seven Arab members, by Mapam, and by the Communists mainly because it appeared to them to undervalue land seized by the government. Furthermore, the opponents of the Compensation Law argued, it prevented the return of certain lands seized from Arab citizens for "security" reasons, while permitting the former owners to lease these holdings from the Custodian.

The Israel daily *Haaretz* opposed the Compensation Law because it legalized seizure of Arab lands by collective settlements desiring to increase their own property. The newspaper commented: "There is no reason to legalize the fact that certain farms exploited the victory of the State in the defensive war against invaders, to seize for their own benefit the lands of their neighbors . . ." The law, according to *Haaretz*, was a threat to the agricultural sector of the Arab community and failed to recognize that "seizure of the minority's property is liable to undermine the foundations of private property rights."[22]

Two principles emerged from government policy relating to Arab property, one regarding the owners, the other concerning use of the property. As it became clear that most former owners who fled the country would not return, steps were taken to end their property ownership in Israel. Because much "absentee" property belonged to Israeli Arabs who resided in strategic border areas, there was, initially, little distinction made between them and the refugees who left the country. Failure to separate management of property taken from Israeli Arabs from property of those who had left the country often resulted in inequitable treatment.

As a result of internal Jewish and Arab pressures, the government was forced to rectify many measures considered discriminatory. The Land Acquisition Law, containing provisions for compensation to Arab citizens, was one measure which attempted to differentiate the Arab minority within Israel from Palestinians in enemy territory. But even this legislation was regarded as discriminatory by the country's Arab citizenry and by several Jewish groups.

Policy relating to use of this property was intimately linked with the influx of new immigrants and their absorption into the country. By using Arab property, the government facilitated the settlement of the hundreds of thousands of immigrants who poured into Israel during its first three or four years. "The new population followed a fundamental law of nature and filled the vacuum left by the Arab refugees" and by the country's own Arab minority.[23]

Other early government policies that reflected disagreements within the Jewish community regarding ways of dealing with the Arab minority relate to: (1) questions of residence and nationality; (2) wage differences between Jews and Arabs; (3) prices paid for Arab agricultural products; (4) Arab labor; (5) membership in the Histadrut trade union federation; (6) service in the Israeli armed forces; (7) education; (8) local government; and (9) taxation. Detailed discussion of each of these subjects is not feasible in this chapter. However, a brief examination of the differing perspectives on these policies within the Israeli Jewish political spectrum might be useful.

The 1950 Law of Return and the 1952 Nationality Law underscored Ben Gurion's perception of Israel as a distinctively Jewish state. They emphasized Israel's unique Jewish character, which was either stated directly or implied in such international documents as the League of Nations Mandate for Palestine and the United Nations General Assembly's partition resolution, as well as in Israel's Proclamation of Independence.

The Law of Return authorized the immigration of "every Jew" to the country, while the Nationality Law bestowed citizenship automatically on any person entering the country under the Law of Return.

Others, such as the country's Arab residents, could acquire citizenship through residence, birth, or naturalization. Legal Arab residents of the country who registered on 1 March 1952 could obtain automatic citizenship if they could prove that they had been Palestinian citizens. Non-Jewish children born in Israel of parents who met these conditions were citizens by birth. Non-Jews (Arabs) born in the country who did not meet these conditions had to be naturalized just like non-Jews entering Israel.

These two laws, the Law of Return and the Nationality Law, stated Ben Gurion, were the "charter" which "we have promised to every Jew in exile, who comes to the State of Israel." They confirmed that Israel is not only a Jewish state, "but a state for all Jews. . . . This right is inherent in his being a Jew." This "right to return," he added, "preceded the State of Israel and it built the state."[24]

While no Arab Knesset member, even those in the Communist party, disputed these principles, they all believed that the conditions required of an Arab to prove his citizenship rights by "residence" were discriminatory. Many Arabs, having lost their identity cards during the turmoil of the war, had no proof of Palestinian citizenship, and many had been bypassed during the 1 March 1952 Registration of Inhabitants. Arab Knesset members and their Jewish supporters believed that all who were born in the country should receive automatic citizenship. Communist Knesset members estimated that the Nationality Law would bar half the country's Arabs from citizenship, although the Minister of the Interior stated that no more than 6,000 would be barred.

Nazareth, Israel's largest Arab community, declared a general strike to protest the new legislation's discriminatory clauses. Additional protest demonstrations were organized in the Arab sections of Haifa and in the Arab villages of Western Galilee. *Haaretz* argued that the law was only further proof of the government's policy of pushing Israel's Arabs into the camp of the extreme left. The newspaper supported granting automatic citizenship to all Arabs with Israeli identity cards. The editors observed that the lesson of how to curtail minority rights had been learned too quickly.[25]

Early state policy towards management of Israeli Arab affairs often reflected a rather paternalistic, if not deeply suspicious attitude. No Arabs were designated as officials in charge of Arab affairs in the various ministries. Rather, responsibility for such matters, even in ministries unrelated to security such as social welfare, agriculture, health, education, and the like, were entrusted to Jewish employees.

Thus a Jew was designated by the Ministry of Religious Affairs to control the religious foundations, *awqaf* (religious trusts), and other functions of the Muslim Supreme Council. This differed from mandatory practice in which such tasks had been managed by the community's own Muslim leaders. This appointment aroused such resentment among the shaykhs, qadis, and imams of the Muslim community that they sarcastically referred to their new employer, the first government-appointed director of Muslim affairs, as "Mufti Hirshberg."[26]

Not until 1952 or after were efforts made to equalize prices for agricultural products and wages of Arabs with those of the Jewish community. The government argued that existing differences compensated for the Arab community's failure to carry its share of the tax burden. Tax officials maintained that they collected almost no income tax and only a negligible property tax from members of the Arab community, and that the government thus became responsible for funding local services such as roads, new wells, irrigation facilities, and schools.

During the first years of the state, the government maintained separate labor offices for Jews and Arabs. Until May 1953, members of the minority were organized in separate Arab labor organizations, the Histadrut's Israel Labor League and the Communist-controlled Arab Trade Union Congress. The Histadrut executive voted to admit Arab workers into its affiliated trade unions in May 1953 and accepted them as full members in April 1957.

Those responsible for Arab affairs in the Prime Minister's Office had little confidence in the ability of the Arab community to manage its own local affairs. Joshua Palmon, one of the first principal advisors to Ben Gurion on Arab affairs, believed it unwise to permit Arab communities to elect their own local councils because:

> Democratic elections will only augment family feuds and are not in keeping with the existing conditions in the Arab community. The establishment of local councils is also bound to lead to bloodshed. In the Arab community, one must choose a "middle road" of not-too-much democracy.[27]

Differences in outlook between Arab village elders and officials of the new state caused major difficulties. During the Mandate, a tradition of self-taxation had developed in the *yishuv* to finance the highly integrated system of social services and education, a tradition that continued after the state was established. However, under the Mandate, the government had provided the Arab community with most local services, especially in rural areas. Such services as education, roads, health services, and water supply were usually introduced by the mandatory government at its own expense. No local levies other than a nominal property tax were imposed. This led Jews and Arabs to develop differing expectations.

Differences caused by these differing expectations were especially bitter in the matter of financing education. Arab villages agreed to pay for their own school buildings, as they did during the Mandate. However, they insisted that the Israeli government, like the mandatory government, cover the cost of school operations, teachers' salaries, supplies, and other such costs, whereas the Ministry of Education insisted that the local communities contribute to these expenses.

Among the many ambiguities in government policy towards the Arab minority was the one resulting from the conflicting perspectives of different ministries. Within the governing coalition, parties with diverse philosophies controlled different government ministries and offices. Consequently, these ministries had different policies for dealing with the Arab minority, although the most powerful ministries were controlled by Mapai and dominated by Ben Gurion. Other parties accused Mapai of using its powerful and privileged position to influence the minority vote in elections to the Knesset. Indeed, Mapai and its Arab-affiliated lists captured 61.3 percent of the Arab vote in 1949, 66.5 percent in 1951, and approximately the same percentage in 1955. Although other parties attempted to undercut Mapai, only the Communists made a respectable showing. Parties like the General Zionist and Mapam charged that, owing to Mapai's control of the military government, it was able to influence the Arab electorate through use of carrot or stick, by promising to improve conditions, or threatening to make life difficult for those who did not vote for the "Government" (perceived by most Arabs as Mapai).

During these early years, most Israeli newspapers were critical of the inconsistencies and ambiguities in government policy towards the Arab minority. Even the *Jerusalem Post*, at the time perceived as an unofficial organ of Mapai, wrote that implementing the government's policy of equality in theory and practice "is complicated both by administrative and security considerations." It further pointed out that the division of Arab affairs among more than one authority often caused confusion. "Nothing is more likely to cause unrest and discontent than divided control," it warned.[28]

The General Zionist daily, *Haboker*, sharply criticized Ben Gurion's Ministry of Defense for its handling of Arab affairs. Even though the General Zionists were members of the government coalition at the time, *Haboker* called for abrogation of the military government and the instituting of a system of elections for Arab local councils. "Citizenship in a democratic country cannot be granted by installments," *Haboker* insisted. It called upon Israel's Jewish citizenry to remember their own treatment as a minority and "not to forget so soon their days under Pharaoh."[29] The Agudat Israel organ, *Hamodia*, complained that the country's political parties, in their struggle for votes, had "turned the Arab villages into political battlegrounds, . . . were issuing promises that they could not keep, and blaming each other for the natural and unalterable situation of the Arabs."[30]

One of the most divisive questions that confronted the government of the new State of Israel was whether to work toward integrating the country's Arabs or maintain a policy of separation. This question has divided those concerned about relations with the Arab minority since the state was established more than forty years ago. The majority, then as now, maintained that Israel cannot be both Jewish and democratic. They argued that if the country's Arabs are integrated into society, it would lead to a binational rather than a Jewish state. As Palmon observed: "I opposed the integration of Arabs into Israeli society. I preferred separate development. True, this prevented the Arabs from integrating into the Israeli democracy. . . . The separation made it possible to maintain a democratic regime within the Jewish population alone."[31]

NOTES

1. Cited in Ian Lustick, *Arabs in the Jewish State* (Austin and London: University of Texas Press, 1980), 37.
2. *New York Times*, "Address by Prime Minister Ben Gurion," 8 January 1961, 52–53.
3. *Israel Government Year-Book 5713 (1952)* (Jerusalem: Government Printer, 1952), 21.
4. Cited in Enzo Sereni and R. E. Ashery, eds., *Jews and Arabs in Palestine: Studies in a National and Colonial Problem* (New York: Hechalutz Press, 1936), 149.
5. Cited in Shabtai Teveth, *Ben-Gurion and the Palestinian Arabs from Peace to War* (Oxford and New York: Oxford University Press, 1985), 181–82.
6. Ibid., 186.
7. Ibid., 191.
8. Ibid., 198.
9. Ibid., 199–200.
10. Cited in Sabri Jiryis, *The Arabs in Israel* (New York and London: Monthly Review Press, 1976), 13–14.
11. *Psaqim shel Bayt ha-Mishpat ha-Elyon be-Israel* (Judgments of the Supreme Court of Israel) (Tel Aviv: Israel Lawyer's Society, 1948–49), booklet no. 4, p. 97, file no. 7/48, cited in Don Peretz, *Israel and the Palestine Arabs* (Washington, D.C.: Middle East Institute, 1958), 115.
12. *Psaqim shel Bayt ha-Mishpat ha-Elyon be-Israel* (Tel Aviv: Israel Lawyer's Society, 1951), booklet no. 13–14, pp. 461–66, file no. 64/61, cited in Peretz, *Israel and the Palestine Arabs*, 116–17.
13. Cited in Peretz, *Israel and the Palestine Arabs*, 117–18.
14. Cited in Jiryis, *Arabs in Israel*, 33.
15. Ibid., 14.
16. Cited in Peretz, *Israel and the Palestine Arabs*, 99.
17. Ibid., 99–100.
18. *Divrei ha-Knesset*, vol. iii, 38–40, 140–42, 153, 155–56, 159–60.
19. *Haaretz*, 20 March 1950; 2 July 1951; cited in Peretz, *Israel and the Palestine Arabs*, 172.
20. Cited in Peretz, *Israel and the Palestine Arabs*, 173–74.
21. Ibid., 178–79.
22. *Haaretz*, 10 March 1953, cited in Peretz, *Israel and the Palestine Arabs*, 185–86.
23. Peretz, *Israel and the Palestine Arabs*, 186.
24. *Divrei ha-Knesset*, vol. vi, 2035–37, cited in Peretz, *Israel and the Palestine Arabs*, 122.
25. *Haaretz*, 3 April 1953.

26. Peretz, *Israel and the Palestine Arabs*, 126.
27. *Al ah-Mishmar*, 13 January 1953; *Ner*, February 1953, p. 21; cited in Peretz, *Israel and the Palestine Arabs*, 129.
28. *Jerusalem Post*, 11 August 1953; 7 September 1953; cited in Peretz, *Israel and the Palestine Arabs*, 106.
29. *Haboker*, 3 and 10 August 1953; 6 September 1953; cited in Peretz, *Israel and the Palestine Arabs*, 107–8.
30. *Hamodia*, 3 September 1953; cited in Peretz, *Israel and the Palestine Arabs*, 107.
31. Tom Segev, *1949—The First Israelis* (New York and London: The Free Press, 1986), 67.

CHAPTER 6

Initial Israeli Policy Guidelines towards the Arab Minority, 1948—1949

ELIE REKHESS

The problem of the Arab minority in Israel came into being at the conclusion of the 1948 War of Independence. The nearly 150,000 Arabs who chose to stay in their homes and become Israeli citizens remained, at the same time, emotionally, nationally, culturally, and confessionally bound to the outside Arab world. This resulted in a serious crisis of loyalty and identity. Against this complex background, Israel set out to formulate its policy towards the Arab minority.

Before 1948, little thought had been given to the possibility that the future state of Israel might harbor an Arab minority. The Zionist movement hardly dealt with the matter. Zionist Congresses did no more than pass noncommittal resolutions couched in generalities on the desirable, almost idealistic, future of Jewish-Arab relations. Equality of rights was mentioned in broad terms, but there was no in-depth discussion of its ideological significance or practical implications.[1]

The initial line adopted by the government was a middle-of-the-road solution, an attempt to find a compromise between two contradictory approaches: one that was security-oriented and viewed the Arabs as an "enemy-affiliated minority"; and another, drawing upon liberal and democratic principles, that argued for the equality of all citizens and for the integration of the Arab minority into Israeli life.

The state's commitment to the principle of equality was first expressed in the Declaration of Independence: "The State of Israel . . . will uphold the full social and political equality of all its citizens, without distinction of religion, race, or sex; [it] will guarantee freedom of religion, conscience, education and culture."[2] The same principle, in a somewhat more detailed formulation, underlay the relevant sections of Israel's first government program presented to the Knesset on 8 March 1949:

> In the law which will stabilize the democratic and republican regime in the State of Israel, total equality of rights and obligations will be assured to all citizens, irrespective of religion, race and nationality, [and] freedom of religion, conscience, language, education, and culture will be guaranteed.[3]

All successive governments reaffirmed these tenets in principle, changes in language notwithstanding.

Attitudinally, the liberal approach had its roots in specific considerations relevant to the past history of the Jewish people. Several Israeli leaders were keenly aware that the Jews—themselves a persecuted minority for many centuries—now had an opportunity to prove, first and foremost to themselves, how they would relate to a minority in their midst. Their treatment of the Arab minority would illustrate, it was contended, that the evolving Jewish-Israeli society was firmly based on the liberal, humanistic, democratic tradition.[4]

This liberal attitude was echoed in the writings of the period and was reflected in some actions. In September 1948, Israel's first Minister of the Interior, Yitzhak Greenboim, made an official visit to Haifa in the course of which he met a delegation of the city's Arab community. From the way he addressed the Arab dignitaries, one could sense how uncomfortable and embarrassed he—a former Jewish deputy in the Polish Parliament—felt. Addressing Hajj Taha Karaman, then a deputy mayor, he said: "For many years I used to speak as the representative of a minority. It is not easy for me now to answer you in the capacity of a representative of the majority, addressing the delegates of a minority in the State of Israel."[5] Greenboim promised the Arabs that there would be "a single constitution for all inhabitants of Israel. The Jews have suffered too much to allow themselves to deal unjustly with Israel's Arab citizens."[6]

Yitzhak Ben Zvi, soon to become the country's second president, addressed the same issue in an essay published in September 1949. "For generations we were enriched by the miserable experience of a [Jewish] minority's attitudes towards the [non-Jewish] majority—but not the other way around. Can we get used to being just rulers?"[7] he asked, and replied: "We shall have to."[8] Ben Zvi suggested that the approach towards the Arabs should be based on study and education.

Referring to the emergence of a new Israeli society, marked as it was by the waves of mass immigration, he wrote: "We must educate ourselves, educate our children, our officials and teachers, our soldiers and policemen, and the new immigrants. . . . We must tell [the new immigrants] that we are not like the Poles in Poland and the Arabs are not like the Jews in Poland."[9] Ben Zvi, himself, contributed to the effort of educating the uninformed Israelis. As a historian of Palestine in the early Arab and Ottoman periods, his articles combined updated political analysis with historical survey and background information on the Muslim, Christian, and Druze communities in Israel.[10]

The issue of moral obligations was also taken up by Pinhas Lubianiker (Lavon), who later became Israel's Minister of Defense. Addressing the new experience of having to live "with a minority, and not as a minority," Lavon stated that this required the Jews to "set an example."[11] Lavon attached great significance to the process of confidence-building between Israeli Arabs and Jews. For him it was an "existential matter" of primary importance. Much like Ben Zvi, he regarded education as the core issue. In his view, there were two groups that needed special educational attention: native Israeli Jews who were growing up with a "simplistic nationalism," and Oriental Jews who had a desire to get even with the Arabs for the long "years of . . . oppression in Arab lands."[12]

Both Ben Zvi and Lavon addressed themselves to opposing schools of thought current in Israel at that time. Lavon, for example, contested the "autonomist" argument offered by some publicists. National autonomy for the Arab minority, he argued, would end up creating a "state within the state" and would encourage constant irredentist trends. Israel must, therefore, combine "centralized" administration with both individual liberties and the "greatest possible freedom for local communities."[13]

Ben Zvi, for his part, was sharply critical of those who advocated a population transfer. "It is unthinkable that the State of Israel should use force to remove the minorities against their will."[14] To do so, he insisted, would "run counter to the entire democratic and *Jewish* character [emphasis in the original] of our state."[15] A solely Jewish Israel was no more than a "theoretical possibility . . . neither just nor realistic nor reasonable," Ben Zvi further insisted.[16] There was only one unequivocal way: to accept the idea of an Arab minority in the state of Israel and to work towards the integration of "Muslims,

Christians, and Druzes as citizens with equal rights and as communities with equal rights in the state."[17]

Others, in those early days, argued on the basis of more abstract principles. Among them was the eminent Orientalist and jurist, H. Z. (J. W.) Hirschberg, who was the first to head the Muslim Department in the Ministry of Religions. He, for example, raised the question of whether the state was entitled to impose Western concepts of social and cultural development on its non-Jewish citizens.[18] Similarly, S. D. Goitein asked whether there should be a centralized approach to education or whether there should be a measure of decentralization which would leave room for local authorities and individual religious communities to lay down educational guidelines. "What should be the contents and the spirit of Arab education in Israel," he asked, "and what should be the underlying principles upon which we can base a 'truly public Arab education?'"[19]

Beyond the theoretical considerations and public debate, practical government policies needed to be worked out and put into effect. All Arabs remaining in the country were granted Israeli citizenship. Some 30,000 Arabs with voting rights participated in the first Knesset elections, held on 25 January 1949, and three Arab candidates were indeed elected to the Knesset. Arabic was virtually granted the status of an official language, although Hebrew was the state language. Coins, postage stamps, and banknotes had Arabic, as well as Hebrew inscriptions. The official gazette was published in Arabic as well as Hebrew. Arabs were free to address government departments and plead in courts in their own language. Arabic remained the language of instruction in all state-maintained Arab schools.

A Minorities Ministry (which will be discussed in detail below) was set up to coordinate the government's activities in the Arab sector, and initial steps in developing the Arab community were practically endorsed. This policy was reflected in several fields.[20] Shortly after the conclusion of hostilities, a social welfare network had been introduced into the Arab areas. By mid-1951, twelve welfare offices were operating. Arabic-speaking Jewish welfare workers were assigned to work in Arab districts, while special courses were organized for training Arab personnel. The social assistance rendered included the distribution of food, clothing, and footwear, and the care of babies, adolescents, and the aged, as well as sick and disabled persons. The Welfare Ministry operated twenty feeding centers at which 3,000 Arab students regularly received meals.

All but ten Arab doctors left the country at the time of the Palestinian exodus. The health authorities assumed responsibility for health care, first under the direction of the Ministry of Minorities and later directly through the Ministry of Health. By May 1949, fourteen clinics had been established in Arab areas; a year later the number rose to twenty-eight. In addition, clinics for mother and child care were opened in several Arab locations. By 1951, four mobile clinics were in operation, including two in remote areas inhabited by Bedouins. Medical services began to be provided in Arab schools. To overcome the severe shortage of Arab personnel in the medical services, district nurses were appointed and courses for Arab nurses were organized.

Following the establishment of the state, immediate efforts were made to rehabilitate the economy of the villages and promote Arab farming. The Ministry of Agriculture embarked on a Special Development Project which included, among others, the following programs: restoration of the olive groves; terracing of hilly regions; supplying five-hundred tons of wheat and barley seeds and expanding the areas cultivating these cereals; offering loans for modernizing the production systems; and installation of mobile units of mechanized agricultural equipment for villages with insufficient work animals. At the same time, the marketing of produce from Arab farms was organized largely on the same lines as Jewish farms.

Special efforts were also made to encourage the formation of Arab agricultural cooperative associations. By mid-1951, eighty-five new cooperatives had been established. The consequent results of these initial steps became evident in the 1950s in the extension of irrigated areas, increased mechanization as a result of increased profitability, increased credit granted, and diversification of crops.

The Arab educational system also underwent significant changes. Direct responsibility for schools was transferred to the local municipal authorities, in keeping with the Jewish system. The Compulsory Education Act of 1949 was fully applied to the Arab sector. Coeducation was introduced and, by December 1950, the number of coeducational schools exceeded the number of schools segregated by sex.

The implementation of these educational measures was not an easy task. Overall, the attempt to rehabilitate the educational system encountered tremendous difficulties and setbacks. There was a limited number of qualified teachers as a result of the exodus of most of the intelligentsia. There was also a significant shortage of textbooks and a lack of suitable schools.

Elementary education, nevertheless, made remarkable progress. While the number of Arab schools in December 1948 was only forty-six, with 180 teachers and some 7,000 pupils, the corresponding figures for the end of 1950–51 were 102 schools, 628 teachers, and 26,000 pupils. The increase in the number of state-maintained Arab schools from the end of 1948 to the summer of 1951 amounted to 122 percent; that in the number of teachers to 238 percent; and that in the number of pupils to 240 percent. By the end of 1951 the government had opened new elementary schools in thirty-five Arab villages which previously had no schools at all.

However, the circumstances of 1948, with the war still raging, greatly complicated the commitment to the principle of equality, and significantly limited the ability to bridge the existing gap between the majority and the minority (or minorities).[21] Consequently, more sober assessments of the process of integration soon appeared. One such assessment was written by Mikhael Assaf. The Arab affairs correspondent of the daily *Davar* and editor of *Al-Yawm*, an Arabic newspaper financed jointly by the government and the Histadrut (Trade Union Federation), Assaf was well versed in all matters concerning the local Arab population.

In 1949, Assaf spoke of integration as "a process turning Arabs into citizens with [no more than the] minimal and obligatory loyalty to the State of Israel."[22] His words reflected the perplexities of the period and the prevailing uncertainty concerning the future, even the immediate future. In particular, they reflected the security-oriented views which were soon to dominate practical policies towards the Arab community.

The security-oriented perspective was based on the assumption that the Arabs were "enemy-affiliated." Under the immediate impact of the battles of 1948 and burdened by the memories of thirty years of violent confrontation preceding the war, many Israelis came to view the Arab presence in Israel as a danger to the very existence of the state.

The impressions of the journalist Jon Kimche, who visited Nazareth in the summer of 1948 shortly after the Israeli capture of the town, were typical of the current security-oriented thinking. "The Arab states," he said, "will use the first opportunity to destroy Israel. Israel will have to live by the sword for many more years. Can it afford to let a large Arab minority exist in its midst?"[23]

A similar perception of the Arab minority as a potential "fifth column" was shared by Knesset member Meir Argov, then chairman of the Knesset's Foreign and Security Affairs Committee, as well as by other public figures.[24] This perception was summed up years later by Yigal Allon, who listed five potential dangers stemming from the presence in Israel of an Arab minority: espionage, sabotage, and terror; guerilla warfare; incitement and intimidation; a political struggle carried forward by demands for autonomy; and unrest and rioting at times of international tension.[25]

It must be stressed, however, that there was no clear-cut division between advocates of a security-oriented approach and supporters of the more liberal views. Rather than divide into two camps, many public figures labored to live with both views at one and the same time. Thus, Ben Zvi, while arguing for integration, also wrote: "We must not ignore the suspicion that the danger of a fifth column might emerge."[26] Similarly, Lavon stated: "It must not be forgotten that the Arabs, though a minority [in Israel], live in a state surrounded by tens of millions of Arabs in their own independent states. Today they are comparatively weak; tomorrow they may well be strong."[27]

Security-oriented policies towards the Arabs were pursued in three areas: the partial expulsion of Arabs from towns and villages during war-time operations and afterwards; the seizure of abandoned property and the expropriation of land holdings; and the institution of military government in areas densely populated by Arabs. The first two measures will not be discussed here; they have recently become the subject of several specialized studies which have aroused considerable public and academic controversy.[28] The third measure, military government, was introduced in order to prevent the return of refugees, to forestall border crossings by infiltrators, and to complete the evacuation of villages or urban neighborhoods partially abandoned during the war.

The military government's authority was virtually unlimited. Legally speaking, it drew on British mandatory emergency regulations issued in 1945, which made it possible to restrict the movements of Arab inhabitants and to seize land and other property. It also became an important means of political control and was soon used as an instrument for recruiting voters and supporters for various political parties, mainly the ruling Mapai party.

It must be noted, however, that just as there was no clear-cut division into ideological camps regarding the Arabs, so also was there no clear-cut government policy. The cabinet did not discuss policy towards the minorities as such, had no recognized process of decision making on the subject, and laid down no detailed guidelines for its agencies to follow. In addition to the need to respond to daily problems which might arise, the agencies were concerned with maintaining a general sense of loyalty to the principles of equal citizenship and integration while at the same time providing security for all.

Five ministries in particular dealt with Arab affairs: the Ministry of Finance, the Ministry of Defense (and the army), the Foreign Ministry, the Minorities Ministry, and the Prime Minister's Office. Our discussion will focus on the last three.

The Prime Minister's Office. Prime Minister David Ben Gurion did not, as a rule, deal personally with Arab minority affairs. Inasmuch as he did, he thought in terms of a "dual approach": equality and security. But he was well aware of the problematic nature of this combination. In 1953, he told the Knesset: "Possibly, here or there, someone is dealt with unfairly, as also happens, possibly, in the non-Arab sector." But, he went on, "I want our Arab citizens and inhabitants to know that our considered and determined policy is that of equality of rights and obligations."

Presumably having in mind the exemption of Arabs from military service, Ben Gurion added that greater strides had been made in equality of rights than in equality of duties.[29] Nonetheless, security considerations, according to Ben Gurion, had to be paramount: "The [present] situation along the borders is not our doing. We must work for security, and sometimes security considerations override the rights of individuals."[30] Ben Gurion's special advisor on Arab affairs, Yehoshua (Josh) Palmon, explained that the prime minister insisted on the principle of equality "as much as was feasible, up to some ill-defined 'red line'—ill-defined because it was liable to be drawn [at any particular time] as the result of specific developments and events that could not be foreseen."[31]

Ben Gurion regarded the situation as tentative and transient, for circumstances were constantly changing. As the war continued, there was much unfinished business, and it was important to be careful not to let matters "congeal" in ways which would make it difficult to change them later on.[32] For the most part, Ben Gurion was content to let the military government take care of security matters and allow the other ministries to deal with civilian questions falling within their domain.

The Foreign Ministry. The Foreign Ministry took a rather active role in the political affairs of the Arab minority. Already on 8 August 1948,

Foreign Minister Moshe Shertok (Sharett) wrote to the Minister of Minorities: "In all these political questions [concerning the Arab community], the Foreign Ministry lays down overall policy, except if the cabinet decides otherwise." Sharett suggested that working relations be established with Arab community leaders of varying political affiliations. He advocated, on the one hand, the integration of groups and individuals "who have worked with us for a long time." At the same time, he called for a "carefully controlled cooperation" with communist activists in Nazareth, members of the left-wing League for National Liberation, and with former opponents who might now be willing to cooperate with the authorities on the basis of recognizing the state of Israel.[33]

There were several reasons for the Foreign Ministry's involvement in minority affairs. First, Arab affairs (as well as the issue of refugees) were considered an important aspect of information efforts abroad, which fell under the responsibility of the Foreign Ministry. Next, it was considered possible at the time that the question of Israeli Arabs might come up in an overall settlement of the Arab-Israeli conflict—again a Foreign Ministry matter. In Palmon's view, Sharett's involvement stemmed from the fact that he (Sharett) was the senior "Arabist" in the inner circles of the ruling Mapai party.[34] His long-standing connections among local Arabs qualified him to deal with them.

Sharett's views inclined towards the liberal and egalitarian end of the scale. He vigorously defended "the principles that have been laid down to govern the status of Israeli citizens—principles of equality and justice and of supplying the needs of everyone without discrimination."[35] Replying in 1950 to a Knesset motion on "discrimination against the Arab minority," Sharett described such claims as "a distortion of the reality," saying that the commitment to the principle of equality was not the exclusive "monopoly" of those factions who criticized Israeli policies. It was equally shared by the government and the ruling party, he hinted.[36]

Elsewhere and at other times Sharett stressed, for instance, the need for the military government to adopt "a more humane attitude and to deal more expertly with economic and administrative questions." He also mentioned the necessity to deal more speedily with Arabs who had become displaced within Israel and to be more forthcoming on matters of family reunification and on regulating the status of the Muslim *waqf* (religious endowment property).[37] But Sharett, too, thought in terms of the "dual approach" and gave unqualified support to the continued existence of the military government.[38]

For all that, Sharett's influence on actual developments in the Arab sector was limited. He passed on directives to other ministries, but these were—to quote Palmon—"rather by way of stating his philosophy." He did not follow through on them to ensure their full implementation.[39]

The Minorities Ministry. The Minorities Ministry was set up in May 1948 as part of the provisional government. Bekhor Shalom Shitrit, who was also Minister of Police, became the first person to head it.[40] It was apparently Shitrit himself who had taken the initiative for its establishment. In a memorandum he wrote shortly before the proclamation of the state, he proposed to concentrate all Arab affairs (security, property, food, trade and economy, and religious affairs) in a single ministry.[41]

Shitrit, a police officer and later a judge under the British Mandate, was a likable figure known for his good connections with many Arabs and his knowledge of their customs and lifestyle. He considered his appointment an opportunity and a mission, and thought of himself as a fitting link between the Arab population and the newly formed institutions of the Jewish state. He hoped to become the guide and advisor to other ministries regarding their contacts with the Arab sector.[42] The ministry set itself the task of convincing the Jewish population that the Israeli Arabs deserved to be seen in a positive light. Shitrit's views were similar to Ben Zvi's and to Lavon's. The ministry's task, Shitrit said, was to make Jews in the Diaspora and in Israel understand the complex situation of the Arab minority and bring them to adopt a "fair and equal" attitude towards the Arabs. This was all the more necessary, Shitrit argued, insofar as many Jews, especially new immigrants, did not know the Arabs and their ways and were prejudiced against them.[43]

As for the Arabs themselves, Shitrit held, they needed "gradually and slowly to get to know the new realities and come to terms with them; to grow to trust the Israeli government; and to acknowledge the concept of the existence of Israel."[44] He further believed that he would become "their mouthpiece,"[45] the "official address" to which they would turn with complaints or requests. The ministry, in cooperation with other government departments, would "see to it that the rights of the minorities were not disregarded and that they would be able to resume, as soon as possible, their normal lives." He further asserted,

"It is our heart's desire for the minorities to be content in our midst."[46] And indeed the main effort of the ministry was directed towards the rehabilitation of civilian life in the Arab sector and towards the rapid restoration of government services for it.[47]

The ministry's budget and staff were small. Its director-general, Gad Makhness, had thirty-three officials at his disposal. The ministry had two regional branch offices, in Haifa and in Jaffa. There were two departments: Rehabilitation and Promotion of Relations with the Minorities, headed by Moshe Erem;[48] and Information, Culture, and Education, headed by the writer Yehudah Burla. For a time, there was also a Legal Department (under Attorney Yisrael Shohat). Shitrit also hoped to add a Research Department to study minority problems not only in Israel, but throughout the Middle East. This department, however, did not come about.

The Rehabilitation Department acted as an intermediary between other government departments and the Arab public. For instance, in cooperation with the food inspector (in charge of the food rationing then in force) and the Ministries of Agriculture, Labor and Welfare, it succeeded (during a period of severe war-time shortages) in arranging for regular food supplies for the Arab sector, in securing the rights of farmers to cultivate lands, in sending agricultural instructors to the Arab villages, and in getting loans for farmers to buy seeds.[49]

Special efforts were made to fight unemployment. Towards the end of 1948, two "employment centers" in central Israel, one in Lydda and the other in Jaffa, were set up to direct Arab job seekers to citrus-picking jobs. Hundreds of other workers from Galilee came there as well. In cooperation with the immigrant offices of the Jewish Agency, steps were taken to employ skilled workers from the Arab sector.[50]

The Department of Information, Culture, and Education devoted its early efforts principally to a review of plans and directives relating to education in the Arab sector. In the practical sphere, it was involved with reopening schools, laying down curricula, and recruiting teachers. Two of its major actions were the establishment of an Arabic daily, *Al-Yawm*, and an Arabic library in Jaffa that stocked tens of thousands of books. It also dealt with the formation of representative committees in the Arab towns and neighborhoods of mixed towns.

The ministry's policy bore the stamp of the liberal approach. Yet, when required to weigh military and political considerations against liberal principles, it came down on the side of the former. Nonetheless, as one researcher put it, Shitrit searched for a compromise designed to protect those liable to suffer from planned military operations, even if he was not always successful in preventing them from being carried out.[51]

Shitrit himself stated that his staff made every effort to arrive in any newly occupied area promptly in order to work for the "restoration of normal life there and the prevention of acts of injustice."[52] The following are examples of such efforts. In September 1948, a ministry representative objected to the destruction of fourteen villages east of Lydda that had been planned by General Zvi Ayalon, commander of the Eastern Front. Instead he suggested the funds allocated to raze the villages should be used to set up a "village of refuge" in the immediate area. Similarly, ministry staff argued the case for higher pay for Arab workers in Nazareth employed by the Custodian of Abandoned Property and took the initiative for setting up new businesses there in order to ease unemployment. In short, the Minorities Ministry was "the only senior official body which consistently displayed a fair approach towards the Arab population remaining in Israel."[53]

But the power of the ministry to change the situation was limited, since it possessed only restricted authority.[54] Shortly after it was established, Shitrit wrote, with a touch of bitterness, that he had no real share in laying down policy towards the Arabs and that the army ignored his recommendations.[55] In the absence of a well-defined overall government policy, jurisdiction and authority were not clearly delineated and room was left for uncoordinated action. However, beyond making verbal protests, there was little Shitrit could do to make the military authorities change their minds. He had no independent power base in the party or the government and, according to Palmon, who, as Ben Gurion's confidant was involved with all the ministry's work, Shitrit felt a sense of inferiority when dealing with the military.[56]

What led to the eventual closure of the ministry, however, was not its troubles with the Ministry of Defense and the army (to whom Shitrit was ready to defer), but rather its relations with the rest of the ministries. Shitrit came to realize that his ministry would not turn into an independent alternative body. The other ministers began fighting for their "territorial rights" as soon as they understood the political and budgetary weight of the Arab sector.[57] The first sign came in December 1948 when the Ministry of Education succeeded in taking away authority over Arab education from Burla's department and appointed its own staff to deal with the matter directly.[58] A similar situation soon arose vis-à-vis the Health Ministry, whose staff began working among the Arab population without coordinating their steps with the Minorities Ministry.

Shitrit came out in defense of his office. In an internal memorandum written early in 1949, he asserted, "It is my opinion that the Minorities Ministry must not be closed down. I am saying this in response to rumors current in the press, among the public at large, and among Knesset members to the effect that the government is about to disband the ministry."[59] In arguing against its closure, he fell back on the reasons that had led to its establishment in the first place, speaking of it as "an important linking tool between the Jewish people and the minorities in our midst." Its abolition, he argued, was liable to undermine "the trust of the minorities in our government." Without his ministry, he insisted, the minorities might fall under the influence of "undesirable elements." Furthermore, closing down the ministry would add to, rather than reduce, budgetary requirements.[60]

After consulting Palmon, Ben Gurion decided that it was preferable to disband the Minorities Ministry and set up separate Arab departments in the other ministries. At the same time, he approved Palmon's recommendation to appoint a special advisor on Arab affairs who would be authorized to coordinate the work of the various bodies concerned with the minorities. The special advisor was to be on the prime minister's personal staff and to report to him directly. Palmon himself, by his own testimony, took the idea from British administrative practice.[61]

The Minorities Ministry was closed down in June 1949. The official reason given was that members of the minorities were citizens with equal rights and their affairs should therefore be seen to by the appropriate government department, just like those of all other citizens. Beyond that, however, a number of considerations seem to have combined to bring about the dissolution of the ministry. The frequent frictions between the ministries were wearying the prime minister, who was often called upon to intervene and come up with a compromise solution. In addition, Ben Gurion seems to have been convinced that minority affairs would be properly taken care of by the relevant ministries. When the ministry was first set up in May 1948, Shitrit and his senior staff genuinely believed that they would turn their office into the principal executive branch concerned with Arab affairs. A year later, it had become apparent that the other ministries would not let him trespass on their domain. What was needed, it turned out, was a coordinated effort rather than a separate, independent executive authority. Once this was understood, the prime minister came to prefer a coordinating advisor close to his own office rather than a constantly disgruntled cabinet minister.

The liberal stamp the ministry had acquired may have been a further reason for its disbandment. Its staff had sometimes been given sobriquets like "defenders of Islam" or "slanderers of the army."[62] Moreover, the ministry's declared policy of speaking out against discrimination and injustice while the war was still being fought had given it a negative image in some quarters, especially among those holding security-oriented views. The fact that some of the ministry's senior staff, such as Moshe Erem, were affiliated with the left-wing Mapam party did not help its image in the ruling Mapai party.

The closing of the ministry was criticized by left-wing circles, who rejected the official claim that since Arab affairs were being attended to by the various ministries, there was no need for a separate ministry. Thus, Yossef Waschitz, a leading member of Mapam's Arab Department, wrote, "The existence of the Minorities Ministry is imperative as long as severe restrictions are applied to the movements [of members of the minorities] and as long as the authorities and the public have not been persuaded to watch over the rights of the Arabs."[63] Within Mapai, senior figures were critical of the ensuing administrative confusion. "So far, it has not been made clear whether [after the demise of the ministry] minority affairs come under the Minister of Interior or Justice, or under the prime minister," wrote Yitzhak Ben Zvi. "No less important," he stated, was the question "which public body; [and] which Knesset committee has the ultimate responsibility [over matters concerning the Arabs in Israel]."[64]

Indeed, Arab affairs were now parceled out between the Defense Ministry, the army, the Custodian of Abandoned Property under the Ministries of Justice and Finance, the Ministries of Religions, Agriculture, Education, and Labor, and the new office of the Prime Minister's Advisor on Arab Affairs. No clear policy evolved, and this unsettled state of affairs characterized the situation in the early 1950s. The various government departments proceeded pretty much as they saw fit, with only a minimum of coordination.

In light of the previous discussion, I find the treatment of Israeli policy towards the Arab minority by scholars such as Ian Lustick and Sammy Smooha to be highly one-sided. In his analysis of Israeli policy

towards the Arab minority in the first years of statehood, Lustick states that the government had the following objectives:
> to prevent the Arab minority from serving as a fifth column or abetting large-scale infiltration; to acquire from Israeli Arabs a large percentage of their landholding; to take advantage of Arab resources for the absorption of new immigrants; to harness Arab economic power for the rapid development of the Jewish-controlled Israeli economy; to aggregate political support among Israeli Arabs for partisan advantage; and to prevent the Arab minority from becoming a burden in the arena of international politics.[65]

Having listed these aims, Lustick then adds the following conclusion: "The regime did not want nor did it strive to achieve the integration or absorption of the Arab population into the Jewish community." Its overriding objective was "to control the Arab community in Israel rather than to eliminate, integrate, absorb, or develop it."[66]

Sammy Smooha arrives at a similar conclusion. In his view, the primary objective of the government was:
> to institutionalize effective control over the Israeli Arabs for an indefinite period of time, thereby neutralizing them as a threat to [Israel's] security and to the Jewish-Zionist character of the state, and to mobilize their resources for the benefit of the Jewish people.[67]

The democratic and egalitarian policy, Smooha asserts, was no more than a verbal "ethos."

Both Lustick and Smooha, ignoring the complex realities of 1948, place a disproportionate emphasis on the security considerations.[68] A more balanced assessment would have taken into account the overall conditions under which policies towards the Arab population were formulated. The decision to establish the Minorities Ministry and to work for the assurance of equal rights for the Arabs was made the day the 1948 war broke out. Basic policy guidelines were worked out over a period of eight months during which the fate of the Jewish state, indeed its very existence, was decided on the battlefield in a prolonged military struggle.

The complex ambience of the years 1948–50 was effectively described by Sharett, a politician known both for his liberal sensitivities and his opposition to applying the security yardstick consistently. Present realities, he said, "were the legacy of war; realities born from most unusual circumstances, resulting from the fact that there is still no peace between us and the neighboring states [and between us] and our turbulent environment."[69]

Given this situation, it was no wonder that the Arab population was perceived by many as "enemy-affiliated" and as a security risk. The institution of military government, the military operations leading to the partial occupation of Arab areas, the evacuation of villages, and the seizure of lands all attest to the primacy given to security-oriented action. Moreover, security matters came to override other considerations.

But at the same time, there existed another set of actions that were motivated by liberal and egalitarian concerns. The views of those who not only hold that such liberal, egalitarian concerns failed to prevail, but that they simply did not exist in the first place, and the views of those who describe them as mere verbiage are highly one-sided and fail to take into consideration the realities such as they were at the time.

Ethical and humanistic codes, liberal and egalitarian tenets not only existed, but were also practically applied from the very early days of the state. We have seen how men like Yitzhak Greenboim, Yitzhak Ben Zvi, and Pinhas Lubianiker (Lavon) stressed that the Jewish people, itself a frequent victim of brutal discrimination, had a special responsibility for practicing fairness, equity, and justice towards the new Arab minority in Israel.

Moreover, the Minorities Ministry was set up to promote the cause of integration, which was also Shitrit's personal aim. Had he not directed his staff to act so as to achieve this goal, they would not have been accused of being "overly friendly" to the Arabs and would not have been mocked as "defenders of Islam." Its subsequent dissolution notwithstanding, the ministry managed to lay the foundations for the progress subsequently achieved by the Arab community and for its considerable economic and social development since then. As short-lived as it was, it made the leadership and the public at large aware of the liberal values that were at stake. Yet Lustick, in his only reference to the ministry—made in the context of his description of the "potential fifth column"—dismisses it by pointing out that "the head of their short-lived Minorities Ministry (May 1948–July 1949), Bekhor Shitrit, was at the same time, Minister of Police."[70]

In contrast to such one-sided accounts, it would be more correct to describe Israeli policy as proceeding simultaneously along two contradictory lines. Neither security concerns nor liberal, humanistic concerns were dominant enough to exclude the other. The two conflicting desires of isolating and integrating the Arab community are as old as the state of Israel itself. Thus, underlying Israeli policy towards the Arab minority in the state was a genuine conflict of values, one which continues to this very day.

NOTES

The author wishes to thank Reuven Aharoni for his significant assistance.

1. For a discussion of pre-state attitudes, see Don Peretz, *Israel and the Palestine Arabs* (Washington, D.C.: The Middle East Institute, 1958), 92–93; Ian Lustick, "Zionism and the State of Israel: Regime Objectives and the Arab Minority in the First Years of Statehood," *Middle Eastern Studies* 16, 1 (January 1980): 127; Charles Kamen, "Aharei Ha'ason: Ha'aravim Bemedinat Yisrael, 1948–1950" (After the catastrophe: the Arabs in the state of Israel, 1948–1950), *Mahbarot Lemehkar U'levikoret* 10 (December 1984): 41. The present attempt to assess the formulation of Israel's policy towards the Arab minority in the late 1940s and early 1950s is based on the analysis of texts and several primary sources which were made available in recent years.
2. "State of Israel Proclamation of Independence," in Walter Laqueur and Barry Rubin, eds., *The Israel-Arab Reader* (New York: Penguin Books, 1984), 127.
3. State of Israel, *Shnaton Hamemshala* (Government Yearbook) (Jerusalem: Government Printer, 1950), 25.
4. Shimon Shamir, "Haperspectiva Hahistorit-Divrei Mavo" (The historical perspective–introductory notes), *Skirot* (Tel Aviv: Shiloah Center, 1976), 5.
5. *Ha'aretz*, 6 September 1948.
6. Ibid.
7. Yitzhak Ben Zvi, "Lebe'ayat Hami'utim Beyisra'el" (On the problem of minorities in Israel), *Davar*, 2 September 1949.
8. Idem, 9 September 1949.
9. Ibid.
10. Ibid. Also see his article, "Be'ayot Harov Bemedinat Yisra'el" (Problems of the majority in the state of Israel), *Davar*, 18 November 1949.
11. Pinhas Lubianiker, "Yehasei 'Amim Vepo'alim Bemedinat Yisra'el" (Peoples' and workers' relations in the state of Israel), *Davar*, 16 June 1948. For a discussion of his writings, see Tom Segev, *1949, Hayisra'elim Harishonim* (1949, the first Israelis) (Jerusalem: Domino, 1984), 58.
12. *Davar*, 16 June 1948.
13. Ibid.
14. Ibid., 25 November 1949.
15. Ibid.
16. Ibid., 2 September 1949.
17. Ibid., 25 November 1949.
18. In response to Hirschberg's dilemma, Yossef Waschitz suggested that

compulsion was justified whenever it served to enhance the local society, whether by prohibiting polygamy or introducing compulsory education (*Hamizrah Hehadash* 1, 4 [July 1950]: 264). For Hirschberg's views, see his article "'Al Irgun Ha'edot Halo-Yehudiyot" (On the organization of the non-Jewish communities), *Davar*, 11 April 1949.

19. "Al Hahinukh Etzel Hami'utim Benedinat Yisra'el" (On the education among the minorities in the state of Israel), *Ha'aretz*, 17 June 1949.
20. The following survey of government activities in the Arab sector in 1948 and 1949 is based on and compiled from the following sources: Mikhael Assaf, "Tahalikh Hishtalvutam shel Ha'aravim Beyisra'el, Nisyon Sikkum Rishon" (The integration process of the Arabs in Israel—an attempt at a first summary), *Hamizrah Hehadash* 1, 1 (October 1949): 2–7; Y. L. Benor, "Hahinukh Ha'aravi Beyisra'el" (Arab education in Israel), *Hamizrah Hehadash* 3, 1 (1951): 1–8; S. D. Goitein, *Ha'aretz*, 17 June 1949; State of Israel, Government Press Division, "The Arabs in Israel," 24 June 1951 (mimeographed); *The Arabs in Israel*, Israel Office of Information, January 1952.
21. See, for example, grievances voiced by Mapai-affiliated Arab Knesset members regarding the lack of sufficient development resources: 'Abd al-'Aziz Zubi, *Divrei Haknesset*, vol. II (13 July 1949): 1009; Amin Jarjura, *Divrei Haknesset*, vol. II (18 July 1949): 1033.
22. *Hamizrah Hehadash* 1, 1 (October 1949): 4.
23. "Hatatir Yisrael Mi'ut 'Aravi Bamedina?" (Will Israel allow an Arab minority in the state?), *Ha'aretz*, 2 August 1948.
24. For Argov's comments, see *Divrei Haknesset*, vol. XI (12 February 1952): 1273.
25. Yigal Allon, *Masakh Shel Hol* (A curtain of sand) (Tel Aviv: Hakibutz Hame'uhad, 1969), 322–23.
26. *Davar*, 25 November 1949.
27. Ibid., 16 June 1948.
28. See Benny Morris, *The Birth of the Palestinian Refugee Problem, 1947–1949* (Cambridge: Cambridge University Press, 1987), and his article "The New Historiography: Israel Confronts Its Past," *Tikkun* 3, 6 (November-December 1988): 19–23, 99–102. For a polemic reply, see Shabtai Teveth, "The New Historians," three articles published in *Ha'aretz*, 7 April, 14 April, and 21 April, 1989.
29. *Divrei Haknesset*, vol. XIV (8 June 1953): 1530. Ya'acov Shimoni similarly contended at that time that the Israeli Arabs were "positively" discriminated against. (*Ha'aravim Bemedinat Yisra'el* [The Arabs in the state of Israel] [Jerusalem: Institute for Zionist Education, 1950]: 52.)
30. Ibid.
31. Interview with the author, 20 March 1988.
32. Ibid. For a detailed discussion of the notion of "temporariness," see

Amnon Linn, Appendix 12, in Ya'acov Landau, *Ha'aravim Beyisra'el* (Tel Aviv: Ma'arakhot, 1971), 313–14.
33. Israel State Archives (hereafter ISA), 307/56.
34. Interview, 20 March 1988.
35. *Divrei Haknesset*, vol. IV (7 March 1950): 449.
36. Ibid.
37. Moshe Sharett, *Yoman Ishi* (Personal diary), vol. I (Tel Aviv: Sifriyat Ma'ariv, 1978), 125–26.
38. Ibid., 150–51.
39. The ministry continued to be involved with Arab affairs throughout the early 1950s. See memorandum prepared by Ya'acov Herzog to the director-general of the ministry outlining policy recommendations, 27 April 1953, ISA, 02/29.
40. The government first named the office "Ministry for Arab Affairs." Shortly afterwards, according to Shitrit, the name was changed to "Ministry of Minorities." The latter reflected the official view differentiating between Muslims, Druzes, and the various Christian sects. See memorandum by Minister of Minorities, 27 February 1949, ISA, 1320/11.
41. Segev, *1949*, 59.
42. He often provided various ministries with background information regarding their areas of responsibility. See, for example, a booklet on the Higher Muslim Shar'i Council prepared by the Ministry of Minorities, February 1949. It included specific remarks addressed to the Minister of Religions.
43. Memorandum, signed by B. Shitrit, 27 February 1949, ISA, 1320/11.
44. Ibid.
45. Ibid.
46. At a press conference held in Tel Aviv on 9 November 1948, *Ha'aretz* and *Haboker*, both 10 November 1948.
47. For a first review of the ministry's activities in the Arab sector, see *Davar*, 27 July 1948. For a supportive description of the ministry's efforts to improve the quality of life in the Arab sector, see Yossef Waschitz, "Hayesh Tsorekh Bemisrad Hami'utim?" (Is the Minorities Ministry necessary?), *'Al Hamishmar*, 29 March 1949.
48. Erem was later elected to the first Israeli Knesset as a member for the left-wing Mapam.
49. For a survey of the department's activities, see report dated 29 September 1948, ISA, 307/24; and *Shnaton Hamemshala* (1950), 118–19. On the activities of the Haifa office, see document dated 20 October 1948, ISA, 1320/11.
50. See report by Erem, *Ha'aretz*, 20 December 1948.
51. Kamen, *Mahbarot*, 35.
52. *Haboker*, 10 November 1948. See also report on Shitrit's visit to Nazareth

on 19 July 1948, three days after the city was taken, ISA, 307/56; and report on a visit to the village of Jishsh (Gush Halav), *Haboker*, 22 November 1948. This should also be compared with a request issued on 16 September 1948 by the ministry's director-general asking the Haifa branch to prepare a list of steps to be taken "*for the sake of* [emphasized in the original] the local Arab population," ISA, 1320/11.

53. Kamen, *Mahbarot*, 35, 39, 61–62.
54. Aryeh Gelblum, *Ha'aretz*, December 1948.
55. Report by Shitrit, *ISA*, 307/24.
56. Interview, 20 March 1988.
57. Segev, *1949*, 58–59.
58. See report by Shitrit, *Davar*, 29 December 1948.
59. Report by Shitrit, 27 February 1949, ISA, 1320/11.
60. Ibid.
61. Interview, 20 March 1988.
62. Waschitz, *'Al Hamishmar*, 29 March 1949. For an opposite view taken by an Arab citizen who supported closing down the ministry, see Kamil Musallam, *Haboker*, 3 March 1949.
63. Waschitz, *'Al Hamishmar*, 29 March 1949.
64. *Davar*, 9 September 1949. In March 1950, the Knesset discussed Mapam's motion on "inequality of and discrimination against the Arab citizens of Israel." Foreign Minister Sharett responded and suggested that the matter be referred to one of the committees. The following committees were mentioned: Security and Foreign Affairs, Interior Affairs, a joint Interior-Security and Foreign Affairs Committee, or a special committee of representatives of the six major parties. No agreement was reached and eventually the Knesset committee was charged with finding a proper solution. See *Haboker*, 8 March 1950. See also a critical assessment of the situation by M. A. [Mikhael Assaf], *Davar*, 17 February 1950.
65. Lustick, *Middle Eastern Studies*, 143.
66. Ibid.
67. Sammy Smooha, "Mediniyut Kayemet Ve'alternativit Klapei Ha'aravim Beisra'el" (Existing and alternative policies towards the Arabs in Israel), *Megamot* 26, 1 (September 1971): 14.
68. For a critical review of Lustick's and Smooha's analysis, see Moshe Sharon, *Middle Eastern Studies* 18 (July 1982): 336.
69. *Divrei Haknesset*, vol. IV (7 March 1950): 449.
70. Lustick, *Middle Eastern Studies*, 136.

CHAPTER 7

Arab Historiography of the 1948 War: The Quest for Legitimacy

AVRAHAM SELA

There is a widespread conviction among scholars of Arab civilization that history written by Arabs in modern times has been generally apologetic. Charged with strong emotion, its primary motivation has been to nourish and glorify a self-image in the face of frustration and a bitter sense of decline. As Wilfred C. Smith put it, "Arab writing of history has been functioning . . . less as a genuine inquiry than as a psychological defense. Most of it is to be explained primarily in terms of the emotional needs that it fulfills (and is designed to fulfill)."[1] A selective and arbitrary use of the past for present needs and purposes is perhaps a universal phenomenon. It is, however, particularly striking in modern Arab historiography, which is fueled by the vast gap between reality and self-image, and between the memory of a glorious past and a dissatisfying present that evokes neither pride nor self-esteem.[2]

This ideological approach to the past is nowhere more discernible than in Arab historiography of the 1948 war, a conflict which had a traumatic impact on the collective Arab memory. That impact is well encapsulated in the terminology used to describe its outcome: *Nakba* (catastrophe), *Karitha* (disaster), and *Mihna* (misfortune). Despite the Arabs' apparent superiority in material and human resources, and contrary to the Arab states' expectations of a quick and easy victory, the 1948 war ended in humiliating defeat for the Arab armies and in outright disaster for the Arab Palestinian population, about half of whom became refugees. Moreover, the Jewish state, the birth of which the Arabs desperately sought to prevent, gained international recognition and achieved territorial gains even beyond those that it had been allotted under the U.N. partition plan. The defeat was especially humiliating because it was inflicted by "armed Zionist gangs," Jews whom the Arabs traditionally despised and held in contempt.[3]

The Arab defeat in Palestine threw the Arab world into turmoil, triggering a series of political assassinations and military coups in Egypt and in the Fertile Crescent states. The defeat fomented political extremism and revolutionary attitudes and contributed to further decline of the West in the Arab world. Instead of serving as a rallying point for the Arab states, the war for Palestine intensified inter-Arab differences and disputes. The Arab League, which had been responsible for formulating and implementing Arab policy on Palestine, suffered an irreparable blow to its prestige. Overall, the loss of Palestine festered as an open wound in the Arab collective consciousness. In the words of Professor Elie Kedourie, these Arab polities "tasted to the full the disappointments and the disasters of the life of politics. Autonomous political action coincided with and led to the disaster of Palestine, a disaster the like of which had never befallen the Arab world when it was governed by the Ottomans."[4]

The Palestine war coincided with the struggle of the fledgling Arab states to build national institutions and to consolidate their authority in the face of economic crisis and political disarray. From the outset, the Arabs' historiographical approach to the conflict was both emotional and practical. Indeed, even before the fighting ended, the desire for self-justification generated Arab histories of the Palestine war. Following the war, two basic modes of Arab historiography emerged: an apologetic mode, geared towards enhancing political legitimacy; and a mode of self-examination that sought to elicit historical lessons and motivate radical social, political, or ideological change in preparation for the "next round" against Israel.[5]

Even today, Arab historiography of the 1948 war consists predominantly of non-scholarly literature based more upon collective memory than critical historiography. This trend has been reinforced by two major factors. The first is the ongoing Arab-Israeli conflict, in which the Arabs persistently refused to recognize Israel, and in which each side has sought to establish its legitimacy and elicit the support of the international community. As a result, Arab historical writing on the conflict's history has been colored by ideology. Second, none of the Arab states has yet made its official archives on the 1948 war available for study even to retired high-ranking officers who saw service at the time.[6]

More recently, the consolidation of authority in the Arab states and within the Palestinian national movement has given rise to greater openness and more freedom for critical research. Nevertheless, the number of critical studies on the war[7] remains relatively small compared with the large number of first-person accounts, textbooks, memoirs, diaries, and polemics, many written by political leaders and senior military officers. Even these critical works, however, often relying on established myths and beliefs in Arab countries, consistently justify or disclaim particular war-time activity.[8]

Few of the new Arab historical studies of the 1948 war have made use of British, American, or Israeli archives.[9] In addition, political and military memoirs and diaries, a primary source for the history of the Arab-Israeli war of 1948, have been used rather selectively by Arab historians.[10] However great the disposition of such memoirs to "apologize, or palliate or embellish or suppress,"[11] their value as a historical source cannot be gainsaid. Historical research into the author's role, his political and social standing, historical accuracy, and the purpose, timing and venue of the work's publication are important factors for understanding the relevance of any particular work, besides deepening one's knowledge of events.

One can treat Arab historiography of the 1948 war according to various motifs:[12] explanations for the defeat; lessons to be learned from the war that can serve present needs and goals; and the regional and international impact of the war. In this chapter, however, we focus on the use of historiography as a means to legitimate authority and enhance collective self-confidence.[13] Arab historiography is marked by a multiplicity of conflicting versions that have been evoked by the need felt to account for the *Nakba*. These histories are replete with mutual recriminations and the search for scapegoats. The centrality of the 1948 war in Arab political consciousness has thus transformed the historical discussions of the war into instruments of political legitimacy.

Egypt

The earliest and most notable example of this kind of historiography is a semi-official booklet published in Egypt shortly before the start of the Israeli offensive in the Negev.[14] Although acknowledging a few setbacks, this publication, on the whole, glorifies the army's performance in Palestine and portrays King Farouk as both courageous and devoted to pan-Arab ideology. In particular, it stresses the efficiency of Egyptian military preparations as well as Egypt's full coordination with other Arab armies.[15] The booklet was obviously a response to the growing opposition to the government and indirectly to the king himself brought about by the unsuccessful and seemingly endless fighting. It also expresses strong criticism of the regime for accepting the truce called for by the U.N. Security Council on the eve of a purported Arab victory.

The acceptance of this truce became a key element in Arab historiography's explanation for the defeat. The reason for the acceptance was alternatively explained by the international mediator's promises, the low motivation for continuing the fighting, and the Arab leadership's treason.[16] Indeed, given the uninformed public's unfounded expectations of a quick victory, there seemed to be no justification for the Arabs' acceptance of the truce. Thus, as the second truce took effect, on 19 July, without a specified time frame, Egyptian historians deemed it urgent to explain the situation in a manner that would preserve the king's prestige, as he bore personal responsibility for deciding to send the Egyptian army into Palestine. The booklet under discussion is a telling indication of Egypt's unrealistic expectations of a quick "disciplinary action" against the "Zionist gangs" and an easy "promenade" to Tel Aviv.[17]

From the outset, the Egyptian government adamantly opposed committing its regular army in Palestine, claiming that by doing so it would expose its rear flank to the British forces deployed in the Canal Zone.[18] The government maintained this stance until three days before the end of the Mandate. However, from 12 April on, there was a growing indication that King Farouk intended to dispatch the regular army. When the king finally ordered Minister of War Haydar Pasha to activate the troops, Prime Minister Nuqrashi Pasha had no choice but to seek formal Senate approval for the army's intervention in Palestine. Post-revolutionary writings criticize Farouk's decision as reckless and motivated predominantly by the pressure of public opinion, by concern about Egypt's position in the Arab world if it failed to intervene in Palestine, and by the king's personal ambitions for Arab and Islamic leadership.[19]

We learn a great deal about the process of Egyptian decision making on Palestine from the memoirs of the then chairman of the Egyptian Senate, Muhamad Hussein Haikal. In these memoirs, Haikal describes the confusion and conflict among Egyptian policy makers and institutions regarding military intervention in Palestine; the pressure from the king to intervene; the influence exerted by public opinion on the government, which, although aware of the army's unpreparedness, eventually succumbed to the pressures; and the Egyptian leadership's underestimation of the Jewish military force and its perception of the invasion as a "political demonstration" intended to bring about the great powers' intervention. Haikal's version is largely confirmed by the protocols of the Egyptian Senate meeting during which the decision was taken to enter the war.[20]

The Egyptian government's underestimation of Jewish strength became a major source of criticism by Arab politicians and historians, who cited it both apologetically[21] and as a lesson for the future.[22] However, Arab politicians were by no means ignorant of Jewish military might, certainly not by the eve of the termination of the Mandate. On 30 April, they had been informed by Arab military commanders that the minimum order of battle needed to defeat the Jewish forces—five divisions and six squadrons—was twice the size of the forces then available to the Arab states.[23] Nevertheless, the continued use of expressions such as "gangs" (*'Isabat*) or "flotsam and jetsam" (*Sharadhim*, or *Shudhadh al-'Afaq*) by Egyptian politicians was meant to belittle Jewish military strength and overcome the politicians' doubts and confusion concerning the possibility of a quick Arab victory. Moreover, such expressions did not indicate their actual assessment of Jewish military capability. Instead, their purpose was to enable them to attribute any future defeat to the great powers rather than to the Jews.[24]

A few years after the Free Officers' Revolt in 1952, Jamal Abd al-Nasser published his own observations about the Palestine war, in which he accused King Farouk and his entourage of immoral and corrupt behavior. In particular, he charged that they had procured obsolete arms for the Egyptian forces in Palestine.[25] In these observations, as well as in his posthumous memoirs of the 1948 war published by Muhamad Hassanein Heikal, Nasser's description contradicted the one offered by the Farouk regime.

Nasser was especially critical of the indeterminate nature of the "political war" which, he believed, lacked clear strategic goals. Nasser also complained about the lack of adequate preparation for war, the poor intelligence, the incompetence of the higher command, and the persistent feeling of the soldiers at the front that they had been abandoned by the country.[26] Nasser's criticisms, for the most part confirmed in the arms trials held in Cairo in 1953, as well as by later studies, provide a useful historical and social context for explaining the Egyptian army's poor performance in the war.[27] Nasser utilized the war to delegitimize the regime he had overthrown and to support his emerging pan-Arabic vision. His case was enhanced by his own combat record which included decorations for bravery and a series of victories. He also endeavored to use the collective memory of the Palestine war as a "battleground of aspirations"[28] and a vehicle to promote his concept of national liberation and pan-Arab security.

The timing of the publication of Nasser's memoirs in the mid-1970s by Muhamad Hassanein Heikal, the late president's spokesman and confidant, is an excellent example of the use of historical memory for the purposes of political legitimation. Heikal's introduction to the memoirs was an unabashed attempt to restore the luster to Nasser's image that had been tarnished by the 1967 defeat and eclipsed by his successor's victory in 1973.[29]

Iraq

Although Iraq's armies achieved no major victories in the 1948 war, its expeditionary force, deployed in Samaria, sustained no major defeat. Indeed, in early June, the Iraqis repulsed an Israeli offensive on Jenin, and they continued to hold the area until their withdrawal from Palestine in April 1949. Yet, despite this record, the Iraqi army was already criticized during the war for failing to initiate any military operations, even though for most of the war it was the largest Arab force operating in Palestine. The Iraqi forces' inactivity was contemptuously encapsulated in the phrase "no orders" (*maku awamir*), an apologetic catchword allegedly used by the Iraqi military command in Palestine during the war.[30]

Troubled by domestic unrest and disappointed by the Arab military failure in Palestine, the Iraqi parliament decided, as early as February 1949, and apparently with the government's consent, to form a commission of inquiry to investigate the course of the war and the reasons for the military failure.[31] The commission's unpublished original report contains military and political documents attesting to Iraq's militant stance on Palestine, especially its declared policies. Despite its obvious bias, selectivity, and strong tendency to present Iraq as the leading force in the pan-Arab effort to rescue Palestine from

Zionism, the report is still the most comprehensive and valuable source regarding Arab deliberations and collective policy making on Palestine in the two years preceding the war as well as during the war itself.

The report's overall finding is that, from the very beginning, Arab collective activity regarding Palestine was characterized by inter-Arab rivalries, conflicting interests, and disagreements. It shows, furthermore, that even a few weeks before the expiration of the Mandate, the Arab states were complacent about Palestine. The report confirms that the politicians decided to invade Palestine despite the Arab states' inability to muster even half of the order of battle stipulated as necessary by the military commanders. Interestingly, the report does not entirely absolve Iraq of all blame for the Arab debacle in Palestine—which may explain why the document has never been published. Further, it discloses that Iraq persistently resisted assigning to the Palestinian leader, Mufti al-Haj Amin al-Husseini, any significant military or administrative role in the collective Arab efforts on behalf of Palestine.[32]

However, the report does emphasize that the Iraqi government repeatedly urged the adoption of two major measures by the Arab states: first, the necessity of deploying regular Arab armies; and, second, the use of oil as a weapon against Britain and the United States.[33] With regard to the latter notion, the report leaves no doubt that the Saudi monarch consistently rejected Iraqi proposals, made in Arab League meetings, to use the oil weapon to further the Palestinian cause. However, the report does not address the question of Iraqi sincerity in this matter.

While stressing that none of the other Arab armies was willing to obey the joint command's orders, the report leaves the impression that the Iraqi army was an exception, possibly because the commander-in-chief of the Arab forces in Palestine was Iraq's General Nuri al-Din Mahmud.[34] Interestingly, whereas most Arab states denounced the behavior of King Abdullah of Jordan during the war and labeled him a traitor to the Arab cause, the report is circumspect about the king's role. Moreover, it ascribes no ulterior motives to Abdullah regarding Palestine and blames John Bagot Glubb, the Arab Legion's British commander from 1939 to 1956, for changing the Arab invasion plan. The Legion, the army of the Hashemite kingdom of Jordan, was established by Britain to serve under the command of the mandatory government and was principally under the control of British officers until the mid-1950s.

The critical tone of the parliamentary commission's report is best grasped when it is compared to the heavily apologetic memoirs of Salih Sa'ib al-Jubouri, Iraq's war-time chief-of-staff. While referring to many of the same documents used in the official report, the memoirs do not always interpret them in the same way. Understandably, Jubouri's memoirs reflect a much more defensive approach, possibly because during a part of the war, he served as commander-in-chief of the Iraqi forces in Palestine.

Besides rejecting the "fallacy of no orders" attributed by others to the Iraqi army, Jubouri argues that of all the Arab states, Iraq was the most dedicated to its military mission in Palestine and most willing to cooperate with other armies.[35] Jubouri blames the Egyptian government for postponing the meeting of the first conference of Arab chiefs-of-staff, which finally convened at the end of April 1948, only two weeks before the end of the Mandate. He further maintains that the Iraqis sent the largest expeditionary force from the outset. However, the mechanized force that attacked Gesher on the first day of the invasion did not exceed 1,700 men.[36] Only later was this unit beefed up with additional forces.

Understandably, Jubouri relates neither the painful failure of the Iraqi force to break through the Jewish defense line, nor the reason for the subsequent deployment of the Iraqi forces in the "Triangle" in the war's second week. Jubouri assigned the blame for the fiasco at Gesher, where the Iraqi flank was exposed, to Glubb.[37] In so doing, he ignores the rapidly changing military situation in Jerusalem that demanded the Legion's deployment there.

Jubouri underscores the lack of arms and ammunition as the major limitation on the Iraqi army's operational capability, criticizing the politicians for committing the army to tasks for which it was not prepared. Jubouri's claims are partly supported by the memoirs of another Iraqi officer, who served as his country's military attaché in London during the Palestine war. While this officer blames Britain for denying to Iraq the necessary weapons and equipment, he holds the Iraqi politicians and the high command equally responsible for the lack of preparedness, arguing that had the army's needs been recognized earlier, the arms could have been obtained from Britain or partly produced in Iraq.[38]

Jordan

Despite the Arab Legion's military successes in rescuing the Old City of Jerusalem and throwing back repeated Israeli attacks at Latrun, by the summer of 1948 the other Arab states found Jordanian policy in Palestine to be intolerable. This policy also aroused overt concern and suspicion among the Arab public. The immediate reason was the fall of Lydda and Ramle, portrayed ever since in Arab historiography as the result of the Legion's abandonment of the cities to Israel as part of the ostensible secret agreement between the Jews and Abdullah on the partition of Palestine.[39] Long before the end of the Mandate, Abdullah's political and territorial aspirations in Palestine, a part of his "Greater Syria" scheme, were no secret to the Arab rulers. The doubts about the king's faithfulness to the Arab cause were intensified by two factors: first, the king's urgent requests for an end to the war during the first truce, which began on 11 June 1948, resulting from the U.N. Security Council resolution of 29 May; and, second, administrative measures introduced in Jordanian-occupied territory which were indicative of Abdullah's plan to incorporate it.

As the Arab war effort ground to a standstill, Abdullah's position in the Arab world, and even in his own kingdom, was gravely undermined. This was mainly the result of the growing inter-Arab dispute over the future of the Arab-occupied territories of Palestine and Palestinian aspirations for national sovereignty. At the end of the war, the king was isolated in the Arab world and attacked and denounced by his Arab neighbors as an imperialist stooge and an ally of the Zionist movement.

In light of Abdullah's delicate position in the Arab world, one would expect the emergence of an official Jordanian history of the war stressing the major role of the Arab Legion, especially until the second truce, which took effect on 19 July 1948 as the result of a U.N. Security Council resolution ordering a cease-fire. During this period, the Legion constituted the main obstacle to an Israeli takeover of the entire city of Jerusalem and its strategic approaches. However, the quantity of such official literature is surprisingly meager.

King Abdullah's war-time memoirs, the only published version by an Arab head of state at the time of the war, remain a leading example for the Jordanian-based history of the war. This might be explained, first and foremost, by the continuity of the Royal Hashemite regime and the traditional values and symbols it espouses.

In the years immediately following the war, two publications appeared with the obvious purpose of enhancing the Jordanian image and legitimacy on both the domestic and inter-Arab levels. The first was the "completion" of the king's memoirs—the pivotal issues of which were the Palestine war and Jordan's relations with the Arab states. The book is marked by the king's arrogance and his deep contempt for his Arab rivals, particularly the Mufti al-Haj Amin al-Husseini, whom Abdullah held responsible for all the disasters inflicted on the Arabs in Palestine.[40] Abdullah describes the invasion as "the Arab military demonstration," an "improvised" decision taken despite the knowledge that the forces available were insufficient.

Besides endeavoring to counter his sworn political rivals' views on Palestine, Abdullah stresses his devotion to Arab unity as well as his historic role with regard to Palestine since the late 1920s. He also emphasizes his sincere and long-standing concern about the Zionist-Arab conflict, particularly in view of the ineptitude of the Palestinian leadership, headed by al-Haj Amin. Abdullah documents this by citing his correspondence with Palestinian and Arab leaders, as well as with the British High Commissioner, about the political problems in Palestine. Abdullah's interest in Palestine during the war and, more important, his move to implement the "unity of the two banks," namely, the annexation of the West Bank, are viewed as a linear historical process.

According to this book, Abdullah, at a time when the leading Palestinian figures had reached a point of bankruptcy, came to the rescue of Palestine, while allowing its people the freedom to assert their own political wishes. The book also defends, on wholly practical grounds, Abdullah's resistance to the Mufti's short-lived, Gaza-based "All-Palestine government," established by the League of Arab States in cooperation with prominent Palestinian leaders. Abdullah named it "the illusory government."[41] In contrast to the recklessness and total absence of statesmanship he attributes to the Palestinian leadership headed by the Mufti, Abdullah portrays himself as a reasonable and responsible leader who bases his policies on a realistic and astute study of the prevailing conditions. In this context, Abdullah candidly admits that he was willing to accept even a separate peaceful settlement of the Palestine problem inasmuch as "peoples are either in an active war or in peace and settlement."[42]

In his memoirs, the king praises the Arab Legion's glorious performance. However, while the British arms embargo was detrimental to the Legion, Abdullah fails to mention it. Abdullah also maintains that his title, Supreme Commander of the Arab Forces in Palestine, was devoid of practical meaning since each government preferred to direct its own forces. The Arab governments, he says, concealed from one another, and from him as well, basic information needed for cooperation, such as order of battle, military plans, and intelligence data. Even when the Egyptians came under heavy Israeli attack in the Negev, this pattern of behavior remained unchanged and the other Arab governments refused to cooperate with the king and come to the help of the forces under attack.[43]

The second postwar publication was a book by Mahmud al-Russan, the man who served during the battle for Latrun as operations officer in the Legion battalion in charge of this sector. The semi-official status of the book is reflected in the fact that its foreword was written by the Legion's highest-ranking Arab officer. In both books, the role of the British officers in general, and of Glubb Pasha in particular, is minimized or utterly disregarded, while much attention and praise are heaped on the role of the king and the Legion's Arab officers. This tendency is perhaps understandable in light of the anti-British mood among Palestinians in Jordan and elsewhere in the Arab world in the war's aftermath. No less important, however, was the regime's need to secure legitimacy in the eyes of young Arab officers in the Jordanian army, particularly in the aftermath of the attempted coup against Abdullah, led by the ex-commander and governor-general of Arab Jerusalem, Colonel Abdullah al-Tal, in 1949.

Although the main theme of Russan's book is the tenacious fighting by the Arab Legion at Latrun, the author also attests to the Legion's active support of the Arab inhabitants of Palestine during the last months of the Mandate.[44] This took the form of training and the participation of senior Legion officers in actions of the local Arab militia. As a Legion officer in Haifa in those days, Russan painted a gloomy picture of the local Palestinian leadership's performance; an extreme shortage of funds and military supplies resulted from the lack of preparations for the imminent showdown.[45]

Following his escape to Egypt, Abdullah al-Tal published his own memoirs in which he attributed the motivation for his participation in the war to his strong anti-British sentiment as well as his devotion to Arab nationalism. However, the book's overt purpose was to expose King Abdullah's treacherous role in the war as an agent of British policy that was practically implemented by Glubb.[46] Tal suggests that

Glubb, as part of the British plot to bring about the partition of Palestine, restrained the Legion from attacking the Jewish areas. He thus prevented the Legion from capturing the whole city of Jerusalem. He also refrained from sending reinforcements to the Egyptian forces under attack in October, exploiting the opportunity to re-deploy his forces in the Bethlehem-Hebron area instead.[47] According to Tal, it was he, not Glubb, who initiated the takeover of the Etzion Bloc by the Legion as well as other attacks in the Jerusalem area.[48] The inclusion of original documents from the secret armistice negotiations between the Israeli government and Abdullah lends credence to Tal's book.

In light of Tal's coup attempt, the publication of these documents was most likely meant to prove his faithfulness to the Arab national cause. Tal implies that, in spite of his knowledge of Abdullah's negotiations with the Jews, he remained with Abdullah for so long to allow time to prepare an opposition movement that would put an end to Abdullah's treason.[49] Tal's purported motivations notwithstanding, the book, which predated the availability of relevant British and Israeli archival material, serves as an invaluable historical source for Israeli-Jordanian relations during the war. The book also provoked accusations, first leveled during the war, of collusion between Abdullah and the Jews, a charge which became a major Arab explanation for the defeat and was later adopted by Israeli leftist historians.[50]

Responding to the denunciations of King Abdullah's role in the war, Jordanian prime minister Hazza' al-Majali published his memoirs in 1960 in an effort "to present to the Arab reader the truth" regarding the king.[51] Majali, the chief court chamberlain and the king's confidant during the war, defends Abdullah's stance on Palestine and his army's behavior in the war as motivated by realpolitik. Abdullah, Majali claims, was willing to agree to a partition as the lesser evil and as a tactical stage only. The king is portrayed as a pragmatic, judicious, and courageous statesman in contrast to those Arab leaders who, in spite of knowing the truth, misled their people with unrealistic promises.[52]

Majali, who was assassinated shortly after the appearance of his book, implicitly reiterates Abdullah's argument that the Arab governments were responsible for the loss of Lydda and Ramle. Fearing domestic repercussions, the other Arab leaders decided not to prolong the truce, although they knew that their armies were incapable of victory given Israel's increase in both arms and manpower achieved during the truce.[53]

However, although mentioning the king's willingness to negotiate a peaceful solution of the Palestine conflict, the book is silent about the political contacts between the king and the Jews both preceding the war and near its end, including the secret armistice talks held at Shune. As for the surrender to Israel of the western slopes of the Jenin-Nablus-Tulkarm triangle, Majali blames the government and Abdullah al-Tal for misleading the king and showing bad judgment and poor knowledge of the terrain in the negotiations.[54] Majali's book is also critical of the Palestinian leadership for relying too much on Arab governments while doing too little itself. He also sees the Palestinians as partly responsible for the panic defeatism ensuing from the "improvised" and exaggerated propaganda following the 1948 Deir Yassin massacre.[55]

A research-oriented and relatively well-documented study of the role played by Jordan and the Arab Legion in the war is found in a book published in the early 1980s by the well-known historian of the Hashemite kingdom of Jordan, Sulaiman Mussa. The book comes to grips with several problematic issues such as the secret talks between Abdullah and the Jews, the loss of Lydda and Ramle, and the failure to assist Egyptian forces under Israeli attack. Mussa's book is the first Arab publication not devoted to vilification and denunciation that admits that diplomatic contacts took place between the Hashemite government and the Zionist leadership prior to the war. Although Mussa says nothing about the king's direct involvement in the talks, the proximate timing he cites for the meetings and his descriptions of them coincide with those of Israeli documents describing the king's participation.[56] Nevertheless, Mussa's book does not accept the contention that Abdullah at any time agreed to divide Palestine with the Zionists or Israel.

The book also seeks to explain the role of Abdullah and the Legion in the war. On the whole, Mussa maintains that limited military capabilities and political constraints lay at the root of the Arab Legion's operational policy in the war. He thus accounts for the four-day delay in intervening in the battle for Jerusalem, even though the city's Arab defenders were on the brink of collapse; the withdrawal of the Legion's token force from the Lydda-Ramle sector in the face of a large-scale Israeli operation; and the failure to help the Egyptian forces in the Negev.[57]

Mussa also emphasizes the political constraints dictated by the British government, whose material and political support was indispensable to the king's plan to take over the Arab part of Palestine. These constraints ruled out a possible Legion attack on the territory allotted to the Jewish state. In addition, Mussa refutes a central argument in Arab historiography that the acceptance of the first truce by the Arabs was a devastating mistake that turned the war in Israel's favor by enabling her to acquire new arms supplies and manpower. Mussa contends that Israel would have acquired these reinforcements anyway. He further argues that their own limitation had already forced the Arab armies to adopt a noncooperative, defensive approach even before the truce.[58]

Syria and the Army of Deliverance

Despite Syria's contribution to the Palestine war effort, it was not until the advent of Assad's regime that publications appeared discussing Syrian activity in the war. This may be explained by the turmoils, revolts, and successive military coups that marked Syrian domestic politics for more than two decades following the Palestine defeat.

Syrian publications say little about Damascus' role in the six-month "unofficial war" that preceded the invasion of Palestine or its political motivations for being the most active Arab state in organizing, financing, arming, training, and supervising the Army of Deliverance, an eight-battalion force of Arab volunteers.[59] However, these publications do praise Syria's leading role in defense of Palestine before the invasion as genuine evidence of the unique historical and geographical ties binding both these parts of natural Syria. (Natural Syria and "Greater Syria" refer to the Arab term *Bilad al-Sham*, which includes today's Syria, Lebanon, Jordan, and historic Palestine.)[60] Regardless of the changing regimes in Damascus, Syria's commitment to the cause of Palestine has always shaped its policies, ever since the Roman invasions. Hence, Damascus' support for the Palestinian revolt in the years 1937–39 and her financial assistance to the war effort in 1947–48. It is further claimed that, unlike other Arab states, Syria sought no particular gains for itself in the war, perceiving it as a total effort to rescue Palestine in its entirety, and thus felt reluctant to follow the other Arab governments in signing an armistice agreement with Israel. Her ultimate decision to follow suit is explained as resulting from Husni al-Za'im's military coup against the Syrian constitutional regime.[61]

Indeed, it is ironic that Syria's role in this phase of the war has been used, under Assad's regime, to legitimize its demand for a decisive role in the Palestinian issue. The concept of "Greater Syria," which, under the aegis of King Abdullah in the late 1940s, was the driving force behind Syria's preventive policy on Palestine, became a useful historic concept for present political aspirations.

The small output of literature on the Syrian army's role in the 1948 war underlines the politicians' mistrust of the army and the striking gap between the Syrian leadership's vociferous enthusiasm to get involved in the war and the state's meager capabilities.[62] Amin al-Nafouri, a former Syrian general, whose article on the Syrian army in the Palestine war was published in an official Syrian military journal, focuses on such military aspects as tactics, order of battle, and capabilities. The article attributes the low level of preparedness at the beginning of the war to Britain's refusal to supply the necessary arms. However, it implicitly blames the army's failure in its first attack on the Syrian politicians' delay in issuing orders and on their failure to provide the necessary means for the attack. Compounding the situation was the lack of coordination with the Iraqi force operating on the Syrian left flank and Abdullah's last-minute changes in the Arab invasion plan, which took the Syrian forces by surprise.[63]

Fayiz al-Qasri, another retired Syrian general, also argues that the dishonest and deceitful behavior of Abdullah and Glubb was detrimental to the other Arab armies. Qasri is critical of all Arab governments for their reluctance to play an active role in the war—hence, their readiness to accept the U.N. cease-fires. He emphasizes in particular the inactivity of the Jordanian and Iraqi armies. These tended to support Abdullah's desire to put an end to the war immediately after the start of the first truce.[64]

Regarding the Army of Deliverance, Syrian historiography has followed the path of general Arab historiography which, until the early 1970s, either ignored or deplored its role in the war. The army, which was established by the Arab League in late 1947 in view of the imminent war, served in Palestine during the 1948 war under Fauzi al-Qawaqji's command. Overall, the army has been portrayed, particularly by the Palestinians, as an aimless mob which harassed the local Palestinian population and has been taken as evidence of the Arab governments' insincere and improvised approach in the Palestine war.[65]

Perhaps in an effort to avoid responsibility for the Army of Deliverance's failures, Syrian historical writings complain about the absence of coordination between Qawaqji's forces and the Syrian army during the latter's battles in Mishmar ha-Yarden. At the same time, however, Syrian historiography ignores the Army of Deliverance's unheeded requests for urgent support when, in late October 1948, it was forced by a heavy Israeli offensive to withdraw from Galilee.[66] Qasri, who served as an officer under Qawaqji's command, underplays the role of the Army of Deliverance and its military capability. He argues that it was merely meant to demonstrate the Arab states' resistance to partition and to exempt them from official intervention in Palestine. Basically, Qasri says, the idea of organizing a military force of volunteers from different countries in such a short time was utterly impractical, and Qawaqji had no experience in commanding regular forces on the scale of the Army of Deliverance.[67]

A critical study on the Army of Deliverance published in 1973 in a Palestinian periodical describes the military and political constraints under which it came into being: the shortage of arms and ammunition; the short time available to turn the volunteers into organized military units; Qawaqji's controversial personality; the fractious discipline among the soldiers and officers of the force; the lack of staff routine; poor control of forces; and estrangement from the Palestinian population. The study, the conclusions of which are largely accepted by the Jordanian statesman Wasfi al-Tal, a former officer and a battalion commander in the Army of Deliverance, blames the politicians for not defining clearly the force's operational goals, thus adding to its inherent weaknesses.[68]

Qawaqji's own memoirs are marked by a strongly apologetic, if occasionally bitter tone and reflect a transparent effort to portray his army's military record as heroic. In spite of the shortage of arms and ammunition, indifference of the Arab League's military committee in Damascus and the Arab governments as a whole, and provocations by the Mufti and his followers in Palestine, the Army of Deliverance was the only force that took the offensive initiative. Qawaqji's main complaints are directed against the military committee in Damascus and particularly against Taha al-Hashimi, the exiled Iraqi leader who served as the inspector-general of the volunteers. Hashimi was a confidant of the Syrian president and the main figure behind the irregulars.

Qawaqji also accuses the Arab governments of being competitive, harboring unwarranted suspicions, misjudging the true capability of the

Arab armies, and being inefficiently organized and unprepared. Qawaqji's descriptions of the Mufti and his armed men, namely, the Holy Jihad (al-Jihad al-Muqaddas), and the behavior of the Palestinian population as a whole are markedly contemptuous, emphasizing their defeatism and lack of will to fight.[69] Although Qawaqji pays lip service to the argument that Britain and the United Nations enabled and encouraged the Jewish aggression and subsequently legitimized its consequences, he is certainly less bitter than his Arab compatriots about Britain's role in Palestine.

Qawaqji assails the widespread contention in Arab historiography that the British withdrawal from Palestine was deliberately organized so as to enable the Jews to take over mixed or mainly Arab-inhabited areas. He records that, upon his arrival in Samaria, the British army recognized his force as responsible for this homogeneous Arab area. Qawaqji also refutes the contentions of both Arabs and Jews that the withdrawing British army supported the other side in supplying arms and providing defense, pointing to the British disposition to always back the stronger side.[70]

The Palestinian Dialogue with the Past

If the Arab regimes were sharply criticized for their inept leadership in the war, the Palestinian national leaders, headed by al-Haj Amin al-Husseini, were more strongly excoriated. The controversy surrounding the Mufti's leadership and the personal responsibility imputed to him by Palestinians and other Arabs[71] is indicated by the absence of any serious scholarly discussion of his role in determining the fate of the Palestine question, particularly during the crucial years of 1946 through 1948.

The results of the war and the consequent criticism against the Mufti and the Arab Higher Committee generated a few apologetic publications shortly after the end of the war.[72] In the 1950s and 1960s, the Mufti was politically on the defensive. Arab and Palestinian efforts to bypass or dispossess the Arab Higher Committee as the only legitimate representative of the Palestinians culminated in the establishment of the Palestine Liberation Organization in 1964. Thus, the Mufti's apologetics were intended not only to justify his past policies, but also to legitimize his continuing claim as chairman of the Arab Higher Committee to the official leadership of the Palestinian people.

The Mufti's struggle for leadership is reflected in the apologetic literature published mainly by his faithful lieutenant Emil al-Ghori describing his active role as leader of the Palestinian national movement under the Mandate and during the war.[73]

This Palestinian literature also aims at falsifying the allegations spread in the Arab world since 1948 assigning the Palestinians responsibility for their own tragedy. These allegations included the charges that the Palestinians failed to fight for their national cause, that they collaborated in selling their lands to the Jews and abandoned it without resistance, and that they were irreparably divided and "negative."[74] In the aftermath of the 1948 war, feeling an urgent need to counter these allegations, Palestinian writers emphasized the long-standing struggle of the indigenous Palestinian Arab population for its homeland and political rights. Thus, the Mandate era was depicted as one in which the Palestinians courageously challenged the mighty British Empire through repeated uprisings and willingly sacrificed their lives for the national cause. This behavior was carried on in the face of the activities of Arab "traitors" and the Zionist-Imperialist plot against the Palestinians.[75]

In these Palestinian writings, the Arab states are basically portrayed as indifferent to the Palestinian's need for material support and lacking a strong sense of national consciousness. Arab governments, it is argued, abandoned the Palestinians, thereby contributing to the creation of the Arab refugee problem that they subsequently exploited for their own ends. In addition, they made possible the emigration of their Jewish populations, thus reducing the Palestinian refugees' chances to return to their homes.

Above all, the Arab governments are accused of virtually implementing the British plans by preventing the Palestinians from assuming any significant political and military role in the struggle for Palestine. Indeed, this point remains a leading complaint against the Arab governments. Moreover, Palestinian writings implicitly criticize the Hashemite states for opposing the Mufti's requests to establish a provisional Palestinian government which would bear sole responsibility for military action and civil administration, and for being content to merely provide material support.[76] Palestinian sources also argue that, given the British control over the Arab Legion, the intervention of the regular armies in the war for Palestine was tantamount to reintroducing a British presence into Palestine. It is even argued that Britain encouraged the invasion of Palestine by the Arab regular armies. A further claim is that the mission of the Army of Deliverance was to undermine the Holy Jihad and that Qawaqji was a British agent.[77]

It is noteworthy that other sources, written by long-standing supporters of the Palestine cause as well as by members of the Muslim Brotherhood who volunteered to fight in Palestine as a religious duty, support the argument that the intervention of the Army of Deliverance and the regular Arab armies in Palestine was fatal.[78] In both Egypt and Syria, the Muslim Brotherhood, which maintained close ties with the Mufti, sided with the Palestinians and criticized their own government's weak and insufficiently patriotic posture.

The literature sponsored by the Arab Higher Committee, as well as Palestinian historiography in general, sharply criticizes the Arab governments for acting during the war according to their own particular narrow interests. They argue that, while the Palestinians were in the midst of a desperate struggle for survival, the Arab governments were involved in negotiations with the imperialists over the building of new oil pipelines in Syria and Lebanon. Because of their subordination to imperialism, the Arab governments refused to invade Palestine before the Mandate terminated. Similarly, Egypt's refusal to allow the Mufti to return to Palestine shortly before the end of the Mandate was an effort to assuage the British, who naturally objected to the Mufti's presence in Palestine. Moreover, when the Mufti finally arrived in Gaza in late September 1948 to attend the Palestinian National Conference, he was forced by the Egyptian government to return to Cairo after a few days, despite his election as the council's president.[79]

The Mufti's memoirs focus on his own painstaking and thorough preparations for war—including the purchase and shipment of adequate quantities of arms and communications equipment. The Mufti also claims that he had sufficient troops and qualified commanders to win the war against the Zionists. Here he implicitly criticizes the Arab League, which forced him to accept the Army of Deliverance commanded by his sworn enemy, Fauzi al-Qawaqji.[80]

In a series of articles published by the Mufti in mid-1973 summing up his political career since the 1930s, he offers no response to the persistent complaints of leading Palestinian figures concerning their lack of success in acquiring arms during the "unofficial war" despite their repeated visits to Arab capitals in search of more military supplies.[81]

Since the revival of Palestinian nationalism in the 1960s, a new trend has been discernible in Palestinian as well as in general Arab historiography. Its basic thrust is to reestablish the Palestinian people's role as an essential element in the Arab-Israeli conflict by rewriting the history of Palestine. These writings seek to legitimate the very existence of the Palestinian people and their political rights in the face of "distorting Zionist propaganda" widely accepted in the West.[82] Accordingly, these writings range over the whole period of the British Mandate and sometimes even reach back to the Canaanite era in an effort to link the present-day Palestinians to the original inhabitants of the country. Recapitulating the land and population situation in Palestine before the 1948 catastrophe, these writings seek to reassert the claims of the refugees and refute Israeli allegations that the Palestinians had left their country in response to calls from Arab states.[83]

In the 1960s and 1970s, a new thrust emerged in Palestinian historiography. Wishing to persuade Western public opinion of Israel's illegitimacy, these writings describe Israel as a state born in sin on the wreckage of the Palestinian society.[84] Zionism is presented as an ideology based on military power which was unjustly used against the unarmed and defenseless Arab inhabitants as part of a premeditated plan under the shield of the withdrawing British Mandate forces.

The role of the Palestinians in the 1948 war is generally portrayed as heroic and crucial to the overall Arab effort, with an emphasis on their struggle in the face of a shortage of arms, lack of military training, and poor command. However, their participation in Arab attacks on the *yishuv* is essentially ignored. Regarding the refugee problem, the more recent Palestinian sources argue that the Jewish offensive alone was responsible for the exodus of about 300,000 Arabs prior to 15 May, that is, before the invasion of the regular Arab armies.[85] Also, the Haganah offensive is usually presented as an independent Jewish initiative, with no mention made of the threat posed by Arab irregular forces to the *yishuv*'s very existence. In other words, these accounts either deny the Palestinians' responsibility for rejecting the U.N. partition resolution or entirely ignore the "unofficial war" engaged in by Palestinians and Arab volunteers alike.

Following the establishment of the Palestine Liberation Organization (PLO), renewed endeavors were undertaken to commemorate Palestinian determination to remain and defend their villages.[86]

Integral to this effort was a systematic attempt to collect documentary material and to sponsor and publish research on the period in question. These studies, emphasizing the rich Palestinian heritage of pre-1948, are particularly attentive to criticism that the lack of a strong institutional infrastructure within Palestinian society was its main source of weakness during the war. The response to such criticism has been to emphasize the leadership and institutions in Arab Palestinian society, the destructive role of the Arab states in the Palestinians' struggle to establish their national sovereignty, the short-lived "All-Palestine government," and the usurpation of Palestinian sovereignty by Hashemite Jordan and Israel.[87]

The most contentious question in the historiography of the war remains that of the Palestinian refugees. Without delving too far into the historical debate as to why the Palestinians left, it is worth exploring Palestinian sources that offer reasons for their departure. The most comprehensive account of the war, written by the Palestinian historian 'Arif al-'Arif, attributes the departure primarily to Jewish military power. 'Arif draws a clear distinction between cases of outright expulsion of Arab populations by Jewish forces and cases resulting from the ongoing hostilities.[88] 'Arif maintains that military and organizational weakness, combined with the early departure of Palestinian notables and political leaders, created an atmosphere of fear among local Palestinians. The ensuing sense of insecurity, heightened by Arab disunity and inept leadership, drove the population to seek refuge elsewhere.

In his memoirs, the Mufti stresses that he tried to halt the mass flight and that, at various stages of the "unofficial war," he unsuccessfully asked Arab governments to turn away Palestinian males seeking refuge.[89] At the same time, however, Palestinian Arab memoirs argue that the panic among the Arab population was aggravated by the ineptitude of local and national Palestinian leaders; their miscalculated propaganda concerning Jewish atrocities such as the Deir Yassin massacre; and their absence from the scene.[90] Palestinian Arabs, particularly from the Jewish areas, tended to view their departure as temporary.

These explanations are heavily supported by other Palestinian and Arab memoirs and research. Although each of these sources accepts the predominant Arab argument that the Zionists expelled the Palestinians deliberately, each provides other reasons for the early collapse of the Palestinian community. These reasons include basic military weakness, an extreme socio-political fragmentation, the lack of an institutional infrastructure, meager military participation among the Palestinians, and above all, the damage caused by the Army of Deliverance, which tended to retreat in the face of Jewish military pressure.[91]

The most important Palestinian historian to take up the refugee issue is Professor Walid Khalidi. His numerous articles dealing with the refugee question try to refute the official Israeli claim that the Palestinians were ordered to leave by Arab broadcasts that promised them that they could return to their homes after the liberation.[92] Significantly, the arguments that the Palestinians were told to leave, were encouraged to do so on humanitarian grounds, or were led to understand that their departure was only temporary are included in several Palestinian and Arab sources, including the Mufti's memoirs.[93] While this explanation neither lessens Israel's share of responsibility for the creation of the refugee problem nor blames the Palestinians for bringing the tragedy on themselves, it is seen as necessary to any explanation of the causes underlying the Palestinian exodus.

However, these sources are almost entirely ignored by Khalidi, who nowhere comes to grips with the historical context of the flight. Moreover, Khalidi does not address the socio-political factors contributing to the Palestinian community's weakness which rendered it totally unable to militarily support the posturing of its political leadership. Indeed, he even argues that the intention to systematically expel the Palestinians was an integral part of the Haganah's "Plan D," launched at the beginning of April.

Like Professor Edward Said, Khalidi argues vehemently that the idea of expelling the Arab Palestinians—the "transfer" concept—was deeply rooted in the ideology of the Zionist movement from its very inception. He thus criticizes Benny Morris for concluding in his book that the Arab exodus from Palestine was not the result of pre-planned Zionist strategy, but of complex factors resulting from the war. Khalidi's contention, however, seems to be based solely on his assumption that a "connection exists between the imperative to 'transfer' the Arab population and seize its lands and the imperative to accommodate the hundred thousands of Jews it was planned to bring to the new Jewish state."[94] This logic suggests that even if the Arabs had not resorted to arms in the six-month "unofficial war," the *yishuv* would still have wielded its power to expel the Arab population.

Conclusions

A major characteristic of a democratic and pluralistic society is its ability to engage in an open and critical discussion of its own cultural and political legacy, undertake a critical inquiry into its past, and critically evaluate its historical myths. However, Arab historical writings on the 1948 war have been shaped by an ongoing concern with the fateful issues confronting the Arab world in our time: how to effect a break with centuries of political and cultural decline, and most of all, how to deal with the painful impact of the West on Arab society and culture. Accordingly, it is particularly difficult for Arab historians to treat the Arab-Israeli conflict in purely academic terms. Not only were the Arabs defeated in the crucial 1948 war, but the Palestinian-Jewish conflict prevents the wounds from healing. Moreover, in the period since 1948, the Arab world has neither been able to cope militarily with the Jewish state nor accomplish its pan-Arab goal of a collective commitment to the Palestinian cause. In short, the history of the 1948 war is an essential part of the "unfinished business" of Arab nationalism.

Recent studies by Egyptian and Jordanian historians may be indicative of a new political self-confidence, a more critical historiographical approach, and a more dispassionate attitude towards Israel.[95] However, there is no reason to anticipate such a critical historiography in the foreseeable future from Palestinian writers. Insofar as the right of return of the Palestinian refugees and the establishment of a sovereign Palestinian state is an essential element of Palestinian nationalism, an unbiased open academic debate of this painful chapter in Palestinian history may not be possible until the resolution of the Palestine problem.

NOTES

This is a preliminary version of a larger research on Arab historiography of the 1948 war.

1. Wilfred C. Smith, *Islam in Modern History* (New York, 1957), 121–24; G. V. Von Grunebaum, "Self-Image and Approach to History," in Bernard Lewis and P. M. Holt, eds., *Historians of the Middle East* (Oxford, 1962), 457–583; Yehoshafat Harkabi, *Arab Attitudes to Israel* (London, 1972), 362. For a similar approach, see Emanuel Sivan, "Modern Arab Historiography of the Crusades," *Asian and African Studies* 8, no. 2 (1972): 142–43. As will become clear in the following pages, I am using the term historiography in its broadest sense to include critical and non-critical historical writings.
2. Elie Kedourie, *Arab Political Memoirs* (London, 1974), 177–78.
3. Ibid., 178; Muhamad 'Izzat Darwaza, *Hawl al-Haraka al-Arabiya al-Haditha* (Sidon, 1950), vol. 4, pt. I, 30; 'Arif al-'Arif, *al-Nakba: Nakbat Beit al-Maqdis wal-Fardus al-Mafqud, 1947–1952* (Sidon and Beirut, 1959), 3–4; Hassan Mustafa, *Mudhakirat Mulhaq Askari fi London Qabl Harb Filastin wa-Athna'ha, 1946–1949* (Baghdad, 1985), 9–10; Al-Sayyid Faraj, *Jaishuna fi Filastin, May–July 1948* (Cairo, August 1948), 39.
4. Kedourie, *Arab Political Memoirs*, 178.
5. The earliest and most prominent examples are: Kustantin Zureiq, *Ma'na al-Nakba* (Beirut, 1948); Musa al-Alami, *'Ibrat Filastin* (Beirut, 1949). For an English version of Alami's booklet, see his article "The Lesson of Palestine," *Middle East Journal* 3 (October 1949): 373–405. See also Walid Qamhawi, *al-Nakba wal-Bina' fi al-Watan al-Arabi* (Beirut, 1962).
6. For examples of complaints over this state of affairs, see Mustafa, *Mudhakirat*, 24, 35; Salah al-Aqqad, *Qadiyat Filastin, al-Marhala al-Harija (1945–1956)* (Cairo, 1968), 111.
7. Such critical works are the comprehensive books of 'Arif al-'Arif and Muhamad 'Izzat Darwaza, *al-Qadiya al-Filastiniya fi Mukhtalaf Marahiliha* (Beirut, 1951), pt. II; Walid Khalidi, "The Fall of Haifa," *Middle East Forum* 35, no. 12 (1959): 22–32; Khalidi, "Why Did the Palestinians Leave?" *Middle East Forum* 34, no. 7 (1959): 21–24, 35; Khalidi, "The Arab Perspective," in William Roger Louis and Robert W. Stookey, eds., *The End of the Palestine Mandate* (Austin, 1986), 104–36; Leila S. Kadi, *Arab Summit Conferences and the Palestine Problem, 1936–1950, 1964–1966* (Beirut, 1966); Bayan N. al-Hout, *al-Qiyadat wal-Muassasat al-Filastiniya, 1918–1948* (Beirut, 1981); Muhamad Fa'iz al-Qasri, *Harb Filastin 'Am 1948* (Cairo, 1961); Hani al-Hindi, "Jaish al-Inqadh, 1947–1949," *Shu'un Filastiniya*, pt. I, no. 23 (1973): 27–58, pt. II, no. 24 (1973): 115–32; Hassan al-Badri, *al-Harb fi Ard al-Salam; al-Jawla al-Arabiya al-Israiliya al-Uwla, 1947–1949* (Cairo, 1976);

Abd al-Wahab Bakr Muhamad, *al-Jaish al-Misri wa-Harb Filastin, 1948–1952* (Cairo, 1982); Sulaiman Mussa, *Ayam La Tunsa, al-Urdun fi Harb 1948* (Amman, 1982); Nafez Nazzal, *The Palestinian Exodus from Galilee, 1948* (Beirut, 1978).

8. See for example: 'Arif, *al-Nakba*, 31, 33–34; Bakr, *al-Jaish al-Misri*, 116; Badri, *al-Harb fi Ard al-Salam*, 3–20; Anis Sayigh, *al-Hashimiyun wa-Qadiyat Filastin* (Sidon and Beirut, 1966), 227–30, 235, 240–43, 247–48; Hout, *al-Qiyadat*, 637, 639; Khalidi, "Haifa," 25–32; Mussa, *Ayam La Tunsa*, 77–9, 532; Kadi, *Arab Summit*, 51–52, 60; Nazzal, *Palestinian Exodus*, 105.

9. Exceptions sporadically using British documents are Mussa, *Ayam La Tunsa*; Bakr, *al-Jaish al-Misri*; and Mustafa, *Mudhakirat*.

10. See, for example, Nazzal, Khalidi's "Arab Perspective," Bakr, and Mussa. None of them or other historians, such as Hout, *al-Qiyadat*, who uses relatively many Arab memoirs, used the diary of Taha al-Hashimi, the prominent figure behind organizing and directing the Arab irregular forces in Palestine. See Khaldun S. al-Husri, ed., *Mudhakirat Taha al-Hashimi*, pt. II, 1942–1955 (Beirut, 1978).

11. Kedourie, *Arab Political Memoirs*, 178.

12. As presented in Harkabi, *Arab Attitudes to Israel*, 362–83.

13. Bernard Lewis, *History, Remembered, Recovered, Invented* (New York, 1975), 18.

14. Faraj, *Jaishuna fi Filastin*. The preface to the book is signed by General 'Uthman al-Mahdi, the deputy chief of staff of the Egyptian army.

15. Ibid., 11, 13, 27–29, 55–57, 119.

16. Ibid., 97. For examples of criticism of the Arab acceptance of the first truce, see Badri, *al-Harb fi Ard al-Salam*, 79; and Bakr, *al-Jaish al-Misri*, 119. Jamal Abd al-Nasser, *Falsafat al-Thawra* (Cairo, 1956), 24, blames King Farouk for committing the "great treason" of accepting the first truce. For the perception of the first truce as a "spectacular mistake," see Sami al-Hakim, *Tariq al-Nakba* (Cairo, 1969), 65–66. For a caveat on this argument, see Mussa, *Ayam La Tunsa*, 298, 304.

17. Faraj, *Jaishuna fi Filastin*, 39.

18. "al-Jalsa al-Sirriya li-Majlis al-Shuyukh al-Ma'quda fi 11 Mayu 1948 'an Mas'alat Filastin," *al-Tali'a* 3 (March 1975), 135.

19. For the Senate proceedings, see "Jalsa Sirriya," 135–44; Badri, *al-Harb fi Ard al-Salam*, 40; Muhamad Hussein Haikal, *Mudhakirat fi al-Siyasa al-Misriya*, pt. III (Cairo, 1978), 41–45.

20. Haikal, *Mudhakirat*, 41–45. The concept of "political demonstration" is also approved by *Taqrir al-Lajna al-Niyabiya fi Qadiyat Filastin* (Baghdad: The Government Press, 1949), 34; Muhamad Faisal Abd al-Mun'im, *Asrar 1948* (Cairo, 1968), 191–93; Qasri, *Harb Filastin*, 157. "Jalsa Sirriya," 135–44. See also Fadel al-Jamali, *Dhikrayat wa-'Ibar* (Beirut, 1965), 33.

21. Faraj, *Jaishuna fi Filastin*, 39.

22. Abd al-Mun'im, *Filastin Qalb al-'Uruba* (Dar al-Ma'arif, Cairo, 1968), 9, 15; Badri, *al-Harb fi Ard al-Salam*, 85.
23. *Taqrir al-Lajna al-Niyabiya*, 34, 191; Salih Sa'ib al-Jubouri, *Mihnat Filastin* (Beirut, 1970), 131–32.
24. I derive my interpretation from my reading of "Jalsa Sirriya," 44.
25. Nasser, *Falsafat*, 24.
26. Jamal Abd al-Nasser, *Mudhakirat Harb Filastin*, ed. Muhamad Hassanein Heikal (Cairo, n.d.), 25–32, 34–39, 42–45, 62, 64, 68.
27. Badri, *al-Harb fi Ard al-Salam*, 45–46, 85, 232, 237; Bakr, *al-Jaish al-Misri*, 63, 65–66, 74–79, 117–18, 153.
28. Quoted from Von Grunebaum, "Self-Image and Approach to History," 475. For examples of Nasser's use of the history of the Palestine war for drawing lessons and enhancing his pan-Arab nationalist ideas, leadership, and legitimacy, see Nasser, *Falsafat*, 103, 110–11, as well as in his *Filastin, Min Aqwal al-Ra'iss Jamal Abd al-Nasser* (Cairo, n.d.), 12–13, 15, 34, 45, 51, 57, 60, 107–8, 120–25, 128, 131, 138.
29. See Heikal's introduction to Nasser's war memoirs, *Mudhakirat Harb Filastin*, pp. 11–18, as well as his concluding essay emphasizing the role of Palestine in the development of Nasser's pan-Arabism, pp. 106–111.
30. Jubouri, *Mihnat Filastin*, 314, 435–44.
31. For the background to the establishment of the Parliamentary Inquiry Commission, see the introduction of *Taqrir al-Lajna al-Niyabiya*. For a different version, see Muhamad Mahdi Kubba, *Mudhakirati fi Samim al-Ahdath* (Beirut, 1965), 267.
32. For example, *Taqrir al-Lajna al-Niyabiya*, 30, 36–37, 67, 69–70. See also Jubouri, *Mihnat Filastin*, 131–32.
33. *Taqrir al-Lajna al-Niyabiya*, 23–28. On the oil weapon, see *Taqrir al-Lajna al-Niyabiya*, 89–91, 116. See also Jamali, *Dhikrayat*, 116; Kadi, *Arab Summit*, 83–84.
34. *Taqrir al-Lajna al-Niyabiya*, 200; Jubouri, *Mihnat Filastin*, 189–201.
35. Jubouri, *Mihnat Filastin*, 311–19, 323–28, 440–41.
36. Ibid., 122, 439. Jubouri himself mentions much smaller numbers at another place in his book, p. 502. See Badri, *al-Harb fi Ard al-Salam*, 616; Bakr, *al-Jaish al-Misri*, 75; Mussa, *Ayam La Tunsa*, 9–10.
37. Jubouri, *Mihnat Filastin*, 173–79.
38. Mustafa, *Mudhakirat*, 26–30, 36, 55–61; Jubouri, *Mihnat Filastin*, 141, 332–33.
39. 'Arif, *al-Nakba*, 602, 607–9; Sayigh, *al-Hashimiyun*, 261–62; Aqqad, *Qadiyat Filastin*, 96–97. See Mussa's explanation on these accusations, *Ayam La Tunsa*, 371–72.
40. Abdullah Ibn al-Hussein, "al-Takmila," in *al-Athar al-Kamila lil-Malik Abdullah Ibn al-Hussein*, ed. Umar al-Madani (Amman, 1979), 295. See also 241–45.
41. Ibid., 263. On Abdullah's position to the Gaza government, see 243–44.

42. Ibid., 242, 259–63.
43. Ibid., 321–22.
44. Mahmud al-Russan, *Ma'arik Bab al-Wad* (Amman, n.d. [1950?]), 30–32. See also Abdullah al-Tal, *Karithat Filastin, Mudhakirat Abdullah al-Tal, Qa'id Ma'rakat al-Quds* (Acre, 1958), 4, 19–22.
45. Russan, *Ma'arik Bab al-Wad*, 30–32.
46. Tal, *Karithat Filastin*, 21, 27, 35–36, 65–73, 100, 344–45, 432, 437–42, 473–97.
47. Ibid., 407.
48. Ibid., 4, 19–22, 31–35, 158–59.
49. See, for example, the author's preface to the second edition, p. 7.
50. Sayigh, *al-Hashimiyun*, 261, 264–65; Israel Bear, *Bithon Israel, Etmol, Hayom, Mahar* (Tel Aviv, 1966), 125–35. For distorted and sometimes invented descriptions of the talks' proceedings between Abdullah and the Jews, see Wahid al-Dali, *Asrar al-Jami'a al-Arabiya wa-Abd al-Rahman Azzam* (Cairo, 1982), 259–88; Emile Tuma, *Yawmiyat Sha'b, Thalathuna 'Aman ala al-Ittihad* (Haifa, 1974), 59–60, 63–64; Simha Flapan, *The Birth of Israel: Myths and Realities* (New York, 1987), 142–44; Avi Shlaim, *Collusion across the Jordan* (New York, 1988), 122–59, 220, 233–38. For a reassessment of the validity of the myth of "collusion" between Abdullah and the Jews, see my "Yahasei ha-Melekh Abdullah u-Memshelet Israel be-Milhemet ha-Atzma'ut - Bhina Mehudeshet," *Cathedra* 57, pt. I (September 1990): 120–25, and *Cathedra* 58, pt. II (December 1990): 172–93.
51. Hazza' al-Majali, *Mudhakirati* (Amman, 1960), 8.
52. Ibid., 52–55, 79.
53. Ibid., 77–79; Abdullah, "al-Takmila," 261; Mussa, *Ayam La Tunsa*, 321.
54. Majali, *Mudhakirati*, 90–92. See Tal's version about his own role in this regard, *Karithat Filastin*, 504–5.
55. Majali, *Mudhakirati*, 62. For a similar criticism, see Ahmad al-Shuqairi, *Arba'un 'Aman fi al-Hayat al-Arabiya wal-Dawliya* (Beirut, 1969), 289; 'Arif, *al-Nakba*, 174. See the critical response, representing the Arab Higher Committee, to Shuqairi's argument about Deir Yassin: Emil al-Ghori, *Al-Shuqairi fi al-Mizan: Abatil Tudhiduha al-Haqa'iq* (Amman, 1972), 114.
56. Mussa, *Ayam La Tunsa*, 76–77.
57. Ibid., 127–44, 281–86, 345–72.
58. Ibid., 479–80, 298–302. Mussa raises the question whether Jewish Jerusalem could have sustained the siege without the truce.
59. For Syria's leadership role in sponsoring the volunteers and the Army of Deliverance, see Husri, *Mudhakirat Taha al-Hashimi*, from p. 151 on; *Filastin fi Mudhakirat Fawzi al-Qawaqji, 1936–1948*, ed. Khairiya Qasimiya (Beirut: PLO Research Center, 1975), vol. II, from p. 124 on; Amin al-Nafouri, "al-Jaish al-Souri fi Harb Filastin 'Am 1948," *Al-Fikr al-Askari* 7, no. 2–3 (1979): 11; 'Arif, *al-Nakba*, 40; Hindi, "Jaish al-Inqadh," 47. On Abdullah's aspirations for Greater Syria and its implications on Damascus' rulers, see

Najib al-Armanazi, *'Ashar Sanawat fi al-Diblumasiya fi Samim al-Ahdath al-Arabiya wal-Dawliya* (Beirut, 1964), 125–29; Husri, *Mudhakirat Taha al-Hashimi*, 158, 166, 180, 182, 217.

60. Muhamad 'Ismat Shikhu, *Suria wa-Qadiyat Filastin* (Dar Qutaiba, Damascus, 1982), 5–6; Nafouri, "al-Jaish al-Souri," 1–2, 4.
61. Shikhu, *Suria wa-Qadiyat Filastin*, 287–90, 98–99, 141–42.
62. Nafouri, "al-Jaish al-Souri," 8, 33, 35; Qasri, *Harb Filastin*, 155–56; see also his *Ma'sat al-'Alam al-Arabi* (Damascus, 1959), 214–15; Husri, *Mudhakirat Taha al-Hashimi*, 151.
63. Qasri, *Harb Filastin*, 155–56; Nafouri, "al-Jaish al-Souri," 13–16, 23, 38.
64. Qasri, *Harb Filastin*, 157, 169–71, 206–8.
65. See, for example, 'Arif, *al-Nakba*, 459; Darwaza, *Hawl al-Haraka*, 19–20.
66. Nafouri, "al-Jaish al-Souri," 38; Qawaqji, *Filastin*, 270–75. On the withdrawal of the Army of Deliverance, see Hindi, "Jaish al-Inqadh," 118. Qawaqji himself argues that both King Abdullah and the Syrian leadership were responsible for the decision to withdraw his forces: Fauzi Al-Qawaqji, "Memoirs, 1948," *Journal of Palestine Studies*, vol. 1, pt. I, no. 4 (1972): 14, and vol. 2, pt. II, no. 1 (1973): 13, 28. See also his *Filastin*, 194–97.
67. Qasri, *Harb Filastin*, 250–52. Hindi, "Jaish al-Inqadh," pt. I, 38–39, 50, disagrees with Qasri on the level of the soldiers. Subhi Yasin, *Harb al-Isabat fi Filastin* (Cairo, 1967), 160, presents Qawaqji as a collaborator with Britain.
68. Hindi, "Jaish al-Inqadh," 35, 42–44, 116–17; Wasfi al-Tal, *Kitabat fi al-Qadaya al-Arabia* (Amman, 1980), 256–57, 261–62; Qasri, *Harb Filastin*, 153, 206–9, 250–51; Husri, *Mudhakirat Taha al-Hashimi*, 185.
69. Qawaqji, *Filastin*, 132–38, 146–49, 151–52, 172–77, 184–85, 233. See also his *Memoirs, 1948*, pt. II, 4–6, 27–28.
70. Qawaqji, *Filastin*, 149; Armanazi, *'Ashar Sanawat*, 208.
71. The most vehement criticism is found in Ahmad Farraj Tayi', *Safahat Matwiya 'an Qadiyat Filastin* (n.p., n.d.), 56–59, 65–68, 71–75, 87–88; and in Husri, *Mudhakirat Taha al-Hashimi*, 152–58, 181, 190–92, 198–202, 208–9. See also, Abdullah, "al-Takmila," 232, 295; Muhamad Nimr al-Hawari, *Sir al-Nakba* (Nazareth, 1955), 96–98, 127, 145–46, 346–50; Wasfi al-Tal, *Kitabat*, 260; Jubouri, *Mihnat Filastin*, 499–501; Qawaqji, *Filastin*, 123–24, 126–27, 236; Shuqairi, *Arba'un 'Aman*, 290; *Taqrir al-Lajna al-Niyabiya*, 149–50; Darwaza, *Hawl al-Haraka*, pt. I, 119.
72. Al-Haj Amin al-Husseini, *Haqa'iq 'an Qadiyat Filastin* (Cairo, 1954), 5–6. The book was published under the auspices of the Arab Higher Committee. Darwaza, *Hawl al-Haraka*, pt. I, particularly 59–62, 74–83, 102–21; pt. II, 9–30.
73. For defense of the Mufti's record, see Emil al-Ghori, *Filastin Ibra Sittin Aman* (Beirut, 1972), 235–38, 244, 247; Muhamad 'Izzat Darwaza, *al-Qadiya al-Filastiniya fi Mukhtalaf Marahiliha* (Beirut, 1951), pt. II, 39. See also Emil al-Ghori, *al-Mu'amara al-Kubra: Ightiyal Filastin wa-Mahq al-Arab* (Cairo,

1955), 199–216, 238–39, 224–27; *al-Mu'adhabun fi Ard al-Arab* (Beirut, 1960), 38, 75–77, 86–87.
74. Ghori, *al-Mu'adhabun*, 5–6, 154–56; Husseini, *Haqa'iq*, 8.
75. Ghori, *al-Mu'adhabun*, 74–75, 156; Ghori, *al-Mu'amara*, 198–99; Akram Zu'aitar, *al-Qadiya al-Filastiniya* (Cairo, 1955), 93–126; Dhuqan al-Hindawi, *al-Qadiya al-Filastiniya* (al-Mamlaka al-Urduniya al-Hashimiya, Wizarat al-Tarbiya wal-Ta'lim, 1964), 69; Husseini, *Haqa'iq*, 9–26.
76. Husseini, *Haqa'iq*, 21, 61, 164; *Taqrir al-Lajna al-Niyabiya*, 67, 149–50. Compare the Mufti's version with Husri, *Mudhakirat Taha al-Hashimi*, 198–202; Qawaqji, *Filastin*, 123–24.
77. Husseini, *Haqa'iq*, 21, 61, 174–75; Ghori, *al-Mu'amara*, 209–12, 236–39, 244–49, 256–66; Ghori, *al-Mu'adhabun*, 80–87. Even Hout, *al-Qiyadat*, 637–38, who depicts the Palestinian national leadership's policies as "negative," joins the argument that had the Palestinians been left alone to tackle their problem by themselves, they would have succeeded. Yasin, *Harb al-Isabat*, 160; Darwaza, *Hawl al-Haraka*, 74–75, 104–5, 107; Mustafa al-Siba'i, *al-Ikhwan al-Muslimun fi Harb Filastin* (Dar al-Nadhir, 1985), 52.
78. Kamil Isma'il al-Sharif, *al-Ikhwan al-Muslimun fi Harb Filastin* (Cairo, 1951), 25–30; Siba'i, *al-Ikhwan al-Muslimun*, 48, 51–52; Muhamad Hassan al-'Uraibi, *Sira' al-Fida'iyin: al-Fida'iyin al-Libiyin fi Harb Filastin 1948* (Tripoli-Libya, 1968), 92–94.
79. Husseini, *Haqa'iq*, 81–84; Ghori, *al-Mu'amara*, 236–38, 244–49; Kadi, *Arab Summit*, 53–55, 83–84; Mun'im, *Filastin Qalb al-'Uruba*, 37–39.
80. Husseini, *Haqa'iq*, 92–93, 97; see also his memoirs in *A'khir Sa'a* 6, 20 June, 1973; 4, 18 July, 1973. See also 'Arif, *al-Nakba*, 45–46, 73; Sharif, *al-Ikhwan al-Muslimun*, 74; Hawari, *Sir al-Nakba*, 119, 121–22.
81. Husri, *Mudhakirat Taha al-Hashimi*, 198–200; Wasfi al-Tal, *Kitabat*, 268; Abdullah al-Tal, *Karithat Filastin*, 14.
82. Sami Hadawi, *Palestine: Loss of a Heritage* (San Antonio, 1963), 4; and his *Palestine: Questions and Answers* (New York, 1966), 1–2; Ibrahim Abu-Lughod, ed., *The Transformation of Palestine: Essays on the Origins and Development of the Arab-Israeli Conflict* (Evanston, 1971), xi–xiii; Badri, *al-Harb fi Ard al-Salam*, 3; Hindawi, *al-Qadiya al-Filastiniya*, 6, 8, 11–13; Henri Katan, *Filastin fi dhou' al-Haq wal-'Adl* (Beirut, 1970), introduction by Akram Zu'aitar (this book is a translation into Arabic from an English version: *Palestine, the Arabs and Israel: The Search for Justice* [London, 1969]).
83. Hadawi, *Loss*, 4, 12–23, 28–29, 50–105; Hadawi, *Bitter Harvest: Palestine between 1914–1967* (New York, 1967), 111–15, 169–89; Hadawi, *Questions*, 24–27; Katan, *Filastin*, 57. See also Khalidi's first two articles cited in n. 7 above.
84. Katan, *Filastin*, the introduction, 53–54, 57; Hadawi, *Loss*, 1–4; and also his *Bitter Harvest*, 1–8; and his *Crime and No Punishment: Zionist-Israeli Terrorism 1939–1972* (Beirut, 1972) 8–9, 20–23, 28–29; Izzat Tannous, *The Expulsion*

of the Palestine Arabs from Their Homeland: A Dark Page in Jewish History (New York: 1961), 15–20. See also Hindawi, al-Qadiya al-Filastiniya, 56–68, 124–25, 139–40.

85. Katan, Filastin, 57; Hindawi, al-Qadiya al-Filastiniya, 139; Hadawi, Questions, 27; Hadawi, Loss, 4; Tannous, The Expulsion, 15–20.
86. For example, Khairiya Qasimiya, "Abd al-Qadir al-Husseini fi Dhikrah al-Khamis wal-'Ishrin," Shu'un Filastiniya 20 (1973); Nafidh Yousuf Abdullah, "Filastiniyoun Yatadhakkaroun: al-Qital fi Sabil al-Birwa," Shu'un Filastiniya 21 (1973); Akram Dairi, "Suqout al-Nasira wal-Jalil: Dawr Fawj Hittin Ajnadin," Shu'un Filastiniya 21 (1973); Muhamad Hisham al-'Azm, "Suqout Safad," Shu'un Filastiniya 46 (1975); Abd al-Rahman Ali wa-Abdullah Muhanna, "Min Dhikrayat 1947–1948: Hakadha Kunna Najma' al-Silah," Shu'un Filastiniya 21 (1973).
87. 'Issa Shu'aibi, "al-Tajriba al-Kiyaniya al-Mahida," Shu'un Filastiniya 90 (1979): 87–114; Hout, al-Qiyadat, pp. ix–xii; Samih Shabib, "Muqaddimat al-Musadara al-Rasmiya lil-Shakhsiya al-Wataniya al-Filastiniya, 1948–1950," Shu'un Filastiniya 129–31 (1982): 72–87; see also his Hukoumat 'Umoum Filastin, Muqaddimat wa-Nata'ij (Nicosia, 1988); Isam Sakhnini, Filastin al-Dawla, Judhour al-Mas'ala fi al-Tarikh al-Filastini (Acre, 1986), 217–36. See also his "Dam Filastin al-Wusta Ila Sharqi al-Urdun, 1948–1950," Shu'un Filastiniya 40 (1974): 56–83.
88. 'Arif, al-Nakba, 178–79 for Jerusalem, 206–23 for Haifa, 259–63 for Jaffa, 300–311 for Safed, 420–23 for Acre. In the case of Beisan, he mentions expulsion, 312; Hout, al-Qiyadat, 623–37. Hawari, Sir al-Nakba, 312–14, argues that expulsion of Arabs from the territory allotted to the Jewish state started only after the first truce. Tayi', Safahat Matwiya, 84-85.
89. Husseini, Haqa'iq, 63–73; Muhamad Nimr al-Khatib, Min Athar al-Nakba (Damascus, 1951), 167, 169.
90. Khatib, Min Athar al-Nakba, 202; Wasfi al-Tal, Kitabat, 260, 269; 'Arif, al-Nakba, 174; Shuqairi, Arba'un 'Aman, 289; Hala al-Sakakini, ed., Kadha Ana Ya Dunya: Yawmiyat Khalil al-Sakakini (Jerusalem, 1955), 379–89.
91. Alami, "The Lesson," 381; Hout, al-Qiyadat, 623–37; Khalidi, "The Fall of Haifa," 24–26; Wasfi al-Tal, Kitabat, 270–71, 273; Nazzal, Palestinian Exodus, 72–77, 79; 'Arif, al-Nakba, 172, 627.
92. Besides Khalidi's articles mentioned above, see also his "Plan Dalet: Master Plan for the Conquest of Palestine," Middle East Forum 37 (1961): 11. On the issue of Arab radio broadcasts to the Palestinians, see also Erskin Childers, "The Other Exodus," Spectator, 12 May 1961, whose conclusions are consistent with Khalidi's "Why Did the Palestinians Leave?" For a different view, based on the same sources, see John Zimmerman, "Radio Propaganda in the Arab-Israeli War 1948," The Wiener Library Bulletin XXVII (1973/74): 30–31.
93. Alami, "The Lesson," 381; Zu'aitar, al-Qadiya al-Filastiniya, 212. Husseini, Haqa'iq, 66, complains about the Arab states' call to women, children, and

the disabled to leave. Khalid al-'Azm, *Mudhakkirat* (Beirut, 1973), pt. I, 386-87; *al-Difa'*, 6 September, 1954; 'Aqqad, *Qadiyat Filastin*, 98.
94. Khalidi, "Plan Dalet," reproduced in *Journal of Palestine Studies* XVIII (1988): no. 1, 5; Eduard Said, *The Question of Palestine* (New York, 1980), 99-102.
95. See Bakr, *al-Jaish al-Misri*; and Mussa, *Ayam La Tunsa*.

III. MYTHS, SYMBOLS, VALUES: THE STRUGGLE FOR NATIONAL IDENTITY

CHAPTER 8

Attitudes of the Young State of Israel toward the Holocaust and Its Survivors: A Debate over Identity and Values

DINA PORAT

In a Tel Aviv street in 1947, two poets were speaking about the ghettos and the Holocaust. The first poet, Abba Kovner, was highly respected as a commander of the Vilna Ghetto underground and of partisans in the forests of Eastern Europe. Nathan Alterman, the second man, was *the* poet laureate of the movement to create a new Jewish state and a new Hebrew person. At the end of their conversation, Alterman said: "Had I been in a ghetto, I would have been with the Jewish Council" (the official Jewish leadership in the Ghetto that was accused, after the war, of cooperating with the Nazis). "But," protested Kovner, "I read your *Simchat Aniyim* [*Joy of the Poor*, a book of poetry that praised the spirit of organized fighting and unquestioning sacrifice]. How could you [say that]!" Alterman retorted: "This [the advocacy of fighting in his poetry] is here, this is specifically here!"[1]

The meeting, which symbolizes the encounter between the *yishuv*, the pre-state Jewish community in Palestine, and the survivors, marked a milestone in the ongoing debate over the self-image, identity, and values of the new Zionist society, particularly as they related to the Holocaust and its survivors. This debate was actually part of a much larger one concerning the relationship between Zionism and the Jewish people, between the *yishuv* and the Diaspora. Accordingly, the debate surrounding the destruction of European Jewry is an important chapter in the debate over values and self-understanding that started with the establishment of political Zionism and continues to this day in Israel.

This debate has been marked by an ongoing internal conflict between those Zionist ideologues who drew a sharp distinction between diaspora Jewry and the Jews of Palestine. The criticism of the official Zionist ideology which viewed the Holocaust as confirmation of the non-viability of Jewish life in the Diaspora came not only from marginal or opposition groups, but also from within circles of Zionist activists who were in direct contact with Jews in Europe. Removed, to a certain extent, from the influence of the prevailing thinking in Palestine, these activists were in a better position to acquire a clearer understanding of the condition of diaspora Jewry.

Criticism of the official Zionist position also came from poets and writers, independent thinkers who exercised enormous influence on public thinking in the *yishuv* and the state.[2] Poets laureate, like Alterman, who were considered moral consciences of their era, constantly re-examined the Zionist assumptions and pointed out the discrepancies between Zionist ideology and reality. Moreover, even among political and social leaders we find opinions critical of official Zionist views on European Jewry and the Holocaust.

In this chapter, I shall analyze the conflict between the proponents of official Zionist ideology and their critics, as it is reflected in the debates over the relationship of the *yishuv* to the victims of the Holocaust, and of the state to the survivors. I shall argue that, in their efforts to shape a clear-cut Israeli identity based on values distinct from those of the diaspora Jews, the leaders of the young state tried to ignore that conflict. However, these leaders were unsuccessful in their efforts; and, consequently, the conflict continues to permeate Israeli society and affects the self-understanding of Israeli Jews to this very day.

I shall examine this conflict through three periods: the years of World War II; from the end of the war to the establishment of the state (1945–48); and the early years of the state. The starting point of the debate, the first expressions of conflict, can be traced to the beginning of World War II. The suffering of Polish Jews, the largest community in Europe, in the ghettos appeared to the Zionists as proof confirming their predictions that diaspora Jewish life would end catastrophically. The contrast between the destruction of European Jewry and the constructive efforts in Palestine to build a homeland seemed ample confirmation of Zionist assumptions. Tragically, it was a far stronger confirmation than the Zionist movement had wanted or needed.

The information gathered in Palestine about the conduct of Jewish communities, councils, and policies in the ghettos in 1940–42 reinforced the Zionists' image of helpless diaspora Jews succumbing to their fate passively. This is evident in the response of prominent Zionist leaders to early reports on the behavior and fate of European Jewry. "The Jews of Poland, and those deported there, lost their human image," proclaimed Yitzhak Gruenbaum, a former prominent leader of Polish Jewry.[3] The poet Moshe Tabenkin, the son of the renowned leftist leader Yitzhak Tabenkin, lamented, "Terrible is our pain over the murder of tens of thousands, but no less terrible is the shame over our helplessness."[4] And David Ben Gurion, later to become first prime minister of the new state, promised: "Dear brothers and sisters tortured in Nazi ghettos, we'll do our best to avenge you. We will not rest until we rescue you both from the Nazi inferno and the decay of the Diaspora and bring you, all of you, to us, to our country that is being built and redeemed."[5]

At the same time, a different attitude was evident in the reactions of other Zionist leaders. Responding to the same news about Polish Jews, Shneur-Zalman Rubashov (later Shazar), who became the third president of Israel, suggested waiting before drawing any conclusions about their conduct because "we all come from there." Indeed, most of the *yishuv* members were born in Europe.[6]

Israel Galili, later commander of the Haganah, the defense forces of the *yishuv*, compared the Jews in Warsaw before the revolt to those in Tel Aviv: "Would they, too, not be [led as] sheep to slaughter if an enemy burst into town? . . . Jewish fate is the same everywhere." Galili's words, echoing the widespread fears in Palestine in the summer of 1942 in the face of the pending invasion of Rommel's armies, acquire greater force when we realize that he made his remarks to a convention of youngsters who were supposedly infused with the Zionist attitude of the "negation of the Diaspora."

These conflicting views are reflected in an exchange that occurred that same summer. Yitzhak Gruenbaum, then a member of the Jewish Agency Executive, reflected the official Zionist decision when he urged fighting to the last man so as "to leave at least a legend of Masada," unlike the Jews in Germany and Poland, who preferred the life of a "beaten dog" to a dignified death. In response, Moshe Shapira, another member of the Executive, predicted that were Rommel to establish ghettos in Palestine, the *yishuv* would be forced into them, although perhaps a saving remnant would remain "to rebuild the House of Israel." In other words, Shapira anticipated that the same pattern of response that European Jews had adopted would repeat itself in Palestine.[7] It should be noted that expressions acknowledging common origin and fate and emphasizing the strong bond between the *yishuv* and the Diaspora were heard both in public speeches of leaders as well as in more intimate closed forums.

By the end of 1942, the *yishuv* was made aware, for the first time, that systematic extermination was taking place in Europe. During 1943, the conflict between the two attitudes toward the victims and survivors of the Holocaust grew sharper. In the *yishuv*, the prevailing opinion was that the members of the Zionist pioneer youth movements, predominately socialists, had not only initiated public welfare, educational, and cultural activities in the ghettos, but had also fomented the uprisings in several of the ghettos in the summer of that year. This opinion coincided with the common assumption that Zionist education brings out the best in every Jew and elevates him or her to moral peaks in times of crisis.

However, as more information reached Palestine about the responsible behavior and personal valor of the members of European Jewish youth movements, it became clear that communist youth, members of the Bund (the leftist, Yiddish-speaking, non-Zionist workers' party), and even religious youngsters had also participated in the uprisings. Moveover, the communists, especially, played a large role in initiating Jewish underground organizations and in establishing contacts with non-Jewish ones.[8] Yet both communists and Bundists, the ideological and practical enemies of Zionism, were denied the status of national heroes.

The *yishuv* leadership knew full well that these revolts were carried out with little, if any, help from Palestine. Contrary to the Zionist conviction that only a Jewish homeland could produce a new kind of Jew who could control his own fate or, in this case, at least the form of his death, heroic Jews materialized in Warsaw, Bedzin, and Bialystok. This was evidence that diaspora Jews, too, were prepared to make unlimited sacrifices for the sake of the nation's honor.

Moreover, while deportations were taking place in Europe, Jewish parties in Palestine engaged in endless bitter disputes, whereas the various European movements put aside their differences and engaged in united actions. These facts clearly challenged long-held Zionist assumptions concerning the superiority of their Zionist enterprise in Palestine. As one *yishuv* leader put it:

> After the war, we'll face a supreme court, represented by Frumka and Zivia [Frumka Plotnicka and Zivia Lubetkin, leaders of the revolts in Bedzin and in Warsaw]; each one of us should prepare himself, heart and soul, all his pioneering force, so that this supreme court may find him pure and worthy to sacrifice himself for the sake of the nation.[9]

Seeking to extricate themselves from this embarrassing situation, Zionists described Zivia and her comrades as "heirs to the Zealots of Masada" and "the heroes of Tel Hai."[10] Indeed, in the summer of 1943, when Zivia was mistakenly believed dead, Alterman wrote an obituary poem for her using the same terms and metaphors he later used in his famous "Silver Plate." Thus, equal places in the pantheon of Israel's heroes were assigned to Zivia and her comrades and the heroes of the Palmach, the elite unit of the Haganah that led the nation in its struggle for statehood.[11]

During 1943 one finds an increase in the expressions of respect for the conduct of European Jews, regardless of their political or ideological affiliations. Reports of self-organization and mutual aid, both within and among the Jewish communities of Europe, and of individual acts of sacrifice by mothers and children and teachers and rabbis reached the emissaries of the *yishuv* in neutral countries and those in Palestine responsible for rescue activities. Writing of the "simple Jews who carry their Judaism with pride and dignity" and of human deeds that "could educate generations,"[12] these emissaries and activists expressed regret that the *yishuv* knew far too little about, and understood even less, the quiet daily and hourly struggles of European Jews, "one of the enormous expressions of resistance to the Nazi regime."[13]

These expressions and the events that evoked them posed a number of challenges to official Zionist ideology. If most European Jews withstood the terrible test while the *yishuv* failed to live up to its self-perception as the heroic avant-garde of the people, then perhaps the *yishuv* could "learn a lot from [the Diaspora] and the many values created there."[14] In the words of one *yishuv* leader, "Do we still have the right to claim the leadership of our people—we who enjoy wartime prosperity and were miraculously saved from the great destruction? Have they not revealed spiritual and social powers superior to ours?"[15] Insofar as these "simple Jews" were not all Zionists, the source of the values that motivated their conduct, whether universal or Jewish, had to be sought in the Diaspora.

The end of the war marked a new stage in the ongoing conflict surrounding the assumptions of official Zionist ideology. First of all, there was the question of the role of the survivors in the Zionist enterprise. As Ben Gurion put it: "Those Jews [that survived], are they a hindrance, an obstacle to Zionism, or a benefit?"[16] As early as mid-1942, Eliyahu Dobkin, co-head of the Jewish Agency's Immigration Department, had described the Jewish refugees from Poland who reached Teheran via the Soviet Union as being mostly "broken in spirit, despairing, lacking in hope. . . . According to past criteria, we would never have agreed to approve them for Aliya."[17] Such negative judgments of the survivors were reinforced by Shaul Avigur, head of the Mossad, the organization for illegal immigration: "They are different. . . . completely different [from the *yishuv* members]. The propensity to inform is widespread among them. . . . in commerce, they engage in everything possible; the children buy and sell dollars; corruption is horrible; . . . prostitution is terrible."[18]

Slowly, the suspicion developed that those who survived had perhaps managed to do so because they had been unwilling to sacrifice themselves in the struggle against the Nazis. Emissaries sent to Europe to help the *She'erit Hapletah*, the saving remnant, and to direct it to Palestine, reinforced this view. To a Zionist emissary in Greece, those who returned from Auschwitz were cynical, lazy, money-grubbing idlers and window-smashers. According to an emissary in France, the survivors believed that the whole world owed them, especially the Jewish people. And in the opinion of emissaries in Germany and Austria: "Five thousand like these [those liberated from the camps] could turn Eretz Israel into a madhouse."[19]

In the *yishuv* and later in the state of Israel, there was a latent feeling that the Jews who survived possessed certain aggressive qualities. In a closed Mapai Central meeting in 1949, Ben Gurion expressed what others dared not say publicly:[20] "Among the survivors of the German camps were people who would not have been alive were they not what they were—hard, mean, and selfish—and what they have been through erased every remaining good quality from them."[21]

Comparisons were often made between the Zionist image of a productive person, imbued with universalist humanistic values, who worked for the common good, and the survivors, who seemed, at first sight, to be the polar opposites of that ideal type. After listening to the emissaries' reports, Ben Gurion concluded that the remnant of European Jews, who, redeemed from exile, should have strengthened the *yishuv*, instead posed an obstacle to Zionism and to themselves. They were, he surmised, not fit for *aliyah* and would not fight for it.[22]

Yet the emissaries and the soldiers from the *yishuv* serving in the British army did not neglect the survivors. As representatives of the *yishuv* committed to Zionism's dual goal of rescuing Jews for Zionism's sake and, if this were not possible, rescuing them for their own sake, they assumed the task of caring for the survivors. Dobkin, his negative evaluation of the Polish refugees in Teheran notwithstanding, concluded: "It is our duty to bring them here because . . . anywhere else they will be lost . . . because there may be no others."[23] And Avigur, while reviling prostitution and corruption, concluded: "Given such an object to deal with, one needs also love, a human approach."[24]

The Jewish Brigade officer referred to above, who feared a madhouse in Palestine, decided, nevertheless, to distribute five thousand immigration certificates he brought from Palestine among survivors. And thousands of Brigade soldiers distributed to the survivors loads of food, medicines, clothing, and fuel they had stolen from the British army warehouses, regardless of the survivors' affiliation or their readiness to emigrate to Palestine. In so doing, these soldiers acted without waiting for instructions from the *yishuv* leadership which, in 1945, had not yet decided on how to tackle the problem of the survivors.

As time passed and contacts intensified, the emissaries from the *yishuv* began to see in the survivors a previously hidden power and energy which only became apparent as they recuperated and regained their strength. In the DP (displaced person) camps of Austria, Italy, and Germany from late 1945 to 1948, survivors published newspapers and debated a wide range of topics. They also married, had children, and identified with Jewish values and Zionist aspirations to the surprise of the *yishuv* representatives.[25]

Thus, Chaim Yahil, head of the Jewish Agency welfare mission was led to write home: "They are Zionist in their very essence";[26] and the emissary to France quoted above announced: "This is human material of the most desirable kind." Even the emissary who had feared that the survivors would turn the *yishuv* into a madhouse now commented on the amazing organizational talent, strength, vitality, and initiative of the survivors.[27]

Moreover, *yishuv* emissaries now perceived the contrast between the tendency toward unity among the youth movement's survivors and partisans, particularly those from Eastern Europe (what Ben Gurion had called "fervor for unity") and the divisiveness within the *yishuv* where political parties fought incessantly with one another in their efforts to win over survivors.[28]

From 1946 to 1951, 66,000 survivors emigrated to the Americas, while, during the same period, 152,000 emigrated to Palestine, most of them illegally.[29] The Zionist aspirations of these survivors were clearly reflected in the enthusiastic reception they gave Ben Gurion during his visit to the DP camps in October and November 1945. Following his visit, Ben Gurion, acknowledging the error of his earlier judgment, proclaimed:

> I found to my astonishment—it would be difficult to say to my delight because there are manifestations of corruption—that there is less corruption than is likely under the circumstances. I found that, despite everything, people are healthy, both in the physical sense and in the spiritual sense. The majority are precious Jews, precious Zionists with deep Zionist instincts, ready to undergo again all troubles—if this is what Zionism requires—with fervor for the unity and the survival of the Jewish people.[30]

Thus, Ben Gurion, apparently sensing the spirit that pulsated within the survivors, realized the possible convergence of their needs with the needs of Zionism.

Witnessing the surge of Zionist feelings among the survivors, some Jewish Brigade soldiers doubted their own capacity to fulfill the survivors' expectations: "What do we have to offer those who consider us the embodiment of their hopes and dreams?"[31] Many in the *yishuv*, especially among the emissaries and activists, now felt that they had not done their best to carry out rescue efforts during the war. Accordingly, now that the war was over and their hands no longer fettered, it was their obligation to "prove that we are ready . . . to show a real sacrifice in fulfilling our pioneering duties" toward the survivors who, while no longer in danger of extermination, were still uprooted and dispersed all over Europe. Indeed, the first emissaries and soldiers to reach Europe urged the leadership in Palestine to send many others to help and to mobilize efforts to provide for the survivors' needs.[32]

From the end of the war until the establishment of the state, 70,446 refugees either reached Palestine or were taken to detention camps in Cyprus.[33] As Ben Gurion anticipated, many more were prepared to board unseaworthy vessels, face violent clashes with the British, and endure long stays in detention camps. At first, the *yishuv* activists, mainly the Palyam (the Palmach sea units) and the Mossad, regarded them as an amorphic crowd of miserable survivors who urgently needed to be rescued by the *yishuv*, "human material that is difficult to deal with."[34] "We liked the *Ha'apala*" (illegal immigration), author Yoram Kaniuk said later, "not the *Ma'apilim*" (illegal immigrants).[35]

However, in late 1945, when the first boats of the *Ha'apala* reached Palestine, Yitzhak Sadeh, the commander of the Palmach, wrote a piece of poetic prose, "My Sister on the Shore," describing a young, dirty, barefoot, barren woman with the words "for officers only" tattooed on her chest. Crying, she doubts whether she has a right to live and endanger young healthy men.

> I embrace my sister and tell her there is a place for you . . . here. Here we love you. To me you are more beautiful than any beauty, holier than any holiness. . . . You'll be our bride, our mother. In front of these sisters of mine, I kneel and when I arise I feel and know—for these sisters of mine—I am strong, brave, I'll even be cruel. For you—everything—everything.[36]

Sadeh also emphasized the readiness of the *yishuv* boys to endanger their lives for the survivors—an expiation for the sacrifice that was not possible during the war. Coming from an admired commander whose followers considered him a moral authority, these words had the force of a moral decree. His words also constituted the first expression, intentional or not, of the view that the Holocaust could serve as a justification of power, and, if necessary, even of cruelty.

In Sadeh's depiction, the *yishuv*, although active and morally superior to the dirty, helpless girl, embraced her despite the shame she had suffered. As far as I can determine, this is a typical theme in *Ha'apala* poems and songs, speeches and writings. There is no poem about a partisan, an experienced fighter, who jumps off the boat, not needing to be "carried on shoulders," and embracing the Palmach people as an equal.

From the summer of 1946, the British seized all *Ha'apala* ships in the Mediterranean, even those close to the shores of Palestine, and sent the passengers to Cyprus. Consequently, the *yishuv* again became a passive spectator, while the *Ma'apilim*, along with the emissaries who organized and accompanied the ships, bore the burden of the struggle against the British. Alterman, denouncing the injustice of the situation, described the Jewish people sleeping peacefully "from Haifa to the Bronx" and "from Canaan to Brooklyn" who did not flock to the shores to help prevent the British from sending the ships away. In his poem "One More Page," the heroes are a woman, an orphan, and a blind man whom "we"—the *yishuv*—sent to fight the nation's battle on the seas.[37]

The discrepancy between the vision of the heroic, moral *yishuv* that saves the weak, needy survivors, and the actual reality became fully evident during the summer of 1947. The *Exodus*, leaving France with 4,500 people on board, was caught at sea and, after a furious battle, brought to Haifa. The passengers who were sent back refused, for three weeks, to disembark in France and were finally taken back to the DP camps in Germany. The *yishuv*, was taken by surprise by the survivors' refusal to leave the ships in France. In their refusal, the survivors demonstrated a lot more of the "Zionist" qualities of stubbornness and fighting spirit than the *yishuv* had thought possible. The *Exodus* passengers thus became heroes and a universal symbol of these "Zionist qualities." In the *yishuv*, the question once again was raised: Would the nation (the *yishuv*) be "worthy to look them in the eye"?[38]

To many in the *yishuv*, the survivors reaching Palestine constituted both a blessing, for they increased its numbers, and a threat. In the words of Alterman, they were different "in language, logic, image, way of walking, line of action . . . reactions of fear and laughter." They were many "and a war between two parties . . . will determine whether the millstone will crush the granules" or vice versa; whether the *yishuv* will absorb them into the new Zionist patterns or be crushed under their exilic existence. "At night . . . when we carry them . . . on our backs [from ship to shore], we feel the cracking of their weak body and their hands closing on our throats."[39]

Between 1946 and May 1948, about 2,000 survivors a month—70,446 in all—reached Palestine. From May 1948 to the end of 1951, 687,000 immigrants, including 350,000 more survivors, reached the country, thus doubling the population, which, in May 1948, numbered 650,000.[40] In other words, in 1951, one out of every two Israelis was a newcomer, and practically one out of four was a survivor.[41] According to recent research, 25 percent of the fighting forces in the War of Independence and 15 percent of the casualties were survivors.[42]

In spite of these numbers, during these same years, it seems as if all talk of the Holocaust and its survivors disappeared from the Israeli scene. The Holocaust was not taught in schools, nor was it a topic of research at the Hebrew University (the only one in Israel at the time). In drama and theater, the Holocaust was hardly mentioned; and when it was, it was mostly as part of the background.[43] In both poetry and fiction, other topics shaped the agenda.[44] In Palmach bulletins and literature, little space was devoted to it.[45]

Even references to the famous sequence of symbols—Masada, Tel Hai, Warsaw—disappeared temporarily, perhaps because it was felt that victory, not suicide, should be emphasized. Yad Vashem, the Holocaust Remembrance Authority, did not yet exist, and although "Yom Hashoa" (Holocaust Memorial Day) was officially declared by the Knesset in April 1951, years passed before it acquired a definitive shape. Very few memoirs of survivors were published, and most of those that were published were written by partisans and ghetto fighters.[46]

Why did the Holocaust, the most traumatic experience in Jewish history, disappear so early from the Israeli scene despite the presence of so many survivors, the proximity of time, and the intensive, complex relationship between the *yishuv* and European Jews during the war and after? There are two possible answers. First, the War of Independence and the newly created state displaced all other experiences. The existence of a Jewish state overwhelmed old-timers and newcomers alike, and the phrase "for the first time after 2,000 years" was repeatedly heard. Religious believers and atheists alike, upon arriving in Israel, feeling as if they were walking in the footsteps of the Messiah, kissed the earth.

The survivors, too, were caught up in that atmosphere. To them, the very existence of a Jewish state was their best revenge on the Nazis. Thousands of testimonies preserved at Yad Vashem attest to this sense of a new beginning. Despite the insults and contempt to which some survivors were subjected following their arrival in Israel, they wanted to belong, to do their share, and to fight. Some of them had fought in Europe, and those who did not wanted to prove that they could be fighters rather than victims. Youngsters who were the last survivors of large families were sent to battle upon arrival, in spite of the guilt feelings that this aroused in the *yishuv*. Wanting to become a part of that same Zionist ethos that had disparaged them, these youngsters sought a new name, a new identity, and a new future. Thus, they welcomed the opportunity to fight.[47]

The silence of the survivors cannot be attributed only to the insensitive remarks and unsympathetic attitudes concerning their passivity or to the reasons offered to explain their survival. Rather, as the writer Aharon Appelfeld, himself a survivor, wrote: "after the war . . . they preferred to be silent," because each one was tortured by feelings of guilt for being alive; each doubted his own memories of a world so totally removed from normal human experience; consequently, there was no common ground on which to build a dialogue with the *yishuv*. Finally, because they found the inner essence of the Holocaust events too intimate to share, the survivors viewed those Israelis who did take an interest and try to understand as intruders.[48] The survivors, tired of being different, needed time to heal and to forget.

Yet another reason for the silence concerning the Holocaust relates not to the newcomers but to the state that absorbed them. The young state, on the verge of losing the War of Independence, was precariously perched between being and not being. Six thousand men and women, 1 percent of its population, were killed in combat. And when over the next three and a half years its population doubled, food, housing, and employment were acutely lacking. Moreover, governmental and army authorities were not yet properly functioning. Accordingly, there was neither time nor energy to devote to the special needs of the different groups of newcomers. So preoccupied was the state with its struggle to survive that there was not even sufficient time to count or register the survivors of the Holocaust.[49]

In the absence of education, research, art forms, and human dialogue on the subject of the Holocaust, concern for the murdered European Jews seems to have been limited to formal state declarations. At this level, too, a double message was conveyed. On one hand, it was assumed that the Jews of Europe did not go shamefully like sheep to slaughter, which would contradict the image of the fighting, independent Israeli. On the other hand, once depicted as fighters, they could become a part of that image.

One example of such a mixed message can be found in the wording of the Declaration of Independence.

> The Holocaust . . . in which millions of Jews in Europe were forced to slaughter again proved beyond doubt the compelling need to solve the problem of Jewish homelessness and dependence by the renewal of the Jewish state in the land of Israel, which would open wide the gates of the homeland to every Jew . . .

Insofar as the Holocaust was now seen as providing a fundamental legitimation for the Jewish state, there was a basic bond between the fate of diaspora Jewry and the new state. Therefore, the Jews of Europe could not be ignored or disparaged. On the other hand, to speak of the "renewal of the Jewish state" presupposed a direct continuity with the Maccabean Jewish state, thereby skipping over the 2,000 years of exile, including the Holocaust. The phrase "forced to slaughter" appears to resolve this contradiction. "Forced" means that they fought and resisted mighty powers, so it was not their fault they were eventually led to slaughter.[50]

And another example: the debate over reparations, at the beginning of 1951. On the state level, Israel demanded $3,000 for the absorption of each person who reached Palestine and Israel from Europe between 1933 and 1951—500,000 in all—or one and a half billion dollars. Other reparations, in much larger amounts, were provided for individuals and various Jewish organizations. Formally, then, the state of Israel was not the heir of European Jews. Yet, symbolically, it received payments from the Germans for Jewish property, or even for "Jewish suffering and as compensation for the death of Jews"—a term used by those who strongly objected to the reparations, an opposition led by survivors. In other words, those opposed to the reparations claimed that the state cannot inherit material assets without inheriting, preserving, and perpetuating the spirit of those on whose behalf it inherits as well.

Accordingly, how could the state belittle the murdered European Jews? Thus, in April 1951, in the midst of the public storm over reparations, the Knesset declared "Yom Hashoa vehagevurah" (the day commemorating the Holocaust and the heroism) on the 27th of Nissan, the date on which the fiercest battles in the Warsaw ghetto occurred. The suffering and the misery of the *Shoah* (Holocaust) were to be officially commemorated, along with the *Gevura* (heroism) of those who fought back.

A third example, which epitomizes this mixed message came two years later, in 1953, when the Knesset decided to establish a remembrance authority, Yad Vashem. Not only is it called the Martyrdom and Heroism Remembrance Authority, but the nine categories of dead Jews to be commemorated include individuals, families, and communities (including all organizations) who, as the Declaration of Independence had stated, were "forced to slaughter." The authority was also to memorialize the bravery of Jewish soldiers, underground fighters, and ghetto fighters. Moreover, another article of the Yad Vashem law endows the six million murdered Jews with "a commemorative Israeli citizenship . . . to signify that they in their death have become a part of their people."[51] Thus, by using expressions such as "forced to slaughter," "Holocaust and bravery," and expanding the number of categories for commemoration, the state elevated the valor of the Jews in Europe to a position equal to their suffering, and thereby resolved the problem of its relationship to them.

But this solution created a far more complicated problem, one that persisted for decades: The emphasis on bravery during the Holocaust prevented a realistic understanding of the desperate situation of the Jews in Europe and of their quiet daily and hourly struggle that demanded no less a degree of spiritual stamina than did the actual fighting.

This brings us back to the meeting between Kovner and Alterman with which we began our discussion. Kovner viewed Alterman's poetry as an embodiment of the fighting spirit of Palestine as well as of the ghetto rebels and partisans. Alterman, however, as early as 1947 and perhaps even earlier, grasped that the Jews of Europe did not go like sheep to the slaughter and that the Jewish Councils were not traitors. They were, instead, lonely and powerless, in a hostile exile trapped between German deceit that caused both despair and illusion, and the terror that petrified all nations of Europe. They were also trapped between the fear of collective punishment and the desire to take revenge.

Therefore, Alterman strongly opposed the manipulation of state authorities and public opinion in order to overemphasize bravery; the depiction of the *yishuv* as having respected and morally supported the rebels and the partisans only during and following the Holocaust; and the way in which the impossible situation of the victims was ignored in order to reconcile their behavior with the image of the fighting state.[52] In insisting that the fighting described in *Simchat Aniyim* was here, specifically here, in Palestine, Alterman was saying how unjust it is to have expected the Jews of Europe to fight and that such expectations belied the reality of their situation. The true Zionist lesson, according to Alterman, is not that fighting is a value in itself, but that one should only expect resistance where it is possible, namely "here."

Alterman's view, which he alone held during the stormy public debate of the mid-fifties precipitated by the Kasztner trial,[53] became increasingly accepted during the late sixties and seventies. Today, it is clearly evident in Israeli historiography on the Holocaust, and in the Israeli's self-image and self-understanding.[54]

The analysis of the attitudes of the *yishuv* and the young state toward the victims and survivors of the Holocaust clearly shows that the Zionist hope of creating an Israeli identity that contrasted sharply with the identity of diaspora Jewry did not materialize. Today's Israelis feel themselves to be both rescuers and survivors, fighters yet ongoing potential victims, Israelis as well as Jews.

NOTES

1. Abba Kovner, *On the Narrow Bridge: Essays* (Tel Aviv, 1981), 111.
2. Until the recent Americanization of the Israeli media, poets and writers have been—and perhaps still are, although to a lesser extent—a main source of intellectual debate and major shapers of Israeli self-image and values. See, for instance, Dan Laor, "Mass Immigration as 'Contents and Subject' of the Hebrew Literature in the Early Years of the State," *Hazionut* 14 (Tel Aviv, 1989): 161–76. See also Tom Segev, *1949—The First Israelis* (Jerusalem, 1984), 271–76, on long conversations between Ben Gurion and Israeli poets and writers in 1949.
3. *Moznaim* 16 (Summer, 1942): 250.
4. *Zror Michtavim* 134 (formerly 199, 30 March 1943): 208–10.
5. Speeches, and speech on 20 November 1942 in the Assembly of Representatives, Ben Gurion Archives.
6. Shazar spoke these words at the Histadrut Convention, 5–7 May 1949; see Histadrut Archives (hereafter referred to as HA), vol. 68. Indeed, three-quarters of the immigrants to Palestine between the wars came from Europe, including most of the leaders of the *yishuv*. About 90 percent of the immigrants in the 1930s (close to 200,000 people and 40 percent of the population in 1939) came from Europe—most notably Eastern Europe and mainly Poland. See Gil Benjamin, *Pages of Immigration: 30 Years of Immigration to Palestine, 1919–1949* (Jerusalem, 1950).
7. Galili spoke at the Youth Facing the Holocaust and the Diaspora Assembly on 15 January 1943. The minutes, under the same name, bear no date or publication information. See p. 37. Gruenbaum and Shapira spoke at a Jewish Agency Executive (hereafter referred to as JAE) meeting on 30 June 1942, Central Zionist Archives (hereafter referred to as CZA).
8. Dina Porat, *The Blue and the Yellow Stars of David, The Zionist Leadership in Palestine and the Holocaust, 1939–1945* (Cambridge, Mass., and London, 1990). It is worthwhile pointing out that insofar as the *yishuv* was mostly labor, or leftist-oriented (75 percent were members of the Histadrut, the workers' union), it was natural that they identify with the struggle of the Soviet Union against the Nazis. Indeed, poems were written expressing the wish to embrace "my unknown brother, a red soldier in the wide fields of Russia" (Moshe Tabenkin, *Poems* [Tel Aviv, 1943], 125).
9. Avraham Haft, a member of Kibbutz Degania B, at the Histadrut Convention, 5–7 May 1943, HA, vol. 68.
10. *Davar*, editorial, 21 May 1943.
11. Yechiam Weitz, "The Yishuv's Self-Image and the Reality of the Holocaust," *Jerusalem Quarterly* 48 (Fall 1988): 85.
12. Venia Pomerantz (later Ze'ev Hadari), an emissary in Turkey, at the Mapai

Center on 24 August 1943, the Labor Party Archives (hereafter referred to as LPA), 23/43. Eliezer Kaplan, the JAE's treasurer, after a visit to Turkey, in a JAE meeting on 28 March 1943, CZA.
13. Melech Neustadt, *A Year of Extermination* (Tel Aviv, 1943), 9–11.
14. Venia Pomerantz, in a Mapai Center meeting on 24 August 1943, LPA 23/43.
15. Eliyahu Dobkin, co-head of the Jewish Agency's Immigration Department, at the 46th Histadrut Convention, 26 May 1942, HA, vol. 41.
16. JAE meeting, 21 November 1945, CZA; and Mapai Central Committee, 22 November 1945, LPA, 23/45.
17. Mapai Central Committee, 2 May 1942, LPA, 23/42; and JAE, 18 August 1942, CZA.
18. Mapai Central Committee, 3 May 1943, LPA, 23/43.
19. Jacob Tsur (Greece), Mapai Political Bureau, 9 September 1945, LPA; David She'altiel (France), Mapai Secretariat, 11 September 1945, LPA, 24/45; testimony of Aharon Hoter-Yishai (Germany and Austria) at the Eichmann trial, *Testimonies* II (Jerusalem, 1974), 1250.
20. For the difficulty that some leaders felt in expressing such ideas, see Chaim Yahil, "Activities of the Palestine Delegation to She'erit Hapletah, 1945–1949," *Yalkut Moreshet* 30 (November 1980): 11–12.
21. The Mapai Center, 22–23 July 1949, LPA, section 2, 11/2/1, quoted by Tom Segev, *1949—The First Israelis* (Jerusalem, 1984), 141.
22. Mapai Central Committee, 18 January 1945, LPA, 23/45. Such views persisted until the late 1980s when Israeli society finally started listening to the survivors. They then began to understand that chance and luck rather than character and behavior determined who survived and who perished.
23. See n. 17.
24. See n. 18.
25. See Ze'ev Mankowitz, "The Politics and Ideology of Survivors of the Holocaust in the American Zone of Occupied Germany, 1945–1946" (diss., Hebrew University, 1987), chaps. 1–4.
26. See n. 20.
27. David She'altiel's letter from Paris, 11 June 1945, S25/2541, CZA. See also *Testimonies* of the Eichmann trial, vol. II (Jerusalem, 1974), 1250.
28. It should be noted that, in June 1950, earlier American immigration regulations were changed, allowing the entrance of any survivor who reached the camps by 1 January 1949. Yet in the first half of 1951, only 6,000 made use of this possibility. (The highest number of survivors to be in the camps at any one time was 250,000.) See Irit Keinan, "She'erit Hapleita—Olim or Immigrants," to be published in the Moreshet Ben Gurion Annual, *Iyunim Bitekumat Yisrael*.
29. See n. 25.

30. Yehuda Tubin, "Personal Testimony and a Retrospective Look," *Yalkut Moreshet* 39 (May 1985): 20.
31. A letter from Yehuda Tubin, then a Jewish Brigade soldier, from Brussels to Palestine, 15 September 1945, quoted by Anita Shapira, *Visions in Conflict* (Tel Aviv, 1988), 330.
32. Ibid., 330–46.
33. *Idan* 1, Immigration B (Jerusalem, 1982), 10, 137–39: March to December 1944, 10 ships, 4,256 people; August to December 1945, 8 ships, 1,032 people; January to July 1946, 11 ships, 10,460 people. To Cyprus: July to December 1946, 11 ships, 11,213 people; 1947, 25,241 people; January to May 1948, 22,500 people.
34. Aviva Halamish, "The Ha'apala—Values, Myth, and Reality," in *Points of Observation: Culture and Society in Eretz Israel*, ed. Nurit Gertz (Tel Aviv, 1988), 95.
35. Yoram Kaniuk spoke in a conference on "The Ha'apala, 40 Years after Exodus," at Beit Hatefutzot, August 1987.
36. Yitzhak Sadeh, *Around the Field-fire* (Tel Aviv, 1953), 51–52.
37. Nathan Alterman, *Eir Hayona* (Tel Aviv, 1978), 30.
38. Idem, "The Nation and Its Messenger," *The Seventh Column* (Tel Aviv, 1948), 110.
39. Idem, *Eir Hayona*, 26.
40. *Hebrew Encyclopedia* 6 (Jerusalem, 1957), 667. Moshe Sikron, *Immigration to Israel, 1948–1953*, Special Series of the Falk Project, no. 60 (Jerusalem, 1958), p. 23. The numbers given here for the survivors are a result of calculations based on these sources, since the survivors were not counted or registered as such upon coming.
41. Since most of the *yishuv* itself was comprised of former newcomers at the end of 1951, 76 percent of all Israeli citizens had been born abroad.
42. Dr. Meir Pail, in a forthcoming research of Yad Fabenkin, at a Beit Hatefutzot symposium on "She'erit Hapleita in the War of Independence," 12 April 1990.
43. Ben Ami Feingold, *The Theme of the Holocaust in Hebrew Drama* (Tel Aviv, 1989), 11.
44. Dan Laor, see n. 2.
45. Aya Shacham, "Face to Face, The Absorption of She'erit Hapleita in the Palmach" (seminar paper, Department of Jewish History at Tel Aviv University, 1989); Shapira, *Visions of Conflict*, 326.
46. The Knesset detailed the contents and form of the day on 8 April 1959.
47. Shacham, "Face to Face," 81 (conclusion).
48. Aharon Appelfeld, *First Person Essays* (Jerusalem, 1979), 43.
49. See n. 40.
50. See David Engel, "'Holocaust' and 'Heroism' in the Consciousness of Israeli Society," *Skira Hodshit* 3 (1990): 19, for a different interpretation.
51. See "The Holocaust and Heroism Remembrance Day" Law of 1953, article

1 (Law Book, no. 132, p. 144) and article 3B (Regulation 2326, December 1968).
52. See Nathan Alterman, *Between Two Roads*, Selections from a Diary, edited, annotated and afterword by Dan Laor (Tel Aviv, 1989), 113–57.
53. Dr. Yisrael Kasztner, a leader in the Zionist-organized rescue efforts in Budapest, was accused of cooperating with the Nazis and withholding information of the mass killings in order to save relatives and friends. In June 1955 in a libel trial against Kasztner's accuser, a district court judge held that Kasztner was indeed guilty of the crimes of which he had been accused. Shortly thereafter, Kasztner was murdered. However, the Supreme Court of Israel reversed the decision on the grounds that the original judgment did not take into account the realities and unique circumstances of the period. During the trial, right-wing groups in Israel took advantage of the situation to accuse Mapai, the dominant party during the 1940s and 1950s, of cooperating with the Nazis and sacrificing European Jews for Zionist gains.
54. The debate over Alterman's views was a public issue during the Kasztner trial in 1954–55. The debate and developments from the 1960s to the 1980s are not within the scope of this paper. See *Hatzionut* 15, Dina Porat on Alterman's *Between Two Roads*, 223–37.

CHAPTER 9

Myths, Symbols, and Rituals of the Emerging State

MYRON J. ARONOFF

> [M]odern nations . . . claim to be the opposite of novel, namely rooted in the remotest antiquity, and the opposite of constructed, namely human communities so "natural" as to require no definition other than self-assertion.
> ERIC HOBSBAWM, *The Invention of Tradition*

The modern state of Israel asserts the historic link of the Jewish people to a land from which it had been exiled for nearly two millennia. As a conspicuously new construct, creating the impression of constituting a natural community has been a monumental challenge for the new state. Perhaps the primary goal of Israeli political culture has been to make the continuity of the ancient past with the contemporary context a taken-for-granted reality. The right to statehood for the Jews which is based on this historic link has been challenged by many, both within and without its borders. Therefore, the challenge to inventing the Zionist tradition has been a daunting one.

Zionism has constituted the dominant paradigm of Israeli political culture since its inception in the early *yishuv* (pre-state Jewish community). It aims to establish the legitimacy of the contemporary state by creating a credible claim to continuity with the biblical past. This has been accomplished primarily through the use of symbols, myths, and rituals which were interpreted differently according to the ideological perspectives of competing political movements and parties. This competition has not only determined which ideological interpretation was ascendent or dominant at different periods, but also which views were marginalized or silenced.

This preliminary examination of some of the sources of Israeli political culture focuses on the analysis of selected symbols, myths, and rituals of the emerging state.[1] Such an examination must begin with an appreciative critique of the important pioneering work of Charles Liebman and Eliezer Don-Yehiya.[2] Their contribution through their perceptive analysis of four major versions of the Zionist vision, particularly as they relate to traditional religion, provides a foundation for all future work on the subject.

Unfortunately, their view of culture is a static one which significantly impairs their analysis. It fails to capture the dialectical tension between processes of institutionalization and constant challenge to the taken-for-grantedness of socially constructed reality. Unlike Roy Wagner who conceives of the invention of culture as a "dialectic through which meaning is and *must be* continually invented," Liebman and Don-Yehiya present a reified view of culture.[3]

> Two contradictory processes take place concurrently in all societies and cultures. On one hand, patterns of collective behavior become habitual and the collective meanings ascribed to them undergo a process of institutionalization or reification during which they tend to become taken for granted as they come to define reality for members of the society. On the other hand, the process of reification (or conventionalization) is never completed. Due to the impossibility of achieving perfect socialization and the unequal distribution of status and power (among other factors), there are always individuals and groups who call into question the taken-for-grantedness of the dominant cultural myths and offer competing definitions of reality.[4]

Paul Ricouer stresses that "social imagination is *constitutive* of social reality" and, he suggests, all systems of legitimation exceed their authority and produce credibility gaps.[5] This is what Max Gluckman called the "frailty in authority."[6] Consequently, I suggest that political culture is inherently subject to challenge, particularly in contemporary pluralistic contexts.

Liebman and Don-Yehiya also fail to distinguish between the general political culture which they call civil religion and the more specific ideological interpretations by the various political movements which constitute competing visions of a shared overall symbolic universe.[7] Whereas they recognize that traces of all approaches existed among different groups in every period, they identify each different historic period with a different dominant civil religion. Thus, labor Zionism was dominant in the *yishuv*; statism (*mamlachtiut*) was the dominant civil religion of the new state until approximately 1967; and, they claim, a new civil religion achieved dominance thereafter (a claim I emphatically refute).[8]

I suggest that Zionism constitutes the root cultural paradigm of Israeli political culture which I elaborate on in further detail below.

> Within the general Zionist framework, socialist Zionism, revisionist Zionism, statist Zionism, and religious Zionism (through the different political movements and parties identified with them) have competed with one another for power and the right to claim their version to be the *true* interpretation of *the* Zionist vision.[9]

This debate set(s) the parameters of legitimacy in Israeli politics. Those who do not accept or even reject its major tenets, e.g., Arabs and non-Zionist orthodox Jews, have historically been politically marginalized.[10]

From the beginning of the modern Zionist movement, there have been deep divisions between groups with competing ideological interpretations of many fundamental tenets. Therefore, it is particularly remarkable that the Labor movement was able to establish the dominance of its ideological version of Zionism and, with varying degrees of success, to marginalize competing versions within the Zionist camp——not to mention its ability to deny legitimacy to worldviews which rejected the civil religion of the emerging state. For example, the voices of the Palestinians and the orthodox Jews of the old *yishuv* were successfully muted in the dominant political debate.

I suggest that the major consequence of the polarized political conflict within the Zionist camp was to establish the parameters of permissible discourse as well as the privileged voice of Labor within it. The identification of the majority of the young nation's intellectuals with what informally emerged as the official interpretation helped to establish the hegemony of this interpretation as the dominant one.[11] The old adage that history is written by the victors is as applicable to internal political struggles as it is to confrontations with outsiders. As George Orwell said in *1984*, "Who controls the past, controls the future. Who controls the present, controls the past."[12]

Zionism contains conflicting, even contradictory, principles which have been interpreted differently by competing groups in changing circumstances to justify their goals and to give legitimacy to their interests. This dynamic, after all, is the essence of cultural production and reproduction. It is exemplified in David Ben Gurion's statement:

"Two basic aspirations underlie all our work in this country: to be like all nations, and to be different from all nations."[13] The tension between such contradictory aspirations contributes to the dynamics of Zionist discourse.

The desire for national normality is a widely shared Zionist aspiration. The perception of Jewish life in the Diaspora as abnormal and undesirable is a basic underlying assumption of all versions of Zionism. The negation of the Diaspora was a far more prominent feature of socialist Zionism in the *yishuv* and even of statism during the first two decades of the state than it was of the so-called new Zionism which is associated by several scholars with the Begin era.[14]

Itamar Even-Zohar[15] points out that influencing the invention of a native Hebrew culture in Palestine was the principle of "the creation of a new Jewish people and a new Jew in the Land of Israel." He argues that the most important motive for the adoption of Hebrew and its Sephardic pronunciation stemmed from their role as cultural opposites to the stereotypes of Diaspora culture against which the Zionists rebelled. These stereotypes, in fact, had an enduring influence on Hebrew language and literature. Similarly, the soldier pioneer who heroically sacrificed his life for his country was the mirror opposite of the Zionist perception of the prototypical Jew of the Diaspora.

The desire for national normality is a widely shared aspiration. Those who share this goal interpret the biblical prophesy of Balaam, "Lo, it is a people that shall dwell alone and shall not be reckoned among the nations,"[16] as a curse. However, others consider it an affirmation of Israel's chosenness. Those who adhere to the latter interpretation deny that the Jewish people can be a normal people. Many reject the desirability of Israel becoming like other nations. Such significantly different orientations shape partisan disputes and interpretations of reality.

The powerful, widely shared aspiration to create a nation that would be "a light unto the nations" also logically contradicts the aspiration for normality. Even among those who argued that the Jewish state should adhere to unusually high standards of moral and ethical behavior, there was strong disagreement whether traditional religious, socialist, or humanist values should be the standard.[17] Both secular and religious ideologies considered Israel to be the fulfillment of messianic redemption.

Not only do different groups adhere to differing and even contradictory interpretations, individuals and groups hold such views simultaneously. Just as individuals compartmentalize logically conflicting notions in order to ameliorate cognitive dissonance, cultures contextualize myths in an effort to reconcile contradictory messages. As conditions in a society change, leaders interpret the meaning of myths in a manner appropriate to the changing context and their changing goals. The core myths of all cultures are multivocal and lend themselves to conflicting interpretations with even contradictory ideological messages.

Nurith Gertz has suggested that the myth of David and Goliath, a myth of the few versus the many, has provided a structure of meaning which has linked past, present, and future in Israel from the years of early settlement to the present.[18] Her analysis of political speeches, election propaganda, and literary and journalistic texts traces the varying treatments of the theme in different historical contexts.[19]

Whereas all Zionist parties shared common assumptions, each interpreted the myth through its ideological perspective. In the process of appropriating and transforming them, they made national myths into party myths, and the Zionist heroes into party heroes. As Gertz has pointed out, "The heroes of the past who populate national myths are thus portrayed as the vanguard of the respective contemporary movements."[20]

Similarly, contemporary leaders and policies were given legitimacy through their symbolic association with mythical heroes. For example, Ben Gurion was frequently associated with one of his favorite biblical characters, Joshua, who had led the Hebrews into the promised land. I would, therefore, contend that through their competitive interpretations, political parties also helped to establish in the public mind the authenticity and centrality of the myth, thereby elevating shared Zionist symbols in spite of partisan differences.

A good example of this is illustrated by the Tel Hai legend. Yael Zerubavel describes this narrative as a national myth which highlighted the theme of collective death and rebirth and "sanctified a new beginning in Jewish history and the emergence of a new type of Jew, ready to fight for his land and die for it."[21] The main theme of the myth was the break with the past and the emergence of a new Hebrew. The defenders of Tel Hai symbolized both the revolt against the Zionist image of the "ghetto Jew" and a heroic defense against "Arab marauders."

Zerubavel traces how the death of six Jewish settlers on 1 March 1920 (the eleventh of the Hebrew month of Adar) defending a small northern settlement was incorporated into a narrative emphasizing commonly held Zionist values of self-defense and self-sacrifice for the national cause. The Tel Hai myth also dramatically illustrated the theme of the few against the many, since the settlers were vastly outnumbered and surrounded. The importance of the myth in Israeli political culture is symbolized by the fact that Tel Hai Day (the eleventh of Adar) is one of only four anniversaries of historic events officially sanctioned as state holidays.[22]

Yoseph Trumpeldor, a former officer in the Czarist army who had lost an arm in combat, was a uniquely appropriate candidate for elevation to folk hero as the New Hebrew Man.[23] His reputed dying statement, "Never mind, it is good to die for our country," could not have been more appropriate had it been deliberately invented for the national myth. In fact, Gertz suggests that the Tel Hai scenario (including such heroic dying statements) fits into a common literary formula of what she terms the literature of the periphery at the time.[24] Ironically, although in a later more skeptical era a counter-folklore emerged and popular opinion regarded this statement as having been invented, Zerubavel suggests that historical evidence tends to support its authenticity.[25]

The competing political camps manipulated the Tel Hai myth for partisan advantage. Revisionist interpretation stressed military activism, heroism, and sacrifice as the central values of the myth, while Labor emphasized the pioneering aspects of settling and working the land, and a restrained defense policy. Labor's interpretation linking settlement with defense and institution building was on the ascent during the 1920s and 1930s. The Labor position on Tel Hai culminated a decade and a half after the fall of Tel Hai in the "wall and tower" (*choma umigdal*) policy of establishing facts.[26] Thus, each party selectively interpreted appropriate aspects of Trumpeldor's life, work, and death to validate its ideological vision and interests. Liebman and Don-Yehiya suggest that for the Socialists, who had yet to represent the Arab as "the other" or as an enemy, the myth also reflected the problematic relationship of the Zionists to the Arabs.[27]

Zerubavel's analysis of the use of oral and written literature inspired by Tel Hai in the political socialization of children illustrates the impact of partisan conflict on the interpretation of historical events. I would stress that the struggle over the interpretation of this national myth was a part of a wider struggle which established Zionism as the dominant paradigm of the political culture of the *yishuv*. Labor's victory gave it a privileged voice within that political culture, helping it to establish political as well as ideological dominance in the face of Revisionist, liberal, and left-socialist alternatives.[28] Labor's victory also firmly established the position of the settlers (eventually the *kibbutznikim*) as the vanguard of the Zionist movement.

A subsidiary theme derived from the Tel Hai myth incorporated into Israeli political culture is the notion that it is indeed good to die for one's country. Apropos of this theme I have written:

> The primary rite of passage that initiates one into full membership in the Zionist civil religion is service in Zahal (the Israel Defense Forces). It is the single most important test, particularly for males, for individual and group acceptance in the mainstream of Israeli society governed by Zionist civil religion. The type of unit in which one (or members of one's group) serves, and even the proportion of casualties suffered by the members of one's group are seen to be proof of the extent of one's commitment and the centrality of the group in the mainstream of society. The fact that *kibbutznikim* disproportionately served as officers and in elite units that suffered high casualties was always cited as evidence of their vanguard role in the Zionist venture. More recently, in interviews conducted during the war in Lebanon this writer was told by leaders of nationalist religious Jews and of Eastern Jews that the higher rates of casualties suffered by their respective groups was evidence of their having moved to the forefront of the national (Zionist) struggle.[29]

Conversely, those groups and social categories who do not serve in the army, particularly Arabs and ultra-orthodox Jews, are marginalized. This is also true, but to a lesser extent, of those who serve in noncombatant roles such as women. In essence, it is the "ownership" of military casualties that provides a group's most dramatic claim of centrality in Israeli society. Consequently, while the funerals for the fallen are their final rites of passage, annual memorial ceremonies are an ongoing source of legitimacy for the groups who claim them as well as celebrations of national solidarity.

Zerubavel notes another aspect of the commemoration of heroic action, the reference to the number of casualties involved through the numerical naming of places, which she calls "numerical commemoration."[30] For example, a main street in a town where I lived was named the street of "the five" to commemorate the five residents of the town who died in the 1967 war.[31]

Memorialization of the dead is a leitmotif in Israeli culture that is rooted in Jewish religious tradition. In fact, it has become so extensive and central in the political culture that I suggest it has evolved into a national cult memorializing the dead. Memorialization of those who died in Israel's wars has led to the construction of a vast number of war memorials and shrines throughout the country and an equally large number of rites of commemoration for individuals. Annual rites are held by each of the underground military organizations, various units of the Israel Defense Force (IDF), and collectively for all of the fallen.[32] Regularized rites institutionalized by the IDF are held at thirty-nine military cemeteries throughout the country and at two major monuments the day before the celebration of Israel's Independence Day.[33]

Every local Jewish community in the country has a Yad L'Banim (Memorial to the Sons), which usually serves as a community center but which also memorializes those who died either in Israel's wars or fighting the ongoing battle against terrorism. There is also a central memorial for all Druze who died in battle. Since these facilities are fully utilized by youth and citizens of all ages, they are constant reminders of the sacrifice of members of the community for the nation's defense.

There is yet another type of memorialization derived from Jewish tradition which is a significant, but infrequently noted, aspect of Israeli political culture. This involves the ceremonial reinterment in Israel of the remains of individuals and groups who had been buried abroad. The patriarch Jacob was the first recorded Jew to have had his remains reinterred in the land of Israel.[34] Burial in Israel also has deep resonance for religious Jews because it guarantees that the souls will be in the holy land on the Day of Messianic Redemption and is necessary for the conservation of souls on the Day of Judgment.

David Ben Gurion, a self-avowed secular Jew, was responsible for the reinterment of the remains of the early Zionist socialist thinker Moses Hess in the region of the Kinneret.[35] This symbolic post-mortem *aliyah* honored the memory of a thinker whose major Zionist work, *Rome and Jerusalem*, anticipated and expressed with considerably greater intellectual distinction ideas which later appeared in Theodore Herzl's more widely-known *Jewish State*. Through this ceremony, sponsored by the Histadrut in 1935, the Labor movement honored the first socialist Zionist thinker as their intellectual forefather.

During the statist period, the remains of Theodore Herzl were transferred to Israel in 1949 and, in an elaborate state ceremony, were buried on a mountain in Jerusalem which bears his name. Mount

Herzl subsequently became a sacred site where other greats of the nation are buried.³⁶ Herzl's grave site became a national shrine during the period of statism's (*mamlachtiut*'s) dominance.

Another notable case of reburial involved the founding leader of the Revisionist movement, Vladimir Zeev Jabotinsky, who died and was buried in the United States in 1940. His will requested that he be reinterred by the government of the Jewish state when it came into being. However, Ben Gurion refused Menachem Begin's repeated requests that the government of Israel provide an official state funeral for the reburial of Jabotinsky, just as it had done for Theodore Herzl, the founder of the modern Zionist movement. Ben Gurion's response was that just as the Histadrut had sponsored the ceremony for Hess, so Jabotinsky's political heirs should sponsor the ceremony honoring him.

Ben Gurion's successor, Levi Eshkol, gave Jabotinsky a full dress state funeral and reburied his remains in an honored spot on Mount Herzl on the twenty-fourth anniversary of his death in 1964.³⁷ This ceremony symbolized both the normalization of relations between Labor and the political descendants of the Revisionist movement, and the beginning of the latter's political rehabilitation and legitimization. This process culminated in celebrations for the centenary of Jabotinsky's birth, sponsored by the government headed by Menachem Begin, from 22 October 1980 to 22 July 1981 (corresponding to the dates of Jabotinsky's birth and death according to the Jewish calendar).³⁸

The most dramatic contemporary illustration of this phenomenon of reburial was the state funeral sponsored by the same Begin-led government for remains reputedly belonging to the fighters and followers of Shimon Bar Koziba (popularly known as Bar Kokhba), who had led the second Jewish revolt against Rome in A.D. 132–35. These remains, discovered by the noted archaeologist Yigal Yadin in March 1960, were reburied on 11 May 1982. I have previously argued that this ceremony was part of an unsuccessful attempt by Begin to establish the Likud's political dominance and the ideological hegemony of what some scholars have called a New Zionism, closely identified with Begin's political leadership of the state.³⁹ The debate over the appropriateness, meaning, and significance for contemporary policy of this controversial ritual reaffirmed a shared Zionist rhetoric at the same time as it expressed polarized ideologies and conflicting policy alternatives. The fact that secular scholars like Professors Yigal Yadin and Yehoshafat Harkabi (both of whom played major military roles in their earlier careers) engaged in public debate with the prime minister and the chief Ashkenazic rabbi over their contradictory interpretations of the consequences and implications of events that took place two thousand years ago implies that they share an underlying Zionist/Israeli worldview that makes the debate over such a root cultural paradigm possible, intelligible, and meaningful.

The minutes of the Ministerial Committee on Symbols and Ceremonies (MCSC) are replete with scores of requests annually for state recognition of and support for the reinterment of the remains of various individuals and categories of people, e.g., illegal immigrants who died in British transit camps in Cyprus and Mauritius, the victims of illegal immigrant ships which sank (the *Rafiah, Mifkora, Pisces,* and *Masada*, among others), and the ashes of Jews of the Lithuanian Brigade, to name but a few. During the term of the MCSC from 9 February to 16 December 1981, for example, thirty-five of the seventy-six decisions taken dealt with such requests and related issues of memorialization. How do we account for the pervasiveness of this phenomenon and what does it mean?

The core myth on which Zionism bases its legitimacy is the eschatological notion of exile and redemption. It is both a "root metaphor" which provides categories for conceptualizing the order of the world, and a "key scenario" which elaborates mechanisms for social action.[40]

> The prophetic promise to the children of Israel of an end to exile and a return to Zion is the central principle that motivates and legitimates Zionism. It is interpreted as a historic right (or duty) by the secularists and a religious right (or duty) by the religious Zionists.[41]

The key operational Zionist scenario derived from this core myth is "the ingathering of the exiles":

> Since Zion (Eretz Yisrael, or the biblical land of Israel) is the key symbol identified with Zionism, *aliyah* (literally "ascent," associated with spiritual ascent to the Temple in Jerusalem or the *bimah* where the Torah is read in the synagogue), the Zionist term for immigration to Israel, is the primary rite in the civil religion for Zionists born abroad. This is considered to be the right of all Jews and the obligation of every Zionist.[42]

I suggest that one of the primary motivations for requests for reinterment of remains, particularly by secular Zionists, is related to their desire to fulfill this obligation on behalf of comrades—even posthumously. While this ritual honors both the individual or group being reinterred, it no less importantly symbolically recognizes the Zionist credentials of the sponsors. I have already mentioned the sponsors who supported the reinterment of prominent Zionists figures like Hess, Herzl, and Jabotinsky as well those soldiers reputedly associated with Bar Kokhba.

Other groups, e.g., associations of veterans of both world wars and associations representing ethnic groups such as North Africans, have initiated or sponsored such rites. Each sought recognition of its Zionist credentials, while simultaneously reaffirming its shared belief in a sacrosanct article of Zionist faith. Even in those most partisan cases where opinions and loyalties were divided, the challenges concerned the appropriateness of a particular case or the appropriateness of state recognition. None, however, questioned the general validity or appropriateness of such rites. On the contrary, as in the aforementioned cases of partisan conflict over the interpretation of myths, the controversial debates confirmed the legitimacy of the dominant Zionist paradigm.

Analyses of the changing symbolic salience and meanings of Masada, the Holocaust, and the Western Wall for Israeli political culture reflect not only the general theme of the few against the many, but a growing emphasis on the notion of "them against us." The historical isolation of the Jewish people and the assumption of hostility of the Gentile toward the Jew acquired a new meaning and salience with the Holocaust. Liebman and Don-Yehiya conclude their chapter on the new civil religion by stressing, "the traditional concepts of Esau hates Jacob and a nation that dwells alone became explanations of reality and legitimations of Israeli policy."[43]

Even the celebration of traditional religious holidays and contemporary secular festivities in Israeli kindergartens emphasize the victory of the Jewish people over enemies who sought to destroy them and their culture in both ancient and recent history.[44] A colleague reported the following story related by his daughter upon returning from kindergarten one day:

> Daddy, I know that on Passover we celebrated our freedom from the horrid Egyptian Pharaoh who wanted to keep us as slaves. On Purim we are happy because brave Queen Esther convinced the King to hang the wicked Persian Hamen who wanted to destroy all of the Jews. On Hanukkah we celebrate our freedom from our Greek enemies. Daddy, tell me—who were our enemies on *Tu Bi-Shevat* [the New Year of the Trees or Arbor Day]?[45]

The twisted interpretation of tradition reflected in this anecdote is indicative of a sense of national paranoia which characterizes the more nationalistic Zionists and reaches its extreme manifestation among the xenophobic ultra-Zionists.

> What fundamentally divides Israeli Zionists is their evaluation of whether or not the Jewish people and its state are capable of being "normal," and whether or not such a condition (if it is possible) is one that should be sought. Essentially the humanist Zionists, even those who aspire for Israel to be a light unto the nations, aspire to normalcy (even if it may be an unobtainable condition). The nationalists believe that the Jewish people, and consequently its state, are fated to be a nation that dwells alone. The ultra-nationalists glory in Israel's abnormality, its isolation, and consider this singularity as proof of providential "chosenness."[46]

I have argued that these orientations are related to different perceptions of security, perceptions of "the other," and temporal perceptions of myth and history. To put it succinctly:

> The humanists tend toward greater security, perceive history as a linear process, and aspire to national normalcy. There is an inverse relationship between degrees of nationalism and perceptions of security. There is a positive relationship between the degrees of nationalism and perceptions of history as myth, or temporal notions of totemic time.[47]

Zionism has contained contradictory aspirations from its inception. Competing groups with conflicting interests and ideological interpretations of the Zionist vision have utilized various symbols, myths, and rituals to interpret social reality in conformity with their respective perspectives and goals. The tension created by the struggle between rival groups debating in terms of contradictory aspirations established dominance of the Zionist discourse and the centrality and marginality of various groups in the political culture which this discourse articulated.

The post-1967 period has seen a sharpening of the divisions within Israeli culture characterized by conflicting aspirations, interests, and ideological perspectives. Although this chapter has focused on the sources of political culture in the emerging state, I shall conclude by briefly addressing current trends in the Zionist discourse which may point to a less functional and optimistic outcome for current debates than was achieved in the earlier period. Rael Isaac suggested that the ideological divisions in Israel essentially contributed to stability until approximately 1967. However, argues Isaac, particularly since 1977, cohesiveness and stability have been undermined by the breakdown of a commonly perceived threat to survival. "And it is the perception of threat itself which now divides the public in Israel. Once the threat is differentially perceived, it pits against each other those who identify different—often contradictory—ways of meeting perceived dangers."[48]

Whereas I agree with this perceptive observation, I completely disagree with her further claim that the parties no longer offer alternative views of Israel's national task. Writing at a time of the signing of the Camp David accords, Isaac was obviously disappointed with what she apparently perceived to have been a betrayal by Begin of Revisionist ideology. Subsequent developments, which have made her first observation even more compelling, have proven her second one to be mistaken. The Palestinian *intifada*, the subsequent changes in the position of the PLO, the Egyptian and United States initiatives to facilitate the implementation of the Shamir/Rabin proposals for elections on the West Bank and in the Gaza strip, and the divided reactions of Labor and the Likud, which brought down the government formed after the 1988 elections, have made it clear that there still are viable alternative views between the major Zionist parties.

Isaac wishes to argue that, "Of all the adverse developments that have beset Israel since her 1967 military triumph, the most serious may have been the loss of faith in the traditional slogan, "There is no choice." It is a slogan a beleaguered state with an ideological culture can ill afford to relinquish."[49]

However, I suggest that the loss of *ein breira* as a slogan is only to be regretted if it accurately portrays objective political realities. Anwar Sadat proved that it did not do so in the case of Egypt. Similarly, there is a strong indication that, in the case of the Palestinians, there is a choice, a chance of political dialogue. However, Isaac's fears as to the impact of the loss of a common perception of the source of threat to the state brought about by the territorial issue are even more seriously applicable to the results of the contradictory conclusions drawn by Israelis regarding the challenge of the Palestinian uprising. Such divisions invite international pressures and contribute to divisions within the Jewish communities abroad.

I suggest that the *intifada* has succeeded in convincing most Israelis that the status quo in the territories is not viable. As Amos Oz aptly put it: "What was will never be again, and what will be, is not what was."[50] The *intifada* has forced many Israelis to confront and to consider the legitimacy of the Palestinian claim to the land and to national self-determination. For some Israelis, it has called into question the taken-for-granted traditional definition of the Arab/Palestinian as "the other." As I have argued:

> In a very real sense the present situation is forcing many Israelis to reevaluate and to redefine the essence of Zionism a century after its beginnings and how it relates to the state of Israel in its fortieth year of independence. Such fundamental challenges to perceptions of reality, which have been taken for granted by so many people for so long, are perceived by those thrust into confusion and self-doubt as a great danger. However, with perspective, this situation can also be seen to be a tremendously liberating one, since it allows for considerable freedom in the reinvigoration or re-creation of cultural paradigms, which may also open up new political options. . . . The old policies have proved bankrupt and the old ideologies have lost their salience. There is no turning back. But the future is rife with as many possibilities and promises as it is with threats and dangers.[51]

NOTES

I am extremely grateful to William Robinson, Yael Zerubavel, and Jonathan Boyarin for their helpful comments on an earlier draft of this chapter.

1. Since I am not a historian, I am sensitive to the limits of professional naivety when working beyond one's fields of professional expertise (in my case anthropology and political science). See Ely Devons and Max Gluckman, eds., *Closed Systems and Open Minds: The Limits of Naivety in Social Anthropology* (Edinburgh: Oliver and Boyd, 1964; Chicago: Aldine, 1964).
2. Charles S. Liebman and Eliezer Don-Yehiya, *Civil Religion in Israel* (Berkeley: University of California Press, 1983).
3. Roy Wagner, *The Invention of Culture* (Chicago: University of Chicago Press, 1981), 59.
4. Myron J. Aronoff, *Israeli Visions and Divisions* (New Brunswick: Transaction, 1989), xii–xiv.
5. Paul Ricouer, *Lectures on Ideology and Utopia* (New York: Columbia University Press, 1986).
6. Max Gluckman, *Custom and Conflict in Africa* (Oxford: Basil Blackwell, 1956), 27.
7. See Peter Berger and Thomas Luckmann, *The Social Construction of Reality* (London: George Allen & Unwin, 1966).
8. See Aronoff, *Israeli Visions and Divisions*, 126–29.
9. Ibid., 128–29.
10. The recent polarization of politics and political stalemate created by the election results have strengthened the orthodox parties and made the Zionist parties somewhat less paternalistic toward the Arab voters. These trends, if strengthened, could lead to future governments dependent on either Arab or non-Zionist religious parties. This, in turn, could result in significant revisions of the Zionist paradigm. See Ian Lustick, "The Political Road to Binationalism: Arabs in Jewish Politics," in Ilan Peleg and Ofira Seliktar, eds., *The Emergence of a Binational Israel* (Boulder: Westview, 1989), 97–123, for an example of one such possible scenario.
11. Michael Keren, *Ben Gurion and the Intellectuals* (De Kalb: Northern Illinois University Press, 1983); Michael Keren, *The Pen and the Sword: Israeli Intellectuals and the Making of the Nation-State* (Boulder: Westview, 1989).
12. It is noteworthy that a Revisionist historical perspective or a reinvention of historical traditions (depending on one's political as well as conceptual preferences) of the *yishuv* has only begun to appear in recent years. It is being written by a younger generation of Israeli historians and historians of Israel.

13. Cited in Daniel Shimshoni, *Israeli Democracy* (New York: The Free Press, 1982).
14. This argument is persuasively made by Liebman and Don-Yehiya, *Civil Religion in Israel*.
15. Itamar Even-Zohar, "The Emergence of a Native Hebrew Culture in Palestine: 1882–1948," *Studies in Zionism* 4 (October 1981): 171.
16. Numbers 23:9.
17. Since this chapter focuses on the historic origins of the political culture, I generally use the past tense. However, it should be noted that there is considerable continuity and that many features of the past shape the present political culture. I shall return to this point throughout the chapter.
18. Nurith Gertz, "The Few against the Many," *The Jerusalem Quarterly* 30 (Winter 1984): 94–104.
19. Nurith Gertz, "Social Myths in Literary and Political Texts," *Poetics Today* 7:4 (1986): 621–39.
20. Gertz, "Social Myths," 625. For example, I have analyzed attempts to transform partisan heroes like Jabotinsky and martyrs of the dissident underground military organizations into national heroes through association with mythical "heroes" like Bar Kokhba. See Aronoff, *Israeli Visions and Divisions*.
21. Yael Zerubavel, "The Politics of Interpretation: Tel Hai in Israeli Collective Memory" (unpublished manuscript dated 1989), 1. See also Yael Zerubavel in this volume (chapter 10).
22. The others are Balfour Declaration Day (2 November 1917); the anniversary of the United Nations resolution leading to Israeli independence (29 November 1947); and the anniversary of the peace treaty with Egypt (26 March 1979). See Aronoff, *Israeli Visions and Divisions*, 46.
23. Yael Zerubavel, "From a Marginal Jew to the New Hebrew Man: National Folklore and Counter-Folklore in Israel" (unpublished manuscript [n.d.] made available by the author). See also Yael Zerubavel in this volume (chapter 10).
24. Gertz, "Social Myths," 629.
25. Yael Zerubavel, "From a Marginal Jew," 27 and n. 20.
26. See Nakdimon Rogel, *Tel Hai: A Front without Rear* (Hebrew) (Tel Aviv: Yariv-Hadar, 1979) cited in Zerubavel, "The Politics of Interpretation." For a report of the debate in the Provisional Committee on 20 February 1920 over the so-called "Tel-Hai affair" and for an analysis of its implications, see Baruch Kimmerling, *Zionism and Territory: The Socio-Territorial Dimensions of Zionist Politics* (Berkeley: Institute of International Studies, 1983): 83–90.
27. Liebman and Don-Yehiya, *Civil Religion in Israel*, 46–47.
28. Obviously the establishment of ideological preeminence was intimately related to the establishment of political dominance, which is a subject well beyond the scope of this chapter. For analyses of this theme, see Yonathan

Shapiro, *The Formative Years of the Israel Labor Party* (Beverly Hills: Sage Publications, 1976); and Dan Horowitz and Moshe Lissak, *Origins of the Israeli Polity* (Chicago: University of Chicago Press, 1978).

29. Aronoff, *Israeli Visions and Divisions*, 132–33. Sana Hasan (*Enemy in the Promised Land* [New York: Pantheon Books, 1986], 222) reports the following observation of a *kibbutznik* friend: "I was patriotic once—I was proud of being called to the army after I finished school. But a year later, when I went back to school to attend a friend's graduation ceremony, the headmaster gave a speech and said, 'More graduates of this school have fallen in wars than those of any other school.' And he was proud of it!"
30. Zerubavel, "From a Marginal Jew," n. 18.
31. Myron J. Aronoff, *Frontiertown: The Politics of Community Building in Israel* (Manchester: Manchester University Press, 1973).
32. For example, the Ministerial Committee on Symbols and Ceremonies in a meeting on 14 October 1981 rejected a request to transfer a memorial for *Machal* (overseas volunteers who fought in Israel's war of independence) from Latrun to Jerusalem because of the proliferation of memorials on private property throughout the country.
33. Liebman and Don-Yehiya (*Civil Religion in Israel*, 118–19) indicate the government decision of 1950 to establish this memorial day prior to Independence Day was institutionalized in law in 1980. They also indicate the 1950 decision to establish military cemeteries was somewhat controversial. The annual memorial ceremonies are attended by members of the government and the Knesset, officers and representatives of units of the IDF, the border police, veterans associations, local councils, and mourning families. Student members of Gadna (a pre-military movement for high school students) conduct the ceremonies at the two monuments.
34. "So Joseph went up to bury his father; and with him went up all the officials of Pharaoh, the senior members of his court, and all of Egypt's dignitaries, together with all of Joseph's household, his brothers, and his father's household" (Genesis 50:7–8).
35. I am grateful to Professor Shlomo Avineri, who related this to me in an interview on 24 January 1983. For an excellent concise analysis of the contribution of Hess to Zionist thought, see Avineri, *The Making of Modern Zionism* (London: Weidenfeld & Nicolson, 1981), 36–46.
36. See Liebman and Don-Yehiya, *Civil Religion in Israel*, 95.
37. There is no record of this decision in the files of the Ministerial Committee on Symbols and Ceremonies. According to the secretary of this committee, Aharon Lishansky (in a personal interview with me), Prime Minister Eshkol decided this matter personally.
38. For a more detailed analysis of these events, see Aronoff, *Israeli Visions and Divisions*, particularly ch. 3, 43–53.
39. For an extended analysis of this case, see Aronoff, *Israeli Visions and Divisions*, ch. 3, 54–64. For works dealing with New Zionism, consult

Charles Liebman and Eliezer Don-Yehiya, *Civil Religion in Israel*; Ilan Peleg, *Begin's Foreign Policy, 1977–1983: Israel's Move to the Right* (Boulder: Westview, 1987); Ofira Seliktar, *New Zionism and the Foreign Policy System of Israel* (London: Croom Helm, 1986); and Lilly Weissbrod, "From Labour Zionism to New Zionism: Ideological Change in Israel," *Theory and Society* 10 (1981): 777–803.

40. Sherry B. Ortner, "On Key Symbols," *American Anthropologist* 75 (1973): 1338–46.
41. Aronoff, *Israeli Visions and Divisions*, 130.
42. Ibid., 30.
43. Liebman and Don-Yehiya, *Civil Religion in Israel*, 166.
44. For a perceptive analysis of such a case, see Leah Shamgar-Handelman and Don Handelman, "Holiday Celebrations in Israeli Kindergartens: Relationships between Representations of Collectivity and Family in the Nation-State," in Myron J. Aronoff, ed., *The Frailty of Authority: Political Anthropology*, vol. V (New Brunswick: Transaction, 1986), 71–130.
45. Myron J. Aronoff, "Introduction," in M. J. Aronoff, ed., *The Frailty of Authority: Political Anthropology*, vol. V (New Brunswick: Transaction, 1986), 7.
46. Aronoff, *Israeli Visions and Divisions*, 156.
47. Ibid., 157. A more detailed analysis is contained in ch. 6, 123–44.
48. Rael Jean Isaac, *Party and Politics in Israel* (New York: Longman, 1981), 207.
49. Ibid., 212.
50. Robert Rosenberg, "'What was will never be again, and what will be, is not what was,' says Amos Oz," *Jerusalem Post*, 19 February 1988, 4.
51. Aronoff, *Israeli Visions and Divisions*, 157–58.

CHAPTER 10

New Beginning, Old Past: The Collective Memory of Pioneering in Israeli Culture

YAEL ZERUBAVEL

Every nation reconstructs its own past and creates its own "myth of beginning," a sacred text about an early event in its history that presents a new paradigm in the life of the nation.[1] When the state of Israel was founded, Tel Hai was established as an Israeli national "myth of beginning," representing the pioneering era in Israeli history. The myth of Tel Hai relates to a specific historical battle at a small settlement in the northern frontier that took place on 1 March 1920. Eight Zionist settlers died in Tel Hai, the most famous of whom was Yoseph Trumpeldor. To the *yishuv*, the Jewish community in Palestine, the battle at Tel Hai symbolized a major transformation of Jewish national character and the emergence of a new spirit of heroism and self-sacrifice. The commemoration of Tel Hai marked the beginning of a new era of Zionist settlement and defense of the land that led to the establishment of the state of Israel.

Prior to the foundation of the state, Tel Hai was an issue of conflict between the Socialists and the Revisionists. This conflict generated two competing subtexts of the myth, both of which challenged an earlier agreement on its interpretation. The originally unifying symbols of the plow and the gun were pulled apart by the rival movements to support their competing ideologies.[2] With the establishment of the state, however, the two versions were integrated into one authoritative text and the symbols of the plow and the gun were safely united in Trumpeldor's single arm.

The reconstruction of a unified meaning of Tel Hai was obviously important to its status as a national myth. Tel Hai could now be used to symbolize national unity which the achievement of statehood was supposed to bring about. Moreover, the recovery of a hegemonic myth of "beginning" was essential to the new state to provide a sense of shared mission and common purpose. The continuing state of war following the proclamation of independence and the massive influx of Jewish immigrants to the new state intensified the need for a unified interpretation of the myth.

It is not surprising, therefore, that in this new phase of development, the narrative of Tel Hai played a major role in the education of the country's youth. The annual commemoration of Tel Hai on the Eleventh of Adar (the date of the Tel Hai battle according to the Hebrew calendar) enhanced public awareness of and commitment to the myth. Public school ceremonies, youth movement pilgrimages to Tel Hai, civil and military ceremonies by the monument of the fallen heroes, and special programs in the Israeli media on this date reinforced the significance of Tel Hai in Israeli national consciousness.

However, during the early years of statehood, we also find the beginnings of a significant shift in the collective memory of Tel Hai. Although its formal commemoration emphasized continuity with the *yishuv* period, there was a noticeable erosion in the popular attitude toward the myth. If the establishment of the state was in itself a proof of the success of the spirit of Tel Hai, it was also responsible, in part, for the decline of the myth. During the pre-state period, Tel Hai was important as a source of inspiration and an educational model for the future. Consequently, a strong *futuristic orientation* imbued the literature relating to Tel Hai. However, the establishment of the state of Israel was a turning point demarcating *the end* of the pioneering period. The emergence of the state created an ambiguous framework for the interpretation of Tel Hai. On the one hand, statehood reinforced Tel Hai's effectiveness as an Israeli "myth of origin." On the other hand, the association of the myth with the pre-state period would eventually undermine Tel Hai's mythical status and shift its relevance from the future toward the past.

The ambiguity resulting from this process of historical transition provides the context for the present study. This essay explores how two different readings of Tel Hai emerged within Israeli society as a result of different interpretations of this process. Whereas one reading of Tel Hai has essentially adhered to the narrative constructed during the *yishuv* period, new counter-texts relating to Tel Hai challenged the cultural hegemony assumed by the myth and reinforced by official publications and educational textbooks. As a result of this development, both the earlier myth text and the new counter-texts exist within Israeli political culture, offering conflicting interpretations of Tel Hai and the pioneering era that it represents.

The Tel Hai Myth: A Sacred Text of New Beginning

The construction of a new "myth of origin" requires a dual emphasis on discontinuity with the past as well as a new sense of continuity with the future. "For something genuinely new to begin," Mircea Eliade notes, "the vestiges and the ruins of the old cycle must be completely destroyed."[3] Thus, Tel Hai was originally prized for symbolizing rupture with the Diaspora past and for representing the new spirit of the future Hebrew nation. The spontaneous response evoked by the events at Tel Hai reveals the Zionist pioneers' immediate recognition of the symbolic significance of this event as a major turning point in Jewish history. Tel Hai was *"the first* sign of the *future,"*[4] which generated "a *new* voice and *new* words."[5] Trumpeldor and his comrades were posthumously praised for being *"the first* to know for what you lived and for what you died,"[6] and as "the *standard bearers* of our great ideal, as those who went *in front* of us and *showed us* the way to Zion."[7]

Trumpeldor's role as a symbol for the future was stressed in both oral and written literature. The poet Yitzhak Lamdan in his epic poem, *Masada*, depicted Trumpeldor as the prophet of promise and hope who changed the course of history at a critical moment. When the protagonist, a fellow pioneer, wonders in great despair "if all of us here, one by one, will not slip away into the abyss," Trumpeldor arrives on the scene, singing a song of victory and reviving the dying fire of Masada.[8] In a similar manner, the poet David Shimoni alludes to Tel Hai as "a vision of hope" that brings out the promise of national redemption.[9]

Trumpeldor's image was used to dramatize the rupture with the Diaspora past. The selection of Trumpeldor as a counter-model to the traditional Diaspora Jew is not surprising. Although proud of his Jewishness, Trumpeldor grew up in an assimilated family with little exposure to Jewish tradition or education. In contrast with the predominant Jewish tendency to evade military service by all possible means, Trumpeldor believed that it was his duty as a Jew to join the Czarist army and prove that Jews could be both committed and courageous. When his left arm was amputated due to a war injury, Trumpeldor insisted he was entitled to remain an active soldier. A recipient of military honors, he was the first Jew in the Czarist army to be promoted to the rank of an officer.[10] Thus, Trumpeldor's stature as an outstanding hero was recognized and affirmed by non-Jews prior to his emergence as a Jewish hero.

The sharp contrast between Trumpeldor and the Diaspora Jew and his resemblance to the ancient Hebrews living in their own land was stressed in the first eulogy for the dead hero that appeared in the Hebrew daily *HaAretz*:

> He fell dead, the hero of Israel! Like a figure of ancient magic this man was, the great-grandson of the ancient heroes of Israel, one of those who joined Bar Kokhba's host, one of those who followed the hero of Gush-Halav. A hero—in the most simple, fundamental, positive meaning. Neither the hero of words, nor the hero of arguments, but a hero of action, a fighter for the liberation of our people.[11]

The juxtaposition of the hero of words and arguments with the hero of action clearly suggests the fundamental contrast between the Diaspora Jew's ineffectual verbosity and inaction and Trumpeldor's practical, heroic activism. One of the most popular songs about Tel Hai, "In the Galilee, in Tel Hai, Trumpeldor fell," which was composed immediately after the historical event, highlights Trumpeldor's role as a symbolic leader who calls others to follow him. It is no less significant that the Hebrew words were put to the melody of a Ukrainian folksong glorifying the death of a Cossack.[12] The choice of this melody associates Trumpeldor's new heroism with the ruthless historical archenemies of East European Jews, the Ukrainian Cossacks, and thereby emphasizes the non-Jewish elements of Trumpeldor's heroic image.

Educational texts from the period following the foundation of the state continue this theme, contrasting the heroic character of Israeli society with that of the Diaspora, and presenting Trumpeldor as a model of the Israeli Jew. The following quote from *Mikraot Yisrael*, the most popular textbook of the "general" (i.e., non-religious) Israeli public schools until the late seventies, illustrates this theme. The story of Yoseph Trumpeldor begins as follows:

> In Russia, a child was born to a Jew and his name was Yoseph. He was courageous and brave. He always hurried to help the weak and defend him from the stronger and the more powerful.
>
> When Yoseph grew up, he went out to his brethren and saw their misery in Exile. He felt their sorrow and shared their pain. In his heart, he thought how to raise his nation's honor and defend it against the enemy. For Yoseph was a brother to all those who suffer and a friend to anyone in trouble.[13]

The textbook narrative is modeled on the biblical story of Moses, the mythic Jewish leader of antiquity. Like Moses, Yoseph went out to see his brethren's suffering in exile, and like Moses, he defended the weak against their oppressors. By adopting specific expressions from the Bible (Exodus 2:11–13), the modern text creates a parallel between "Moses" and "Yoseph" and implies that the modern-day hero too is a figure of mythical dimensions. Like Moses, who led his people from Egypt to the Land of Israel, Trumpeldor is portrayed as a symbolic leader of the modern Zionist resettlement of this land.

This use of biblical verses also highlights the contrast between Trumpeldor as a new breed of Jew and the "Jews of Exile." Although Trumpeldor himself was raised in exile, "he went out" to defend his brethren against their enemies, like his predecessor, Moses. Perhaps this is the reason why the narrative begins with the rather awkward formulation "a child was born to a Jew" rather than "a Jewish child": for Trumpeldor was symbolically no longer the Jew of the Diaspora, but rather a New Hebrew, a descendent of the ancient Israelites.

The frequent reference to Trumpeldor by his first name, Yoseph, reinforces his New Hebrew image. While making the hero more easily accessible to young children, the use of his Hebrew first name also emphasizes the Hebrew dimension of Trumpeldor's public image. "Trumpeldor," while a difficult name to pronounce, is also a foreign name that indicates Trumpeldor's tie to the Diaspora. The use of the first name also makes Trumpeldor resemble legendary biblical figures, such as Abraham, Moses, or David, who have been known to generations by their first name. Unlike the modern use of a family name, the frequent addition of an epithet ("Yoseph the hero," "Yoseph the Galilean," or "Yoseph the amputee, or the one-armed") follows the ancient model of "Judah the Maccabee" and "Yiftah the Giladi," thereby reinforcing the mythic resonance of Trumpeldor.

The contrast between Trumpeldor and the Jews of exile is also reflected in a popular children's biography by Uriel Ofek. In the author's description of the young Trumpeldor's first encounter with traditional Jews, the latter are stereotypically portrayed as elderly religious men who continuously sigh as they talk. The old men describe to Trumpeldor the historical persecution of their community that accounted for hundreds of graves on a nearby hill. Trumpeldor, upset by their story, criticizes the Jewish passivity and helplessness in the face of persecution and proclaims that he would always fight to defend himself and others:

> "But we live in exile," the elderly men replied and sighed again. "We are Jews and we depend on others' goodwill. Don't forget . . ."
>
> "Nonetheless," he argued against them, "we have to educate our children so that they know how to defend themselves. We have to send them to serve in the army so that they know how to hold up arms, fight back, and protect their lives."[14]

Trumpeldor's last words, "It is good to die for our country" (*tov lamut be'ad arzenu*), became the climax of the myth that concisely expressed the heroic spirit of the new era. "Your words, 'It is good to die for our country,' split our night like the rays of a proud sun," the poet Shimoni wrote in obvious admiration.[15] The custom of putting up posters in schools with Trumpeldor's famous dying words around the Eleventh of Adar highlighted their centrality to Tel Hai's legacy. Trumpeldor's last words were seen as a strong, patriotic statement that elevated sacrifice for the national cause to an ultimate act of patriotism. Readiness to die for the country and the nation was in itself considered to be a positive departure from traditional Jewish religious martyrdom. Moreover, while the death of Jewish victims in the Diaspora was condemned as pointless, the death of the Tel Hai defenders was praised as a means of reviving Jewish national honor that had disappeared in the Diaspora.[16] This is evident in the reiteration of this praise by Ben Gurion in the forties during the Holocaust.[17]

Trumpeldor's amputation added to his heroic image and became an important theme of his myth. Names such as "the one-armed hero" (literally, the amputee hero, *hagibor hagidem*) or "Yoseph the one armed" (literally, "the amputee") were often used to glorify him. Moreover, the mystifying epithet "the enigmatic hero" (*gibor hidah*) is directly associated with his "single arm" (*zeroah yehidah*), quite possibly because the two expressions rhyme in Hebrew.[18]

While the accepted image of the Zionist pioneer portrayed him holding the plow in one of his arms and the gun in the other,[19] Trumpeldor held the plow and the gun in his single arm, and managed both. His ability to perform complex tasks in spite of his handicap evoked great admiration. A highly popular song for Tel Hai Day, for example, describes the hero working and singing about his plow: "my plow is my work, my plow is my flag, my plow is with me, with me."[20] Another children's story describes how two lumps of soil, upon seeing Trumpeldor's enormous effort while holding the plow, willingly jump into its turning blade thus helping him to perform his mission.[21]

The Tel Hai literature also emphasized the New Hebrew's newly achieved harmonious relations with nature.[22] Thus, Trumpeldor's work in the fields became another important theme of the new beginning. The hero's closeness to the land and nature contrasted with the situation of the Diaspora Jew who lost touch with both. It also made him similar to the ancient Hebrews who worked the fields of this same land. At the end of the story about the two lumps of soil mentioned above, the blood of the dead hero falls upon the two lumps of earth and they, in turn, produce radiant red flowers. Like a male-female union, the union of the New Hebrew Man and Mother Earth then bears a common fruit, a symbol of their renewed bond.

Just as the New Hebrew Man redeems the land of his ancient forefathers, the land redeems him. The transformed Jew thus becomes symbolically a part of the landscape of his country.[23] The story also shows that Earth itself identifies with the hero and follows his example of devotion and self-sacrifice. This theme has a deep resonance in Jewish tradition, echoing the Aggadic-Midrashic literature of the *akedah* ("the binding of Isaac") and other Jewish tales of martyrdom.[24] But while the focus of the traditional tales is death as an expression of devotion to God, the new tale elevates the land as the object of worship.

Accounts of the blood spilled there become a sacred symbol of the renewed bond between the new nation and the ancient land.[25] Thus a few days following the battle, Moshe Smilansky, sharing with the readers of *HaAretz* his concern about the lack of holy places for the young, announced excitedly: "And now a holy place has been created. Every year, on the Eleventh of Adar, teachers and students from all over the free country will flock to the Upper Galilee, to Tel Hai and Kfar Giladi (settlement to which Tel Hai defenders withdrew after the attack of 1 March 1920)."[26]

The myth of Tel Hai provided a model for Israel's future struggle for national independence. By stressing the theme of "a few against many," it portended the state's future experience. Thus, the educational narrative in *Mikraot Yisrael* describes how "one day a mob of armed Arabs attacked Tel Hai. Trumpeldor and his brave comrades resisted them heroically, a few against many attackers." The story further elaborates on this theme, describing how Trumpeldor fought against the enemy, "one hand against many hands."[27]

Tel Hai's significance as a myth of heroism and firm commitment to Jewish settlement and defense is spelled out in the following educational text of the Israel Defense Forces:

> From this, we can learn about the courage, the readiness, and the self sacrifice of these people who wished to hold on to these settlements. They knew well that the enemy outnumbered them ten fold and that they did not have any hope of receiving real aid from the rear, which was also very poor and weak. Nonetheless, they were not discouraged.[28]

The educational message of Tel Hai was further emphasized in a brochure for the annual commemoration on the Eleventh of Adar, Tel Hai Day, published in 1943. Offering a wide variety of materials for the commemoration of Tel Hai in Hebrew nursery schools, the brochure states as its goal "to turn this tale of heroism into an educational treasure for the young."[29]

These educational materials attempt by various means to enhance the children's identification with the defenders of Tel Hai and, particularly, with Yoseph Trumpeldor. Among other things, the brochure suggests concluding the nursery school's ceremony for Tel Hai Day with the presentation of Trumpeldor's photographs to the children, accompanied by the injunction: "Try to be like him."[30] The didactic tone is typical of children's literature for Tel Hai Day, which, through stories and poems, transmits moral messages to the young in the name of the hero: "Yoseph the Galilean / Left us his legacy / To work and to guard / The Land of Israel,"[31] or "The whole Galilee carries his tune / Singing his last words: 'It is good to live and good to die / For the homeland, for freedom.'"[32]

In one children's play, when three children get lost during a school trip to the Galilee, an image appears to them at night. The image, dressed in grey clothes, including a military shirt with its sleeve hanging loose, instructs the children as follows:

> *The image*: If you wish to get rid of snakes and enemies . . .
> *The three*: Then what?

The image: You must make the wilderness blossom . . .
The three: . . . what can we do, for we are still young?
The image: Don't say young. Everyone must do the best they can. The most important thing is willpower. I have only one, single arm, and with it I plowed the mountains and I also expelled the enemy.
Yossi: Oh, oh, I know who you are!
The two others: You are the hero, Yoseph the Galilean![33]

The monument of "the roaring lion" that was erected on the tomb of the Tel Hai defenders is yet another symbol of the hero that links him to the ancient past. On the one hand, the lion provides a vivid visual image and serves as a universal symbol of power and domination. But the lion also serves as the emblem of ancient Judea, thus associating Trumpeldor with that glorious past. Moreover, the literature often portrays the stone lion as coming alive again and roaring, thereby communicating Trumpeldor's message to contemporary Israelis.[34] In other places, the monument is presented as the legendary lion of Bar Kokhba, the leader of a Jewish revolt against the Romans in the second century A.D. The lion, who freezes after Bar Kokhba's death, is brought back to life upon hearing about Trumpeldor and his friends. But upon learning about their death, it froze again on their tomb and has remained there ever since.[35] This glorification of the lion sees it—and by extension, Trumpeldor—as beyond historical time and beyond the natural limits of life and death.

Following the foundation of the state of Israel, educational texts perpetuated the same themes of the Tel Hai myth that had become crystallized during the pre-state period.[36] Thus, these educational texts preserved the ethos of settlement and defense, the importance of fighting until the end, and the spirit of self-sacrifice. Tel Hai Day, also called "the Day of Defense," provides an opportunity to explore the theme of Jewish heroism from a historical perspective.[37] The importance of Tel Hai as the symbolic beginning of Israeli heroic history is manifest in the unique status of Tel Hai Day, the Eleventh of Adar, as the only day for commemorating Israeli heroes besides the national Memorial Day for Israeli soldiers. Whereas the commemoration of the Memorial Day for Israeli soldiers treats the soldiers collectively and anonymously,[38] Tel Hai Day singles out one particular historical episode and tends to center around the singular image of Trumpeldor.

The emphasis on Trumpeldor as a role model for contemporary Israeli soldiers appears in a children's story by a well-known educator and writer, Levin Kipnis. The story, entitled "The Strong Arm," focuses on Trumpeldor's legendary arm which was amputated in exile. During the War of Independence, when Israeli soldiers found themselves in a critical situation, a mysterious object appeared and chased the enemy away. The astonished Israelis learned that this was Trumpeldor's amputated arm, which finally fulfilled its vow to come to the Land of Israel and to continue to fight for its own people.

This rather gruesome story, while emphasizing the intimate bond between Trumpeldor and contemporary Israeli soldiers, also portrays the dead hero as greater than the Israelis who fought in 1948. It is interesting to note that the guidelines issued for seventh-grade teachers define the educational themes of this story as follows: (1) tales of heroism are remembered forever; (2) Yoseph Trumpeldor will be remembered forever; and (3) the Land of Israel will always be the most prominent concern of Jews.[39]

Tel Hai as a Representation of an Old Past

Although after 1948 the educational narrative of Tel Hai conformed to the pre-state interpretation of the historical event, the myth has gradually begun to lose its popular appeal. Like any cultural process, it is difficult to point out a specific beginning for the decline of the myth. The early signs of its weakening can be associated with "the 1948 generation," the generation of Israeli youth who were born in the twenties, were brought up within the *yishuv*'s emerging Hebrew culture, and later fought in Israel's War of Independence. This generation (also known as "the Palmah generation"), educated on the Tel Hai myth, admired Trumpeldor and, as young children, dreamed of becoming heroes like him.[40]

However, the political and social developments in the forties began to change youths' attitude toward Trumpeldor as a role model. Thus, a brochure for Tel Hai Day, published by Betar in 1945, refers to a claim by the youth that, since Trumpeldor has become obsolete, they need new symbols.[41] During this period, Tel Hai began to be associated with a much different past. Tel Hai was now seen as a metaphor for "old," and the expression "from Trumpeldor's days" (*miyemei Trumpeldor*) was taken to refer to something archaic or obsolete.

The 1948 generation also generated new humorous interpretations of Tel Hai that inverted its heroic meaning. These humorous interpretations perceive Tel Hai as a symbol of an "old past" and challenge the earlier glorification of Trumpeldor as the prototype of the New Hebrew Man. As we shall see below, these texts transform the heroic myth into an anti-heroic tale, the glorified event into a ridiculous story, and the model of the future into a symbol of an archaic past. The crude humor employed in these texts suggests a deliberate effort to desecrate the Tel Hai myth.

One *chizbat*, a humorous narrative of the 1948 generation, recorded by Dan Ben-Amotz and Hayim Hefer,[42] describes how the sculptor Melnikov created the monument of "the roaring lion" in Tel Hai:

> When they asked Melnikov to make the statue of the lion on the grave of Trumpeldor, they said that first of all he would have to see a real lion. They said to him, "Find yourself a lion." And in those days there wasn't one lion in the country.

The initial request for a "real lion" as a model seems quite appropriate for a hero of Trumpeldor's stature and is consistent with the glorifying myth. But at this point the *chizbat* departs from that myth and begins its own sequence of symbolic inversions: Since no "real lion" exists in the country, the sculptor has to go to Egypt, an Arab country, to look for a living model. Once there, Melnikov goes to the zoo to sketch the lions, but must first buy a ticket and pay a bribe in order to get permission to sit and sketch. In this less-than-heroic setting, Melnikov confronts his inability to faithfully fulfill his mission:

> By the time he started sketching, all the lions had fallen asleep. He told them to roar, they didn't roar. He said to them, "Tzzzzz." They didn't bat an eyelash. He went "zrrrr" and all the donkeys in the area started braying. But the lions—nothing. They were finished. He saw that he had no other choice. He approached the cage and started to stick his hands in. One lion saw a hand, he got up and tore his shirt, with the chest. But he didn't roar. Blood started to flow. Great God! Melnikov left the zoo and ran to the pharmacy.

After receiving first aid from the pharmacist, Melnikov, following a lead, goes to an Arab who has "a big cat, like a lion, who roared like a leopard." Melnikov buys the cat, starves it, and when the hungry cat roars, he finally makes his sketch of "the roaring lion." The narrative concludes as follows: "And anyone who doesn't believe it can go to Tel Hai and see if the lion there doesn't resemble a cat roaring like a leopard."

The *chizbat* aims its humor at the monument and portrays it as a gross misrepresentation: a cat which is raised as a pet cannot possibly be an appropriate model for a real lion, the symbol of power, mastery, and freedom. Furthermore, to glorify the New Hebrew Man's stand against the Arabs[43] by a model borrowed from "Arabs" undermines the symbolic message of the monument. In contrast to heroic tales in which the hero who faces a series of challenges but succeeds in fulfilling his goal, the *chizbat* offers an anti-heroic figure who, following a series of failures, fails to achieve his goal. While heroic tales often present heroes who overcome fierce wild lions, this narrative describes Melnikov's defeat by caged lions. Seeking the advice of a German Jew and a rabbi, Melnikov chooses to find his solutions through payment and manipulation. Thus, rather than the New Hebrew, the sculptor resembles more closely the stereotype of the Diaspora Jew. With his mishaps, Melnikov may remind one of the *schlemiel*, the humorous "antihero" of Yiddish folklore, a rather unlikely choice for constructing Trumpeldor's monument.

A comparison of the *chizbat* with the *Encyclopaedia Judaica*'s account of Melnikov's monument of the roaring lion is instructive. According to the *Encyclopaedia*, Melnikov's work, "inspired by the sculpture of the *ancient* East, was *the first modern monument* in the country."[44] This statement, emphasizing both the novel character of the monument and its link to the ancient past, affirms its appropriate representation of Tel Hai.

It is quite telling that the first indications of a changing attitude toward the Tel Hai myth are found among those considered the elite of the first generation of New Hebrews for whom Tel Hai was to serve as a major educational model. According to Oring, the *chizbat* lore reflects the Palmah members' need to explore the issues of collective identity and reconsider the attitude toward the exilic past:

> The first truth [of the *chizbat*] which exists at the level of content, implies a reaction to the past, a dissociation from the old Jewish experience, an emphasis upon new values and new experiences. . . .
> The second truth, however, lies at a deeper level within the structure of text and repertoire. It asserts that the dissociation from the old and the adoption of the new is not genuine. The transformation is not complete nor can it be completed. The identity of the native-born remains a paradox whose only solution is laughter.[45]

The humor of the *chizbat* is generated by the juxtaposition of Trumpeldor's heroic and much-glorified image and the profoundly unheroic and unglorified portrayal by Melnikov. This contrast challenges the power of Tel Hai as a myth of *new beginning* that breaks with the past. Instead, the *chizbat* establishes a *direct continuity* between the historic Diaspora mentality and the Tel Hai myth. The humorous text also undercuts the dramatic inversion of the Jewish national character that the Tel Hai myth symbolizes. As the *chizbat* implies, the founding fathers who glorified Tel Hai were themselves immigrants who came from the Diaspora and were constrained by their own past. What they saw as an "authentic" model for the future, the 1948 generation redefined as a symbol of the past.

A similar inversion of the myth appears in other humorous texts relating to Tel Hai.[46] For example, members of the youth movement culture joked that the lion of Tel Hai used to roar every time that a virgin would pass by but, alas, in recent years it has had no opportunity to roar. Like the *chizbat* discussed above, this joke pokes fun at the lion that the myth glorifies. Instead of guarding the nation (as the Tel Hai literature suggests), the lion guards the mores of Israeli youth. But since the previous sexual norms are outdated, it is no longer "the roaring lion."

Another example of "youth movement folklore" is the following song which has several slightly modified versions: "Trumpeldor was a hero / The whole day long he was a hero / With one arm he held the plough / With the other he was a hero." This song is hardly as innocent as it may appear to one unfamiliar with Israeli folklore. It is a take-off on Israeli "youth movement folklore" that describes the pioneer holding the plow with one of his arms and hugging a woman with the other (itself an inversion of the glorifying lore about the pioneer holding both the plow and the gun). The song, therefore, suggests that Trumpeldor could not hug a woman because of his amputation. The joke thus reduces Trumpeldor's much-glorified amputation to a "disability" and makes fun of it. The melodies to which this song is sung—a heroic folksong originally sung about Bar Kokhba as well as other cheerful children's folksongs—suggest another level of parody.

Other examples of jokes about Trumpeldor's amputation reveal a similar transformation of this venerated heroic attribute:

Q. Why didn't they play poker in Tel Hai?
A: Because they missed one hand.

Q: Why did Trumpeldor's plow have a white license plate?
A1: Because he was disabled.
A2: Because he was both disabled and a Russian immigrant.[47]

A very popular one-liner relating to Trumpeldor is: "I was Trumpeldor's right hand!" This joke, which plays on the absurdity of the literal meaning of this statement, is based on the erroneous impression that it was his right arm that was amputated. Another joke begins with the famous glorifying verse "with his one arm Trumpeldor held both the plow and the gun" and then adds that "with his leg he gave himself a hand-job." Some jokes are visual, demonstrating how Trumpeldor's disability prevented him from clapping hands, playing the guitar, or using the Israeli officer's famous gesture of "follow me."

Perhaps the most popular humorous text about Tel Hai is the new version of Trumpeldor's famous last words, "It is good to die for our country." The new version suggests that before he died Trumpeldor actually uttered a juicy curse in Russian, often identified as *iob tvoiu mat* (i.e., "fuck your mother"). The juxtaposition of the myth text with this modified version obviously suggests the depth of the symbolic inversion that transforms a highly patriotic statement into a curse and emphasizes Trumpeldor's status as a Russian immigrant who could not have uttered the famous saying in Hebrew.[48]

The very association of jokes with the once-sacred hero suggests, in itself, a symbolic transgression. The following exchange from an interview I conducted with an Israeli woman (herself a war widow) illustrates how the humorous lore can become the first association with the hero:

I: Let's move on to Trumpeldor.
She: Hmmm . . . This reminds me of a joke. Can I tell a joke? [She laughs and turns to her son whom I had already interviewed in school.] Should I tell her, Danny?
I: Sure, sure, go ahead. [The son also nods in agreement.]
She: It's an awfully nice joke about Trumpeldor . . .

The hero who was raised to the status of a *unique* figure in Israeli history has also been occasionally reduced to a *generic* category. Such was the case, for example, in a rehabilitation ward of a hospital where soldiers who lost an arm were collectively referred to as "Trumpeldors."[49] Several informants also mentioned naming a pet or a toy with a broken limb "Trumpeldor." Such generic usage contrasts with the earlier use of the name Trumpeldor as a sign of glorification.

Of more recent texts that symbolically invert the Tel Hai myth, I would like to mention a cartoon that targets the story from *Mikraot Yisrael*'s which I quoted earlier. In the tradition of Talmudic commentaries, the original educational narrative is placed side by side with the cartoon's visual exegesis. Contrary to the original myth text that emphasizes Trumpeldor's dissociation from his Diaspora brethren, the cartoon shows Trumpeldor the child surrounded by images of traditional Jews and displays the "mythical" hero in oversized dimensions dressed as a Russian soldier. Moreover, the cartoon ridicules the hero's glorified amputation by drawing amputated arms on the monument of the roaring lion as well as the buildings of the city named after the Tel Hai defenders.[50]

The humorous lore thus satirizes the key elements of the Trumpeldor myth: the amputation of his arm, his military experience, his famous last words, his plow, the monument of the roaring lion, his "Hebrew" character, and his function as a role model. The jokes poke fun at his once-admired amputation, shed doubts about his sexual performance, show that he falls short of any contemporary Israeli officer, and focus on his Russian, immigrant status. The humorous lore removes Trumpeldor from his elevated position as the prototype of the New Hebrew Man, viewing him either as a representative of the pioneers of the second and third *aliyot*, or as an East European immigrant.

Conclusion

The Tel Hai humorous lore deliberately violates the cultural expectations developed by the Tel Hai myth. The humorous texts subverting the myth's message suggest the inappropriateness of Trumpeldor as the symbol of the New Hebrew Man and the forerunner of contemporary Israelis. Because of their macabre character, many of these texts belong to the contemporary Israeli genre of "horror jokes" (*bedihot zeva'ah*). These "horror jokes" have developed as a cultural response to the tense atmosphere of frequent wars and military actions, economic hardships, and internal political frictions. The jokes, targeting such issues as war, the Arab-Israeli conflict, hospital wards, death, and emigration from Israel, poke fun at otherwise sensitive and painful problems currently facing Israeli society. By channeling their ambivalence and criticism through humor, contemporary Israelis attempt to cope with the widening gap between the founding fathers' glorified vision of the future and the present pressures of Israeli life. The humorous framework only thinly disguises the latent function of these texts as a form of protest.[51]

The underlying themes of these humorous texts about Tel Hai reflect Israelis' reaction to the excessive glorification of the pioneering past in Israeli educational and political discourse. The new cynical attitude toward this cultural style is best expressed in the emergence of a new concept, "Zionism in quotes" (i.e., *zionut bemerkhaot*). This term conveys a sense of disenchantment with the platitudes and preaching of Zionist rhetoric in which pathos and pomp override substance.[52]

Thus, the first period of Israeli statehood in which the story of Tel Hai was established as a unifying myth of origin also gave rise to a new cynicism and skepticism regarding the pioneering ethos that Tel Hai represents. This ambivalent cultural stance to Tel Hai continues to operate within contemporary Israeli culture. The more formal, educational texts present Tel Hai as a myth of new beginnings of a period of settlement and defense that characterizes modern Israel and distinguishes it from the Diaspora past. The myth is still embraced by many Israelis as a meaningful legacy from the pioneering period. This may explain, in part, the angry response to Nakdimon Rogel's critique of the political implications of Tel Hai.[53]

At the same time, the new subversive texts have become part of contemporary Israeli folklore. As in the early state period, this lore is now generated among native Israelis who, although shaped by the Tel Hai myth from early childhood, now challenge the excessive glorification that informs the Tel Hai literature. These subversive texts suggest that the Tel Hai myth neither provides an accurate account of the past nor serves as an appropriate model for the present.

The current Israeli trend of de-mythologizing the past may be a way of coming to terms with the present. The glorified image of the pioneering past makes it more difficult for Israelis to accept the present social, political, and economic strain in their lives. As long as the pioneering past looms large, Israelis will continue to see the present situation as one of alarming, continuing decline. Challenging the romantic-heroic image of the pioneering past, these new texts demonstrate that the pioneers, too, suffered from weaknesses and limitations, not the least of which was their "inferior" immigrant background. Thus, these new texts invert the relationship between the present generation and the pioneers by elevating the former.

A practical joke that one of my informants described to me illustrates some of the underlying themes discussed above: In the middle of a party, when people sit and have a casual conversation, one suddenly says, "Have you heard that they cut off Yoseph's arm?" When the company becomes alarmed and everyone cries out "Yoseph who?" one says "Yoseph Trumpeldor," and everyone cracks up. The juxtaposition of an otherwise alarming piece of news with the unexpected reference to the overly used Trumpeldor is the source of the humor. But the laughter is also an expression of relief from the deeply rooted anxiety that pervades a society in which news reports about violence and injuries are dreaded everyday experiences. The subtext of this story is that the teller of this joke, a man known for his sense of humor, is also a public school teacher who formally participates in the transmission of the educational myth. This illustrates how the glorification and the subversion of Tel Hai can be simultaneously incorporated in the repertoire of individuals as well as of the society at large.

The recent scholarly trend to re-examine the pioneering generation by emphasizing their European background indicates the broader cultural context for the emergence of humorous lore relating to the pioneering period.[54] A recent Hebrew novel, entitled *A Russian Novel*, unmasks the two-dimensional, mythical image of a fictitious group of pioneers and presents a colorful and engaging description of their lives and work, loves and hates. The Hebrew title of the book, *Roman Russi*, alludes both to the founders' Russian origin and to the rekindling of a pioneer's old love from his youth in Russia.[55] The novel thus highlights the Russian roots of the pioneering experience of Israeli society but also shows that eventually the "Russian love" was more significant for this pioneer than all his life experience and commitments in Israel.

Both the myth and humorous narratives that Tel Hai has generated in Israeli society disclose the inherent ambiguity in the process of cultural transformation. The myth text, typical of a society in its early formative years, highlights the rupture with an earlier, discredited past and defines a new beginning that provides a unified charter for the future. In contrast, the later humorous texts highlight the continuity between the Diaspora past and Israel's pioneering age. The humorous lore is indicative of a society ready to critically examine its collective identity and acknowledge its cultural continuity with the past. The growing historical and cognitive distance from the pioneering period on the one hand and the increased openness to the Diaspora past on the other undercut the effectiveness of Tel Hai as a myth of new beginnings and a symbol of the break with the experience of exile.

The current focus on Trumpeldor's identity as a "Russian Jew" also acknowledges the limited effectiveness of his public image in a society in which ethnicity has become a major political factor. This modified view of Trumpeldor conflicts with the deliberate "native" Hebrew dimension of the myth of Tel Hai, thus diluting its force as a sacred myth of beginning. The Tel Hai myth presents Trumpeldor as a unifying collective symbol of the pioneer, the forerunner of the New Hebrew. But the greater sensitivity to ethnicity in contemporary Israeli society challenges Trumpeldor's appropriateness as a collective representation of "The Israeli." His elevation to a national symbol can thus be seen as a function of the cultural hegemony of East European Jews during the pre-state period. Similarly, the perpetuation of his mythic status in the educational and political discourse in Israel can be viewed as part of the predominantly East European establishment's attempt to maintain its hegemony. As an Israeli of Middle Eastern origin told me in an interview, "Honey, if Trumpeldor had been a Yemenite, no street would have been named after him."

NOTES

1. See Mircea Eliade's discussion of the origin myth in his *Myth and Reality* (New York: Harper & Row, 1963), 21–53, and Barry Schwartz's elaboration of this concept in his study of the collective memory of American social origins, "The Social Context of Commemoration: A Study in Collective Memory," *Social Forces* 61 (1982): 374–402.
2. For further discussion of this political controversy on Tel Hai, see Yael Zerubavel, "Politics of Interpretation: Tel Hai in Israeli Collective Memory," *AJS Review* 16, 1 (Spring 1991); Charles Liebman and Eliezer Don-Yehiya, *Civil Religion in Israel* (Berkeley: University of California Press, 1983), 74–75.
3. Eliade, *Myth and Reality*, 51. For similar examples, see Eviatar Zerubavel, "Easter and Passover: On Calendars and Group Identity," *American Sociological Review* 47 (1982): 284–89; and Eviatar Zerubavel, *Hidden Rhythms: Schedules and Calendars in Social Life* (Chicago: University of Chicago Press, 1981), 82–95.
4. A. L., "leZekher Ahai sheNaflu baGalil" (In memory of my brothers who fell in the Galilee), *haPoel haTsair* (26 March 1920): 17; emphasis added.
5. Hadash, "miSaviv: al Mot Lohem" (Around: the death of a fighter), *haPoel haTsair* (12 March 1920): 26; emphasis added.
6. Yoseph Klausner, "Hem Naflu Halalim" (They died), *HaAretz* (9 March 1920), 2; emphasis added.
7. Max Nordau, "haKapitan Trumpeldor" (Captain Trumpeldor), *Yoseph Trumpeldor: Hai Shanim leMoto* (Eighteenth anniversary of his death) (Tel Aviv: Keren Tel Hai, 1938), 50; emphasis added.
8. Yitzhak Lamdan, *Masada* (original Hebrew publication, 1927), trans. Leon I. Yudkin, *Isaac Lamdan: A Study in Twentieth Century Hebrew Poetry* (Ithaca: Cornell University Press, 1971), 230–31.
9. David Shimoni, "Tel Hai" (original publication 1935), reprinted in his *Shirim* (Poems), vol. II (Tel Aviv: Massada, 1954), 258–59.
10. The biographical data is based on Shulamit Laskov, *Trumpeldor: Sipur Hayar* (Trumpeldor: a biography) (Haifa: Shikmona, 1972).
11. *HaAretz* (5 March 1920), 1.
12. A program on the history of songs for Tel Hai Day, edited by Hedva Szold (16 March 1967) on Israeli national radio. The Hebrew words were composed by Abba Hushi.
13. Almost the same text appears in Z. Ariel, M. Blich, and N. Persky, eds., *Mikraot Yisrael leKhitah Beit* (Textbook for the second grade) (Jerusalem: Massada, 1965) and in the revised edition by Natan Persky, ed., *Mikraot Yisrael Hadashot leKhitah Beit* (The new textbook for the second grade)

(Jerusalem: Massada, 1975), 238. The following text is quoted from the latter source.
14. Uriel Ofek, *Gibor Hidah* (The enigmatic hero) (Tel Aviv: Shreberk, 1975), 12. This description of Trumpeldor's attitude is supported by a story that Trumpeldor himself wrote, "Wertheimer," in which he glorifies an observant Jew's transformation into a secular man during his military service in the Zion Mule Corps, in *HaAretz* (21 March 1921), 2–3. On Trumpeldor's encounter with traditional Jews, see also Dov Rabin, "Yoseph Trumpeldor veSipurei Perez" (Yoseph Trumpeldor and Perez's stories) in *haPoel haTsair* (20 March 1962).
15. David Shimoni, "leTrumpeldor" (To Trumpeldor) (original publication 1929), reprinted in his *Shirim* (Poems), vol. II (Tel Aviv: Massada, 1954), 226–27.
16. See the special *yizkor* prayer for the dead, *Kuntres* 29 (11 March 1920): 1; Hadash, "miSaviv," 26; Klausner, "Hem Naflu Halalim," 2; Vladimir Jabotinsky, "Kaddish," (original publication 1928), reprinted in his *Ketavim: Zikhronot Ben Dori* (Collected works: memoirs of my generation) (Tel Aviv: Ari Jabotinsky, 1947), 105; Shimoni, "Tel Hai"; Haim Harrari, *Moadim leSimhah* (Festivals and holidays) (Tel Aviv: Omanut, 1941), 282.
17. David Ben Gurion, "Zav Tel Hai" (The legacy of Tel Hai), *Kuntres* I, no. 381 (1944): 3.
18. This epithet may have originated in Avraham Breudes's famous song "baGalil" (In the Galilee) (original publication 1932), reprinted in Ariel, Blich, and Persky, *Mikraot Yisrael leKhitah Beit*; Uriel Ofek later used this epithet as the title for his children's biography *Gibor Hidah*.
19. This idiom was based on a biblical verse from Nehemia (4:11) and became part of the folklore of the Hebrew pioneer.
20. Sara Levy, "baGalil Yoseph Harash" (In the Galilee Yoseph plowed), reprinted in *leYom Tel Hai: Hoveret Ezer laGanenet* (For the day of Tel Hai: a reader for nursery school teachers) (Tel Aviv: Histadrut, 1943), 26. For further discussion of the political implications of this theme, see Zerubavel, "Politics of Interpretation."
21. Fania Bergstein, "Rigvei haGalil" (The soil of the Galilee), reprinted in M. A. Levi and D. Zamran, eds., *Ogdan laMadrikh beTenuot haNoar* (An anthology for youth movement councilors) (Jerusalem: Ministry of Education, the Youth Department, n.d.)
22. See, for example, Anda Amir, "beYom Yod-Alef baAdar" (On the eleventh of Adar), reprinted in *leYom Tel Hai*, 1943, 27; S. Shalom, "Ah, Bneh haGalil" (Brother, build the Galilee), in Harrari, *Moadim leSimhah*, 284.
23. The idea that man is shaped by the landscape of his country was also expressed by Shaul Tchernikhovsky, one of the most prominent Hebrew poets of the *yishuv*, in his poem "haAdam Eyno Elah" (Man is not but), reprinted in his *Mivhar Shaul Tchernikhovsky leVatei haSefer veLa'am* (Shaul

Tchernikhovsky's selected writings for school and the nation) (Tel Aviv: Dvir, 1962), 208–11.
24. Shalom Spiegel, *The Last Trial, On the Legends and Lore of the Command to Abraham to Offer Isaac as a Sacrifice* (New York: Behrman House, 1967).
25. See also Liebman and Don-Yehiya, *Civil Religion*, 44.
26. Moshe Smilansky, "Makom Kadosh" (A holy place), *HaAretz* (14 March 1920), 1.
27. Ariel, Blich, and Persky, *Mikraot Yisrael*.
28. *haHaganah* (The defense), 3rd ed. (Israel Defense Forces, Education Headquarters, 1973), 36. I am not analyzing here how Tel Hai was presented as a successful story of heroic defense. For a further discussion on the issue of success, see Nakdimon Rogel, *Tel Hai: Hazit lelo Oref* (Tel Hai: a front without rear) (Tel Aviv: Yariv-Hadar, 1979); Yael Zerubavel, "The Last Stand: On the Transformation of Symbols in Modern Israeli Culture" (Ph.D. diss., University of Pennsylvania, University Microfilms, Ann Arbor, Michigan, 1980), 189–99.
29. *leYom Tel Hai*, 1943, 3.
30. Ibid., 13.
31. Avraham Breudes, "Yoseph haGelili" (Yoseph the Galilean), ibid., 24; the Hebrew original rhymes.
32. Amir, "beYom Yod-Alef baAdar," ibid.; the Hebrew original rhymes.
33. H. Tehar-Lev, *Kol miheHarim* (Voice from the mountains) (Jerusalem: Sifriat Adama, 1959).
34. Yoseph Nahmani, "Aggadat haGalil" (The legend of the Galilee) (Graetz Educational Library, Tel Aviv, Trumpeldor file, n.d.); S. Meltzer, "baGalil haElion" (In the Upper Galilee), *leYom Tel Hai*, 1943, 5; Levy, "baGalil Yoseph Harash."
35. Levin Kipnis, "Ari haEven" (The stone lion), *leYom Tel Hai*, 1943, 23–24.
36. A recent study by Bakalash based on observations of school commemorations and review of textbooks confirms that these themes were used by the educational system as late as 1987. See Rivka Bakalash, "Mitos Trumpeldor 'Adam, Dam, Adama' beVet Hasefer haYesodi" (The Trumpeldor myth, "man, blood, earth," in the elementary school) (Masters thesis, Beer Sheva, Ben Gurion University of the Negev, 1988).
37. *Masekhet Gevurah leYom haHagana, Yod Alef baAdar* (The story of heroism for the day of defense, the eleventh of Adar) (Israel Defense Forces, 1949); *Magen vaShelah: Shloshim Shana leHaganat Tel Hai* (The shield and the weapon: thirtieth anniversary of the defense of Tel Hai) (Histadrut, 1950), 79–89; *Zekhor Yemei Tel Hai* (Remember the days of Tel Hai) (Tel Aviv: Teachers Council for the Jewish National Fund, 1960), 23.
38. See also Liebman and Don-Yehiya, *Civil Religion*, 98. The emphasis on the anonymity of military heroes resulted in what I would call "numerical commemoration," i.e., the commemoration of a heroic action through the reference to the number of casualties involved. Consider, for example, the

choice of naming Israeli settlements "The Thirty-Five Kibbutz" (*Kibbutz haLamed Heh*) or "The Hill of the Five" (*Ma'aleh haHamishah*) in commemoration of specific heroic events.

39. *leYom Tel Hai, Yod Alef baAdar: Homrei Hadrakha leMorim beVatei haSefer haMamlakhti'im* (For the day of Tel Hai, the eleventh of Adar: educational materials for public school teachers) (Jerusalem: Ministry of Education, the Center for Developing Jewish Awareness, n.d.)

40. See Hanoch Bartov's autobiographical novel *Shel Mi Atah Yeled?* (Whose child are you?) (Tel Aviv: Am Oved, 1970), 188, 211, 241; and a teacher's 1930 survey of the most admired historical personalities by high school students, Y. Paporish, "Al Idi'alei haNoar beEretz Israel" (On the Israeli youth's ideals), *Hed haHinukh* 5 (21 November 1930): 52, quoted in Yonathan Shapiro, *Ilit lelo Mamshikhim* (An elite without successors) (Tel Aviv: Sifriat Poalim, 1984), 83.

41. A. Ramba, "haSemel Lo Nityashen" (The symbol has not become obsolete), *haAryeh haGlili* (The Galilean lion) (Tel Aviv: Betar, 1945), 3–4.

42. The *chizbat*, a specific genre of Israeli humorous narrative, was generated by members of the *Palmah* underground in the forties. The following text, based on an unpublished manuscript by Dan Ben-Amotz, appeared in Elliott Oring's *Israeli Humor: The Content and Structure of the Chizbat of the Palmah* (Albany: State University of New York Press, 1981), 126–28. The English translation quoted here is Oring's.

43. Although the first references to the enemy in the early texts identified it interchangeably as "robbers," "Bedouins," or "Arabs," the enemy's identity was later established as "Arab." See also Liebman and Don-Yehiya, *Civil Religion*, 46.

44. *Encyclopaedia Judaica* (Jerusalem: Keter, 1974) 3:606; emphasis added.

45. Oring, *Israeli Humor*, 129–30.

46. During the fieldwork and interviews I conducted in Israel in the late seventies, I collected a wide variety of humorous texts about Tel Hai. It is impossible to date the origin of these jokes, which are primarily in oral circulation. Some of these texts were told as "youth movement folklore," and it is quite possible that they in fact originated around the same time of *chizbat* discussed above. It appears that during the seventies these jokes became more popular among native Israelis brought up within the secular national Israeli culture.

47. A white license plate indicates that a car has been purchased with a considerable discount which the Israeli government provides to new immigrants and disabled persons.

48. For a further discussion of this inversion, see Yael Zerubavel, "The Historic, the Legendary, and the Incredible: Invented Tradition and Collective Memory in Israel" (unpublished manuscript).

49. Yaakov Haelyon, *Regel Shel Bubah* (A doll's leg) (Tel Aviv: Am Oved, 1973), 181.

50. B. Michael et al., *Zoo Eretz Zoo* (This land is a zoo) (Tel Aviv: A. L. Special Edition, 1975), 162–63.
51. D. Alexander, "Political Satire in Israel: Different Views of Zionism," in Avner Ziv, ed., *Jewish Humor* (Tel Aviv: Papyrus, 1986), 137–47; Avner Ziv, "Humor in Israel," *National Styles of Humor* (Westport: Greenwood Press, 1988), 113–31; Aliza Shenhar, "Liheyot Sham: Shirei Meha'ah Shel Hayalim biLevanon" (To be there: protest songs by soldiers during the war of Lebanon), *Hetz* I (April 1989): 34–43.
52. Dan Ben-Amotz and Netiva Ben-Yehuda, eds., *Milon Olami leIvrit Meduberet* (World dictionary for spoken hebrew) (Jerusalem: Lewin Epstein, 1972), 196.
53. Rogel, *Tel Hai* (1979). See my discussion of the political controversy over the myth in the late seventies and early eighties in "Politics of Interpretation."
54. Consider, for example, Anita Shapira's current inquiry into "The Russian-Jewish Sub-Culture in Palestine" (public lecture at the University of Pennsylvania, 1989) or Yonathan Shapiro's analysis of the influence of Polish nationalism on the early origins of the Israeli Herut party in *leShilton Behartanu* (Chosen to rule) (Tel Aviv: Am Oved, 1989).
55. Meir Shalev, *Roman Russi* (A Russian Novel) (Tel Aviv: Am Oved, 1988). The Hebrew word "roman" means both "novel" and "love affair." The tremendous success of this novel (seven printings within the first six months of its publication) demonstrates the popular appeal of this lively and humorous portrayal of the pioneers.

CHAPTER 11

At Half-Mast—Myths, Symbols, and Rituals of the Emerging State: A Personal Testimony of an "Israeli Arab"

ANTON SHAMMAS

In the watchfire-lighting ceremony that opened the celebrations of Independence Day in Israel in 1990 (on the eve of 30 April), somebody came up with an ingenious idea for a sign to fit the occasion. As you know, 1990 in Israel marked the first centennial of the revival of the Hebrew language. The establishment of the Jewish state as the national home for the Jewish people was considered by Zionism, to a great extent, as the territorialization of the Hebrew language after two thousand years of uprootedness. Yet, for most of the Israeli Jews, or at least for those who maintain the prevalent cultural tone, as for most of world Jewry, Hebrew still is a Jewish language, not an Israeli one, and all indications show that it is going to remain that way in the foreseeable future.

To celebrate the revival of the tongue and the establishment of the state, and with no apparent intentions of tongue-in-cheek, the tomb of Herzl, the site where the central Independence Day ceremony is held annually, was flanked by a two-part sign, each part carrying two words from a famous biblical verse: "And the whole earth was of one language," according to the King James translation. However, insofar as the Hebrew word for "earth" (*haaretz*), being more humble, implies "land," what the sign meant was that Israel speaks Hebrew; this insinuated, without saying overtly, that Arabic is deterritorialized and its connections to "*haaretz*" are severed.

I saw the picture in *Haaretz* afterwards, and as an amateur but devout reader of biblical narratives, I immediately recognized the verse, as most of you would: Genesis 11:1. And indeed, the caption read: "In the Bible it did not end well." It ended of course in Babel, with the confusion of the tongues and the scattering of the people.

In his *De Vulgari Eloquentia*, in which he set out to establish his vernacular, Italian, as a literary language, Dante described Hebrew as "the language of grace," as opposed to Babel's "language of confusion." The Jewish Kabbalists argued that God's actual speech, the idiom of immediacy known to Adam and common to men until Babel, can still be decoded, partially at least, in the inner layers of Hebrew and, perhaps, in other languages of the original scattering—the "original scattering" in this case being, of course, the biblical scattering in the Book of Genesis.

The original deterritorialization and scattering of the Palestinians in 1948 was done in the language of grace. Exile for the Palestinian refugees was a language of confusion. There was no grace in being a confused refugee.

A beautiful midrash has it that "the ruins of the Tower can be seen to this day; but he who sets eyes upon them is cursed with the loss of memory. All the people on earth who go around saying: Who am I? Who am I? are those who have seen the ruins of the tower of Babel" (*Midrash Rabbah*). So I will avert my eyes now and fumble in my memory.

I was born in a small village in the Galilee, two years after the original scattering of the Palestinian refugees. The inhabitants of Fassuta were spared the fate of the wanderers, so there is always a feeling of shame lurking in their memories; the shame of having been privileged, of having been left on their lands, while the others had to carry the land in their memories and go. It was not a tangible feeling which a child could have sensed, but it was there all right, hovering silently above the mourning heads.

My father, those days, was continuously and pensively struggling with the new language that had invaded his small world and ours, imposing upon him confusion and a new type of illiteracy. He needed a special permit, like all the fathers of his generation, to move around in the scenes of his homeland which had turned overnight into "the homeland of the Jewish people"; but no such permits were available for moving around in the cultural scenes.

The permits to travel to Haifa from Fassuta, under the military administration of the 1950s, were written in Hebrew. Wanting to decipher his limits, as it were, he was learning Hebrew for beginners, as if he were an "*Oleh Hadash*," a new immigrant to his own country. He was learning Hebrew with the aid of books which were illustrated with water towers and plowed furrows, depicting a lifestyle in which he had no share, depicting a new set of arcane symbols whose significations were beyond his grasp and beyond his horizon.

I remember standing in line with him in the scorching sun in front of the nearby police station, for hours on end, waiting for his travel permit to Haifa to be issued inside. I say hours on end, using apparently a childish sandglass. As a matter of fact, even now as I commit these memories to paper, I miss those lines because the short journey to the police station in nearby Tarsheeha was our only outing in those days.

I hardly remember seeing the desired permit; apparently I couldn't have cared less about it. But I do remember the silent, scolding looks of my father, blaming me for having so much fun out of a dubious, extremely tedious, and humiliating trip. And I do remember that around that time I started to realize the utter importance of paper.

Besides the official papers, there was another kind which seemed to attract the attention of the occasional police patrols in the village. These were the small, tender, transparent bound batches of cigarette paper, which found their way to the village in mysterious ways from faraway Damascus. The policemen would confiscate these papers on the spot and sometimes even invite the criminal to a friendly interrogation in Tarsheeha.

On the inside cover there were two lines of poetry in praise of the brand, "The Damascene Paper." My uncle taught me how to decipher the calligraphy so I could recite the lines. These were the first two lines of poetry I ever memorized. And there was another charming quality attached to these cigarette papers: the vendors were women whose identity was no secret, let alone their occupation. They were the local informers who were recruited by the *Shin-Bet* (Security Services) to provide the emerging state with little gossipy secrets of the inhabitants of Fassuta, their alleged political convictions and subversive inclinations, including the number of cigarette papers purchased.

One can talk about the "Myths, Symbols, and Rituals of the Emerging State" in this regard only tongue-in-cheek; retrospectively, that is. After all, the life of Fassuta in the fifties was no tongue-in-cheek matter. True, for the villagers the "emerging state" was an unpredictable being, controlling their lives with a few strings and devices, filling the air with benignly threatening, unequivocally coded messages. My father was determined to decode the messages that had filled his world with a strange—at times even tantalizing—buzz. So he set out one day to single-handedly change the school system in the village. Disenchanted with the management vicissitudes of the private elementary school (run by the local priest who was the local representative of the Catholic Archbishop in Haifa), and weary of the tuition demands, he convinced a group of parents and a couple of teachers to join him in a subversive PTA, contacted the Ministry of Education, and converted the "School of the *Mutran*/Archbishop" into a public school. This hardly pleased the young students. My father fell from grace and his image was irrevocably tarnished in their eyes, since they had not previously been forced by law to attend school.

At the end of my first year of primary school, which happened to be the second anniversary of the founding of the public school in my village, we children were sent to bring laurel branches from the tree shading the village spring to decorate an enormous star of David which one of the teachers had built from six planks (it was not even Independence Day). Our principal wished to make a good impression on the Jewish Inspector of Schools who had, apparently, invited himself to have a close look at the achievements of the young new school. The huge star of David, covered in laurel branches, was hung carelessly and loosely above the stage front. As it swayed, it frightened the children taking part in the program, and also frightened their proud parents in the first rows, who thought it might topple down on them. (It didn't.)

I sometimes wonder whether we were not seared by that star, whether it wasn't a branding iron after all—a branding iron to all the Arabs who were left, for some reason or another, inside the borders of Israel, in the year of our Lord Balfour 1948, henceforth to be referred to as the Green Liners. And when you brand someone, you are actually telling him two equally painful things: first, that he belongs to you, that he must abide by your laws, wander only in the regions that you had put under his disposal and keep away from the ones that are out-of-bounds; second, you're telling him that this searing of the skin is just a searing of the skin—you are not after his heart. When he, too, realizes that you do not seek his utter loyalty, then you both break even, confining yourselves to a position lacking any mutual anticipation. You both acquiesce in the rules of the game: Don't call us and we won't call you.

Be that as it may, in those days we were referring to Independence Day as Independence Holiday; special songs, written in Arabic and set to music by Arab composers, were practiced for the occasion. And when the special occasion arrived, blue-and-white flags were fluttering in the timid village wind. And when a special guest was expected (usually a Jewish Inspector of Schools from the big city, flanked by his Arab entourage), we were busy all morning cleaning the unpaved street which led to the school. And when he arrived, we stood on both sides of the street, waving our little flags in his honor. However, we didn't even know what "Hatikvah" (Israel's national anthem) was.

Little did we know then that the state whose flags these were, was not ours. Come to think of it, nobody knew, not even the young teacher who had taught us the Arabic translation of the Israeli Declaration of Independence, from a brand new *Reader*, which also had a relatively detailed biography of Herzl. We were told, through some outlandish reasoning, to learn those texts by heart, and to this day some sentences of the Declaration will occasionally pop up out of the blue inside my head.

So even according to the Arabic translation of the Declaration, the state was defined as a Jewish state, but nobody seemed to pay any attention to that trivial fact. You see, we had the flags in our hands, so declarations did not matter, nor did the fact which we discovered later—that there was an utter rift between the signified and the signifier; those flags did not signify a single thing. They were meant by the state to be utterly void of any symbolic meaning and were cynically used as mere decorative objects, completely detached from their statism. And we were hung there at half-mast, like a mourning flag: too high to touch the receding Palestinian ground, but still not high enough to have a sense of the Israeli skies.

Years later, after my family had moved to Haifa, I came across an astonishing piece of information which had eluded my childish village attention in the 1950s. It turned out that many of the restrictions placed on Arab residents were lifted come Independence Day, so they could travel freely to the "celebration sites." One of these sites was in the city of Haifa, where Abba Hushi, the then mayor of the city, and whose name became *Abu* (father of) Hushi in the mouths of the villagers, was practicing his games of power over some of the Fassutites for whom this annual "free" trip to Haifa to take a semi-forced part in the "celebrations" was their only chance to erase the borders and limits of their travel permits. I did not pay much attention to these highly publicized trips at the time because I had thought, apparently, that they were fully covered in the permits.

But now that I had learned that reality was not always bleak, and that there were full Days—uppercase *D*—of freedom, it only made me the more disoriented. This also meant, incidentally, that those Arabs who had cars could travel as far as they wished to see the otherwise prohibited scenes of "their" countryside, so to speak, provided they came home to roost at the end of the Day; provided they were fully aware that movement, in whichever direction, is a privilege granted by the state—the movement of the body in this case being a mere reflection of the movement of the soul. Otherwise, nobody went anywhere. Besides, in Fassuta there was only one car.

We were the static element in the dynamic formula of the state. We were visited, called upon, by really privileged people— those who had a whole year of 365 Independence Days. Fassuta was an occasional night-stop in the ritual called "From Sea to Sea" (*miyyam el yam*): the hiking trip of the high school members of the *Gadna'*, which started near the Mediterranean and ended at the Sea of Galilee (Lake of Tiberias), passing through some Arab villages on the way. They would spend the night in our school, a matter-of-fact business, and the principal of the school, a congenial man of manners, would offer them hot tea.

One of my brothers, who used to have a great partiality for tea, was the assistant in the mission. He would be offered some slices of bread in return; and this was no frivolous matter. We were sick and tired of the monotonous *pita* bread at home and would expect father to come home from his few trips to Haifa with a couple of crispy, swollen, shiny loaves of *franji* bread; *franji* meaning ceremoniously non-Arab. So for my brother, those three slices were worth even three years of slavery in Egypt, and he would come home and tease us for hours on end with the magic smell of the *franji* bread, then brew himself a large pot of tea and savor every single crumb against our drooling mouths.

These were the big attractions of the outside world for us, the world that started in the nearby *moshav* (settlement) whose name, Elkosh, had supplanted the Arab name Deir el-Qasi. The Muslim inhabitants of Deir el-Qasi had left their homes and lands as a part of the great Palestinian Exodus of 1948, and for new neighbors we got a special mixture of newcomers (Jewish) from the Arab world. Elkosh at the time was a unique melting pot. Some twenty families of newcomers were brought to settle in the *moshav*—Iraqi and Yemenite Jews together.

They were not even able to understand each other's Arabic dialect, let alone address their problems and disagreements in the holy language of the Bible. They would come to my father's cobbler shop, and later on they would come and visit our home as friends and practice their survival Hebrew with my father. So everybody was happy and understanding, and the lurking, unpleasant memories of the past which belonged to our neighbors' faith and religion were gradually covered up by the endeavors of all parties concerned to master the new language of the new state.

The melting pot in Elkosh was brimming over in no time; the social structure of the newly born *moshav* was falling apart. More and more of the newcomers would come to the Fassutites and suggest a partnership in tilling the soil of Zionism. Agriculture for them was harsh, and harsh was their life and their attempt to get started in what was supposed to be their own state. The Fassutites, a practical bunch and masters of pragmatism, would plant the seedlings of tobacco—their national product of sorts—in the newly conquered land of their new neighbors, and eventually get better prices in the deal. If you happened to be an Arab grower of tobacco in those days, cultivating a plot of land adjacent to an Elkoshite's, you would get some 70 percent of the price he would get on his tobacco. He was subsidized by the Jewish Agency, and that was his state.

We did not only plant seedlings of tobacco in the newly conquered land, we also took part in the "national" operation to cover the mountainsides with trees. On the fifteenth of *Shvat* (*Tu bi-Shvat*), our second-grade teacher led the whole school to a nearby mountainside, with little trees provided by the Ministry of Education in every hand, and after lecturing us about the unequivocal benefits of trees in nature, practically and otherwise, we then contributed our little tiny share in making the desert bloom. Tree Day became a much-awaited holiday in the years to follow; but we never thought of going back to the planting site to check the results of our little green thumbs. We were merely expected to plant trees—so we did. But apparently we were not expected to conduct the follow up; just vegetate.

Then mysterious fires erupted in the surrounding mountains. At least once a month there would be heard a cry for help raised in the village after someone had seen the smoke. Policemen would come in a jeep, carrying brand-new fire extinguishers, and take some of the men to lend a hand. Nobody knew what had caused the fire, and nobody knew who had set the fire, and nobody knew how the jeep arrived always on time. Or maybe the whole thing was just a weird coincidence in a villager's smoking head.

Then there were a couple of hand grenades thrown, exploding in unexpected places, near unexpected houses. And there were some time-bombs exploding near out-of-the-way houses. Nobody was seriously injured, but outside walls were scorched and sooted, and so were the minds of the new citizens on whose fears, bafflement, and puzzle the military government thrived. And so did Mapai, the precursor of the Labor party, through its puppet, Arab Knesset members.

My family, though, had a brief, enlightening affair with the Mapam party. My elder brother, in his corner at Father's cobbler shop where he had been serving as an apprentice, hung a *Time* magazine cover of Fidel Castro, challenging my father's huge poster of Ben Gurion. He was recruited by one of our cousins to go to work in Kibbutz Kefar Massarik, near Haifa, three months before the elections of 1959. They both joined forces in order to run a well-organized election campaign for Mapam among the young, enthusiastic, first-time voters, including parades with flags of many colors—red, blue, white—and all Mapam, the United Laborers Party, enjoyed a smashing victory in Fassuta that day. Three days later, a group of Fassutites, my elder brother included, were given the sack in Kefar Massarik. And since that day, my elder brother has been a very lapsed socialist. That was also the year in which he got rid of his astonishing stamp collection, and for a couple of weeks even contemplated growing a beard, but then changed his mind. I wonder if the idea of mourning over a defunct civil religion might have crossed his mind.

The second-grade teacher who led us that Tree Day to the mountains used to surprise us every now and then with some of his artifacts: a three-dimensional map of the village, a white rabbit of cotton balls inside a box and, at one point, a gruesome, still beating heart of a bird; except the bird had flown. But the work I admired most was a framed three-portraits-in-one of President Ben Zvi, Prime Minister Ben Gurion, and Benjamin-Ze'ev Herzl, the Big Founder. He set the picture of Herzl, in one piece, as a background on which he mingled the respective glazed-in strips of Ben Gurion and Ben Zvi in such an undulating way that if you looked at the picture from the left you could see Ben Gurion, from the right—Ben Zvi, and Herzl *en face*.

This was sheer magic for us, and our class became "a point of interest" on the otherwise dull map of our dull school. Pupils would come from all grades, at every time imaginable, to look at this new Trinity, this new Wonder of Fassuta.

That same year a painter from Haifa was commissioned to paint a huge work for our local church depicting the prophet Elijah, the patron saint of Fassuta. When the painting was unveiled, there was certainly a stir, a commotion of the devout. But that was nothing compared to the new cult which was emerging around our teacher's triple icon. That icon is one of the most recurrent images of my childhood. I think of it often as the most impressive icon of my school days. But I can no longer see the respective portraits as distinctly and clearly as I could then. All I can see now are some broken lines of faces and glass; and a bird's tiny beating heart.

IV. CONFLICTS WITHIN AND CONFLICTS WITHOUT: DIPLOMACY AND FOREIGN POLICY

CHAPTER 12

Israel's Global Foreign Policy, 1948–1956

URI BIALER

The partial declassification of political and diplomatic papers in Israel has made it possible to engage in Israeli historical research in a way that is similar to the British, American, and French practices. This declassification has provided the necessary means for the historian to focus on the basic parameters and elements of continuity or discontinuity in Israeli foreign policy, rather than be satisfied with case studies of dramatic events such as the Reparations Agreement with Germany, the Sinai Campaign, or the reprisal actions. The purpose of this chapter, therefore, is to present some findings of a study on Israel's global foreign policy orientation in the early years after the establishment of the state and, more specifically, on the diplomatic road the state established for itself in the international arena where the two superpowers competed for allies. Rather than elaborate on the obvious, in concrete terms I shall elaborate on three basic factors which pulled Israel towards a policy of nonalignment at that time and on the distinct and highly important barriers which later prevented a drastic and public departure from this posture: the internal political, the Soviet, and Western considerations.

Having spent several years in various archives studying historical records, I have little doubt that, during the early 1950s, Israel's foreign policy was, to a large extent, determined by the domestic context within which that policy was formulated and carried out. This becomes clear especially when attention is paid to the highly important papers deposited in the Mapai's archive, particularly when these are correlated with the extensive newspaper coverage of the same period. The material shows that the issue of nonalignment had been a matter of intense discussions within that hegemonic party long before Israel made her "Korean decision" in mid-1950. Affecting a wide range of political and ideological subjects, these discussions generated controversies which were often bitter and clearly articulated in terms of internal considerations. Significantly, matters culminated in a series of important party decisions before and after July 1950.[1]

There were two basic dimensions of these controversies: internal ideological and interparty political. As to the former, one has to give adequate weight to the fact that within Mapai debate arose in two related areas: one pertaining to general perspectives on the world and society, the other to specific foreign policy issues. Two different conceptions concerning the link between party ideology and foreign policy formed the background for this debate—one which regarded the link as essential and a second, the pragmatic view, which greatly minimized its significance.

The divergence of views led to a multifaceted debate. In the ideological sphere, it focused on the concrete question of alignment. Did the party as a socialist movement constitute a contender in the international, social, and spiritual battle dividing mankind, or was it merely a neutral bystander? Some factions within the party demanded the adoption of a neutral position in the great ideological struggle then being waged between Bolshevik communism and democratic socialism. This demand stemmed from their distinct and highly significant sense of alienation from and disappointment with the process by which socialism was implemented in the West. Others, emphasizing the oppressive character of the Soviet regime, insisted that it obliged the Zionist socialists to support the members of sister social democratic movements elsewhere in the world.

Both factions at times used the term "nonalignment." They defined this posture as a condition of independence from the positions of other states and powers and as an *a priori* noncommitment to a defined course of action in any given international situation. However, having so defined nonalignment, both factions very often rejected it. The discussions in Mapai's central bodies on the issue of formal links with international socialist organizations bring to light the gradual and rather slow change which took place between 1947 and 1953 in the position of Mapai from a point somewhere in between the two extreme positions to final rejection of the policy of nonalignment.

The second internal facet of the internal debate over Israel's global foreign policy was the debate within Mapai on relations with Mapam. Long before the first Knesset elections of early 1949, Mapai had considered Mapam to be its most dangerous political rival. Were the two camps from which the latter was formed, Hashomer Hazair and Ahdut Ha'avoda, to unite (as they did in 1948), Mapam might even constitute an alternative to the government. The fear was not unfounded; in 1946 the two factions had won almost half the votes in the Histadrut Convention. The elections for the Knesset and the Seventh Histadrut Convention held in January and May 1949, respectively, showed that Mapam still constituted the second most important political party in Israel. At a time when the political affiliations of numerous new immigrants were still undefined, this fact was particularly weighty.[2]

Moreover, the danger from the left was not merely electoral, but also ideological. Mapai's leaders were well aware that Mapam was ideologically very attractive to at least part of their electorate. Although most Mapai members had recovered from their initial intoxication with the Russian Revolution long before 1948, few were able to forget its allure. Mapam's attraction also derived from its justification of its foreign policy platform on the grounds of Soviet political support for the creation of a Jewish state. In short, Mapam seemed to have the ability to successfully outflank Mapai from the left.

One of the most important manifestations of the struggle Mapai waged against Mapam was Mapai's categorical refusal to consider the latter as a potential partner in the government coalition.[3] Foreign policy issues, more specifically Mapam's loyalty to the Soviet Union's cause, were central justifications for this attitude. As Mapai's Secretary-General Lavon once phrased it, "in our relations with the USA we have in that country a fifth column whereas in our relations with the Soviet Union they have a fifth column here."[4] Moreover, the inclusion of Mapam in the government would solidify the opinion that Israel's nonalignment in fact concealed a pro-Soviet orientation, a dangerous impression as far as Israel's relations with the United States were concerned.

Nevertheless, it should be noted that several of Mapai's leaders questioned David Ben Gurion's policy of vicious and sometimes brutal confrontation with Mapam during the first three years of Israel's independence. These leaders were concerned that Ben Gurion had prematurely "closed the door" to any possibility of political cooperation with that party, believing that Mapam's internal dynamics might lead the party to abandon its extreme line. Accordingly, the moderate elements within it should be encouraged.

Much of this more moderate thinking within Mapai can be explained by the unmistakable danger of civil war which a dramatic split of the Histadrut could precipitate.[5] Another consideration which militated against an all-out battle against Mapam was the common belief that it would create the impression within the Eastern bloc that Israel had definitely aligned itself with the West against the Soviets. Concern for the fate of *aliyah* from Eastern Europe, it should be noted, was in the minds of all.

Mapai's internal debate on this subject had two implications for Israel's global foreign policy. First, as long as there seemed to be the slightest hope of moderating Mapam's ideological and political program, Ben Gurion faced a not-insignificant opposition to his conception of Israel's foreign strategy and his stance towards Mapam. Ultimately, it was only Mapam's extremism, after May 1950, which weakened the hand of Ben Gurion's opponents within Mapai. More important, the evidence concerning Russia's hostility towards Israel and Zionism which emerged during the Prague Trials (show trials held in Czechoslovakia under Stalinist influence, which were the first occasion on which anti-Semitic accusations of a world-wide Jewish conspiracy were openly proclaimed by an authoritative communist forum) two years later deprived Mapam of one of its most effective foreign policy arguments and invited attack and denigration on the domestic front.[6] In short, the records documenting Mapai's struggle against Mapam are invaluable for explaining the process of change within Israel's foreign policy and for easing that process, especially for those who opposed the pace and nature of change. The second implication is no less significant. The records support the conclusion that the danger from the left was critical in the removal of the entire notion of an anti-Soviet military alliance with the West from the public national agenda, at least in the late 1940s and early 1950s.

A major consideration affecting much of Jerusalem's attitude towards contacts with the outside world has been, since very early on, the prospects of Jewish immigration to Israel. In April 1949 Ben Gurion told Defense and Foreign Ministry officials that

> internal and external policy is always determined by a state's core interest, which may change; and although we are an especially young country, we have experienced change. . . . Before the state was

established and, upon its establishment, our core interest was defense. . . . The question is, what is now the core interest of the state of Israel? It is Aliyah. . . . The fate of the state depends on Aliyah.[7]

With regard to this central goal of *aliyah*, the East was perceived as central for two reasons. First, when the state of Israel was established in 1948, some two and a half million Jews remained behind the Iron Curtain. However, it was certainly not only numbers which mattered to Israeli leaders. In December 1948, Moshe Sharett, Israel's Foreign Minister, for example, passed on to Andrei Vyshinsky, the Soviet Union's Deputy Foreign Minister, a widespread opinion concerning the quality of Eastern European Jews which, for obvious political reasons, was rarely expressed publicly:

> [The problem of *aliyah*] is not so much a question of quantity as of quality. . . . Our task in Israel is a pioneering one and we need people who have [already] been forged. We are greatly interested in bringing the Jews of Morocco to Israel and we are making great efforts in that regard. But we cannot depend on the Jews of Morocco alone to build Israel, because they are not suitably gifted for it. We do not know what awaits us, what military and political disasters lie ahead. Therefore, we need people who will withstand all difficulties and who can bear suffering. In the past there were the Jews of Russia. . . . After the conditions of Russian Jewry changed in the wake of the Second World War, the Jews of Poland and Rumania filled this role.[8]

Indeed, after independence, one of the central goals of Israeli foreign policy was the maintenance of ties with Eastern European Jewry. In addition to being concerned for their well-being, Israel, above all, wanted to ensure the possibility of their *aliyah*. In the early years of the state, immigration efforts showed partial, but nevertheless quite impressive success. Some 180,000 immigrants from Eastern bloc countries came to Israel between its independence and the end of 1949. In 1950, 75,000 Eastern bloc Jews immigrated; the next year, 45,000; in 1952, 4,700. However, from 1952 until 1956, annual *aliyah* from the Eastern bloc declined to no more than a few hundred. The high immigration figures in the 1948–52 period underscore how important it was to maintain good political relations with those countries when so many Eastern bloc Jews immigrated.

Moreover, it is not difficult to appreciate why, even after mass *aliyah* seemed to come to a halt at the end of 1952, the issue of immigration from Eastern Europe continued to occupy the minds of Israeli policy makers. They clearly realized that there existed a vast reservoir of potential *aliyah* in the approximately 200,000 Jews left in the Soviet bloc countries and in the two million Jews in the Soviet Union itself. Thus, the deep and utterly sincere sense of responsibility for the fate of the Jewish people behind the Iron Curtain and the aspiration that they be permitted to come to Israel precluded drastic deviations from the policy of nonalignment, even when such moves seemed justified by sound reasons of state.

Cordial political relations with the East were essential for other admittedly less important reasons as well. It will be recalled that the Soviet bloc's political support was crucial for securing Israel's independence.[9] On one occasion, Israel's Foreign Minister reported to Jerusalem that "in the Security Council the Russians act as if they were our emissaries."[10] The continuation of this support was no less essential after July 1949 when the young state had to defend the military and territorial achievements of the War of Independence at the United Nations.[11]

Moreover, besides political support, during its hectic early history Israel also needed arms. It is a well-known fact that the state received crucial military assistance from Czechoslovakia during the early phases of the 1948 war.[12] Some less-known aspects of the story become evident through recently declassified documents. Thus, for example, the estimated value of Israel's purchases from the Czechs up to mid-May 1948 was more than $12,000, about 60 percent of the *yishuv*'s total arms purchases in Europe, which was the major source of its military supplies. Another $9,000 was spent by Israel to acquire Czech weapons during the second part of that year.

Far more important than the size of the transaction is the fact, revealed in these documents, that the purchases continued beyond the period of the 1948 war, and only terminated in 1951. The conventional historical wisdom is that the Russians' primary concern was the successful establishment of the state of Israel, and that, beyond that goal, they had little interest in providing Israel with arms. Had this been the case, however, then Russian-backed military aid to Israel, in the form of Czech armaments, would not have continued beyond 1948. However, a significant fact which the newly released documents bring to light is that arms, including heavy weapons, continued to come from Czechoslovakia until early 1951, through the activities of Israel's only full-scale arms purchasing ("Rechesh") mission in the Eastern bloc. The cost of planned Israeli acquisitions from Czechoslovakia in 1950 comprised no less than 25 percent of the total budget for arms imports at that time.

It is, I would argue, inconceivable such large quantities of arms could have left Czechoslovakia (inter alia via Poland) without Soviet knowledge and approval. Furthermore, it is inconceivable that the activities of the Rechesh mission in Prague would have escaped the attention of Soviet intelligence.

Finally, while my thesis must remain speculative, the documentary evidence now available suggests that the Soviet attitude towards Israel changed substantially only when Israel publicly supported the American position on Korea late in 1950 and when other signs of her growing reliance on the United States became evident. In other words, Soviet aid was related to Israel's foreign policy to a larger degree than has hitherto been assumed. It now seems likely that the USSR rewarded Israel for her identification in 1949–50 by approving the Czech arms deal and that she withdrew that support once Israel seemed to alter her foreign policy.

The revival of the military connection seemed to again become a possibility late in 1955, a time, paradoxically, when Czech arms supplies began to stream into Egypt. The newly revealed documents describe the little-known internal debates in Jerusalem which lasted no less than six months over whether or not to submit a formal request for Soviet weapons.[13] No such request was submitted. What deserves to be noted, however, is that the idea of approaching the Soviets for military aid was not rejected out of hand, and the issue was discussed seriously by policy makers in Israel for an extended period, and ultimately there was even a probe in that direction. In retrospect, those months of debate seem to have been the last occasion when there was still a possibility that Israel might strike a balance, however fragile and tactical, between East and West in her foreign policy.

In addition to its need for new immigrants and arms, Israel, during the period under discussion, also lacked energy sources. In the wake of the 1948 war, it had been deprived of the major sources of Middle East oil.[14] By September 1953, this deprivation became total when the British-Persian Oil Company and Shell decided to cut oil supplies to Israel from Middle East sources to avoid protests in the Arab world. This resulted in a 40 percent loss in Israel's crude oil supply and left the country with a severe shortage.

In the wake of the oil companies' announcement, Israel made the decision to purchase a "certain amount" of oil from Russia, an amount whose measure grew considerably. It is a remarkable fact that for three years, until oil deliveries from the Soviet Union were halted following the 1956 Sinai Campaign, Russia supplied Israel with more than 30 percent of her oil consumption, 30 to 70 percent of which was paid for through Israeli exports—a boon to Israel's balance of payments.

In addition to immigration, arms, and fuel, there was a strong emotional factor drawing Israel towards the Eastern bloc. First, the overwhelming majority of Israel's political elite after independence was of East European or Russian origin.[15] Diplomatic positions in Eastern Europe could, therefore, be easily staffed by persons born in the countries to which they were accredited, fluent in their languages, and deeply and personally acquainted with their cultures.

An additional factor was the profound memory of the tragic course of recent Jewish history in that part of the world. Israel Barzilai (born in Neszawa, Poland), the first Israeli Minister of that country, expressed this in a touching dispatch which he sent to the Foreign Ministry the day after presenting his credentials in Warsaw early in October 1948:

> Yesterday we laid wreaths on the grave of the unknown soldier and on the monument of the ghetto uprisings. They played "Hatikvah" [the Israeli national anthem] and there was an elegant military service. When we reached the ghetto the sky darkened and rain poured down, the heavens cried, the people cried. . . . You will probably find it strange, this sentimental report from a governmental representative—but please do not forget that we are talking about the Warsaw ghetto and that our hearts have experienced much.[16]

These emotional ties with countries in the Eastern bloc played a significant role in helping to nurture the feeling and hope, based admittedly on certain undeniable political facts, that Israeli policy makers stood on the verge of a significant turning point in the traditional Soviet attitude towards Zionism, and that Israel could perhaps help to facilitate the process.

Bearing in mind all these forms of contact, especially the *aliyah* connection, there is little wonder that Israel declined to publicly align herself militarily or strategically with anti-Soviet defense arrangements, even in the wake of the Egyptian-Czech arms deal of late 1955. What deserves to be noted, however, is the considerable but, at the same time, little-known efforts devoted by Israeli diplomats to secure the state's vital interests in the Eastern Hemisphere of the emerging bipolar world. Israel had little success in securing *aliyah* from the Soviet Union itself during the period under discussion, nor could she be described as really working for it. Indeed, it is my contention that as a result of explicit decisions made by policy makers in Jerusalem during the late 1940s and early 1950s, decisions which were not changed until 1955 when the real struggle for Soviet *aliyah* started, Israel backed off from asserting any pressure for permission for Jews to emigrate.[17] One reason was their view that such pressure could be unproductive and might even harm Israel in other matters.

On the other hand, conditions for *aliyah* seemed to be more propitious outside the Soviet Union. Israel's successes in securing *aliyah* from Eastern European countries confirmed several assumptions: that the Soviets had not banned *aliyah* from these lands outright; that the leaders of those countries were perhaps less rigid regarding *aliyah* than was the Kremlin itself; that the Eastern bloc possessed no concerted line on the issue; and that the Israeli freedom of maneuver was therefore not as restricted as had initially been thought. Moreover, these factors were buttressed by the economic incentives that Israel could hold out to Eastern bloc countries and which, to a certain degree, evoked a response.

One of the most important tools used by the Israelis to facilitate *aliyah* from Eastern Europe had been forged during the three years in which the "Mossad Le'Aliyah Beth" (The Organization for Illegal Immigration) had been active in the Eastern bloc immediately following World War II. At that time, the organizers of Eastern and Central European *aliyah* had learned the effectiveness of bribery, euphemistically referred to within the "Mossad Le'Aliyah Beth" as "lubricating expenses."[18] These consisted of enormous sums of money which Mossad agents paid to senior police or military officers, border guards, and even politicians for turning a blind eye to Jewish immigration from their countries. In other instances, bribes were paid as part of quasi-official "arrangements" with governments who, especially in Eastern Europe, were in desperate need of foreign currency after World War II. A significant success proved to be the Bulgarian case, one of the first instances after the Second World War where a "poll tax" plus transit expenses for each Jew were paid by the Jewish Agency to East European governments in order to make immigration possible.

It is hardly surprising that the technique employed before independence was viewed as promising after May 1948 as well. The past success of the *modus operandi*, the complexities of *aliyah* from the Eastern bloc, which Israel's statehood did not reduce, and the continuity of personnel and of organizations involved all contributed to the view that bribery be employed as a legitimate means of promoting Israel's fundamental interest. The files of Israel's Foreign Ministry for the first years of statehood prove unequivocally that there were tremendous efforts to apply the Bulgarian model to other East European countries. The achievements were perhaps not impressive and were confined to Hungary, but aspirations persisted for several years.[19]

A second tool applied by Israel to promote *aliyah* was trade agreements which for Israel were partly based on non-economic considerations.[20] At the heart of the matter was the fact that Israeli purchases from the Eastern European bloc outweighed her sales there. Thus, Israel paid for the surplus with foreign currency, which the Eastern bloc vitally needed. This provided Israel with a means of applying pressure for *aliyah*.

Moreover, abandoned Jewish capital lay frozen in Eastern Europe as a result of large-scale immigration. Although she gave little publicity to the fact, Israel had a distinct interest in using this Jewish capital to pay for part of her purchases. Her aim in this arrangement, which was termed "transfer," was to save foreign currency and, far more important, to preserve the finances and property of hundreds of thousands of Jews which otherwise would have been lost. Agreements to this effect were made with Hungary, Poland, and Czechoslovakia.

Notwithstanding the objective economic difficulties that prevented the development of large-scale trade between Israel and Eastern Europe (especially the absence of essential credit facilities in that part of the world) and kept imports from that region to between 5 and 10 percent of Israel's total, an additional economic conduit between the two sides was created. The Soviet bloc countries were in need of industrial products and raw materials which they could not obtain in the quantities and quality required from Eastern Europe or the Soviet Union. The United States' imposition of severe restrictions on trade between her allies and the East had virtually closed the West to the Soviet bloc. One way for the Eastern bloc states to get around the virtual blockade was to purchase such items via "transit" transactions with non-communist countries. Unrestricted by American supervision, several countries imported the goods from the United States or from her strategic allies ostensibly for their own use and immediately re-exported them to the East. By virtue of her geopolitical position, Israel constituted a potentially ideal "transit" country. Soon after her independence, policy makers in Jerusalem were quick to see the advantages in such transactions. The price Israel demanded was cooperation in matters concerning *aliyah*. Intensive transit activity to that effect lasted until late 1951, when the United States tightened its economic control over the West through a regulation known as the "Battle Act."

Efforts to secure Soviet cooperation were not confined to the economic sphere. From 1948 onwards, Israeli leaders initiated a long list of moves which were designed to show the Kremlin that Israel's foreign policy was independent and that she was not bound to Western interests.[21] These actions were undertaken notwithstanding Israel's great dependence on the West, which necessitated extreme caution in her international behavior at the height of the cold war and despite the constraints imposed by her sparse resources and relatively limited global interests. Israeli efforts were concentrated on two main areas: first, her votes and postures at the United Nations and, second, her approach towards the establishment of military-strategic alliances in the Middle East and her decisions to avoid participation in them. The Foreign Ministry records clearly attest to these efforts. In spite of the grave disappointment which Israeli leaders felt over Russia's reaction to her overtures, the basic thrust of the strategy analyzed above remained relatively intact throughout the early 1950s. The effects of the Soviet factor on Israel's global policies will become even clearer as we turn our attention to her relations with the West.

Throughout the first years of her independence, Israel's foreign policy was formulated against a backdrop of chronic economic stress, the primary reason for which was massive immigration.[22] The arrival of some 600,000 new immigrants between 1948 and 1955 doubled the Jewish population of Israel. The absorption of such a large population influx in so short a period of time entailed enormous expenses, particularly since most of the new arrivals were economically destitute, and many were physically handicapped. Furthermore, after 1948 the country was prevented from trading with her neighbors in the Middle East, a region which had provided Palestine with 15 percent of her imports during the 1930s and over 50 percent during World War II. As mentioned above, the difficulties and expenses involved in the import of oil were particularly harmful. Consequently, Israel's enormous trade deficit made the country extremely dependent on external sources of finance.

The fact that about 55 percent of capital imported to Israel in the first decade of her existence stemmed directly from the United States made her extremely dependent on the decisions of that country.[23] It thus becomes clear that Israel, if for no other than economic reasons, had to develop special political ties and bonds with the United States. Jerusalem also depended on the West for military reasons. After 1950, however, she was only able to acquire weapons and military instruction in that part of the world. Moreover, the threatening Arab rearmament (until 1955 exclusively with Western weapons) explains Israel's crucial dependence on Washington, Paris, and London for securing a favorable military balance in the region. If only for these reasons, deviation from the policy of nonalignment was thus a foregone conclusion. What must be explained, however, was the considerations which, in the context of Israel's relations with the West, often militated against deviation from nonalignment.

Military perspectives were prominent among these considerations. Influential circles within the Israeli defense establishment were altogether opposed to a strategic agreement with Washington. A binding connection of that sort, they feared, would give the United States control over Israel's defense forces and thereby curtail Israel's freedom of action. Ben Gurion, himself, was an influential advocate of the position that nothing be done to hamper Israel's independence in that sphere. That position was a cardinal principle of faith to which a proposed and much-debated defense pact with the United States had to take a second place.[24] Moreover, Israel's basic desire was to be provided with, rather than to render, direct strategic assistance.

Furthermore, Anglo-American relations with the Arabs made it unrealistic for both London and Washington to include Israel in an overall Middle East command, an idea which had been on the agenda for several years at that time. Whenever that idea was even tentatively broached, Ben Gurion and Sharett had felt compelled to note its drawbacks. Any such constellation, they claimed, would emphasize Israel's regional inferiority; it would also lead to a local arms race; and, finally, it would run the grave security risk of unavoidable intelligence leaks. The fact that London was, until very late in the period under consideration, at least as responsible as Washington for Middle East defense merely strengthened the force of these arguments. Moreover, Ben Gurion's almost pathological resistance to any association with the British was another important factor influencing some of his more crucial decisions in the early 1950s to reject plans for strategic cooperation submitted to him by London.[25]

Finally, and perhaps most importantly, many of the internal debates in Israel on military connections with the West were ultimately made futile by decisions taken in Washington. The United States government showed a consistent and unmistakable reluctance to enter into any exclusive military relationship with Israel. Israel's futile efforts to change this state of affairs and to alter what was perceived as a clear pro-Arab bias in the State Department exerted a discouraging effect on her leaders.

As is well known, Israel gradually abandoned nonalignment during the early 1950s. That was a result, inter alia, of Russia's adherence to the Arab cause, the decline of the political power of Mapam within Israel, and the growing economic dependence on the West. However, the newly released documents tell a far more complicated story, which sheds new light on the nonalignment period of Israel's foreign policy. As Jerusalem continued and still continues to try to steer a course between Washington and Moscow, the complexities involved in the process during the late 1940s and early 1950s provide a historical perspective for this crucial element in her foreign policy. Furthermore, the historical evidence which has become public in the basement of the Prime Minister's office in Jerusalem challenges the popular image of Israel as an alien creation of the imperialist West, designed and always ready to serve its interests in the Middle East.

NOTES

This article is based on the author's recent *Between East and West: Israel's Foreign Policy Orientation, 1948–1956* (Cambridge: Cambridge University Press, 1990).

The archival sources for this article are the Labor Party Archive (hereafter LPA), the Central Zionist Archives (hereafter CZA), Israel State Archive (hereafter ISA), and Ben Gurion Archive (hereafter BGA).

1. The following is based on U. Bialer, "Our Place in the World: Mapai and Israel's Foreign Policy Orientation 1947–1952," *Jerusalem Papers on Peace Problems* 33 (Jerusalem, 1981).
2. See David Horowitz's comments at a meeting on 12 April 1949, ISA 2441/7.
3. For Mapam's perspective, see Z. Tsur, *Partnership as Opposition: The Partnership of Mapam in the Government, 1949–1954* (Hebrew) (Efal, 1983).
4. Protocol of a meeting with Mapam's leaders, 3 November 1949, LPA.
5. For a typical exposition, see Sharett's remarks at a meeting of Mapai's Secretariat with the party's members of the Knesset on 14 September 1949, LPA.
6. For Mapai's perspective, see D. Ben Gurion, *Concerning Hashomer Ha'Zair's Communism and Zionism* (Tel Aviv, 1953); for Mapam's, see Y. Ben-Ahron, *In the Eye of the Storm* (Tel Aviv, 1972), 47, both in Hebrew.
7. Protocol of a meeting on 12 April 1949, ISA 2441/7.
8. Protocol of a meeting on 12 December 1948, ISA 2493/12.
9. See Y. Ro'i, *Soviet Decision Making in Practice* (London, 1980).
10. D. Ben Gurion, *The Restored State of Israel* (Hebrew) (Tel Aviv, 1969), 302.
11. For an analysis of one aspect of the diplomatic effort, see U. Bialer, "The Road to the Capital: The Establishment of Jerusalem as the Official Seat of the Israeli Government in 1949," *Studies in Zionism* 5, II (1985): 273–96. For a recent analysis of the military dimension see D. Tal, *Israel's Response to Infiltrations to its Territory from Jordan and Egypt, 1949–1956* (Hebrew) (M.A. thesis, History Department, Tel Aviv University, 1990).
12. The following account is based on U. Bialer, "The Czech-Israeli Arms Deal Revisited," *Journal of Strategic Studies* 8, II (1985): 307–15.
13. The following account is based on documentary evidence in LPA (protocols of the meetings of Mapai's Central and Political Committees on 6 May 1954 and 16 October 1955, respectively), ISA 2384/15, ISA 2479/8, ISA 2410/18; and M. Sharett, *Personal Diary* (Hebrew) (Tel Aviv, 1978), 1021, 1206–7, 1214, 1231, 1272–75, 1319–20, 1336, 1337, 1348, 1351, 1358, 1372.

14. The following is based on documentary evidence in ISA 2420/2, 2599/8, Y. Govrin, *Israeli-Soviet Relations 1953–1967* (Hebrew) (Ph.D. thesis, The Hebrew University, 1983), 111–12, and Sharett, *Personal Diary*, 130, 391.
15. For an analysis, see M. Lissak, *The Elites of the Jewish Communities in Palestine* (Hebrew) (Tel Aviv, 1981).
16. 2 October 1948, ISA 2492/20.
17. See protocol of a meeting of the Jewish Agency Executive on 13 December 1948, CZA, ISA 2502/8, 2492/16, 2493/13, 2507/12; Ben Gurion's Diary, entry for 1 June 1950; and Govrin, *Israeli-Soviet Relations*, 131–59, 186–209.
18. For an authoritative exposition, see Z. Hadari, *Refugees Defeating a Great Power* (Hebrew) (Tel Aviv, 1985), 53–54, on which the following account is based. For the use of bribery in other parts of the world, see U. Bialer, "The Iranian Connection in Israel's Foreign Policy, 1948–1951," *Middle East Journal* 39, II (1985): 292–315. For a general analysis of the state's secret diplomacy, see A. Klieman, *Statecraft in the Dark, Israel's Practice of Quiet Diplomacy* (Tel Aviv, 1988).
19. See U. Bialer, *Between East and West: Israel's Foreign Policy Orientation 1948–1956* (Cambridge: Cambridge University Press, 1990).
20. Ibid.
21. Ibid.
22. On the subject, see H. Barkai, *The Beginnings of the Israeli Economy* (Jerusalem, 1990). For an illustration of the way Israel's approach to contacts with the outside world during that period was greatly determined by urgent economic needs, see U. Bialer, "Financial Diplomacy and Post-Colonialism: The Sterling Balances and Claims Negotiations between Britain and Israel, 1947–1952," *Middle Eastern Studies* (forthcoming 1992).
23. See M. Avidan, *Principal Aspects of Israel-USA Relations in the 1950's* (Hebrew) (Jerusalem, 1982), 93–95.
24. See Sharett, *Personal Diary*, 894–99, 1018, 1355, which is the source for the following analysis.
25. See Ben Gurion's Diary, entries for 20 January 1950, 27 January 1951, and 29 January 1951, ISA 37/10, ISA 30/16, ISA 2479/9; and U. Bialer, "Ben Gurion and Israel's Foreign Policy Orientation in the Early 1950's" (Hebrew), *Cathedra* 43 (March, 1987): 145–72.

CHAPTER 13

Zionist-Arab Diplomacy: Patterns and Ambiguities on the Eve of Statehood

NEIL CAPLAN

In the years immediately following the Second World War, political decision makers in the *yishuv* (the Hebrew community in Palestine) and in Zionist leadership circles had to relate to actors and events in three domains: physical security and military realities on the ground; political support and legitimacy to be consolidated internationally; and relations with the regional and local Arab population. With regard to the latter, all efforts were mobilized towards neutralizing hostility and avoiding the likelihood of Arab military intervention. When hostility could *not* be effectively neutralized through diplomatic and political means, Arabs and Israelis met on the battlefield. If the creation of the state and its consolidation during its first difficult years can, upon re-examination, be deemed an overall success achieved against heavy odds, the same cannot be said with regard to the realization of the specific diplomatic goals which were formulated on the "Arab front" in the late 1940s.

In late 1947 and again in May 1948, Zionist officials sought to convince King Abdullah of Transjordan not to join in the expected invasion of Palestine by the neighboring Arab armies. The secret meetings between Golda Meyerson and the king are relatively well known to the American public from colorful published accounts as well as from a popular NBC television dramatization.[1] Scholarly interest in these negotiations and their wider context was recently popularized by the publication of the works of Avi Shlaim and Uri Bar-Joseph, but this interest dates back to the mid-1970s.[2] The so-called "collusion" between these "best of enemies," despite any modest achievements during the years 1948 through 1951, did not culminate in the expected treaty of peace, and other scholars (including Avraham Sela and Itamar Rabinovich) have offered their detailed assessments of these futile Israeli-Jordanian political negotiations.[3]

The failure of the Meyerson-Abdullah talks to prevent Transjordan's involvement in the first Arab-Israeli war was the final episode in a long series of futile attempts made during the Mandate period by Zionist leaders who wished to resolve their differences with the Arabs through diplomacy. Let me mention briefly two other episodes that illustrate the state of Zionist-Arab diplomacy during the final years of the Mandate. One was a lesser-known, but equally serious, attempt made by Eliahu Sasson in late summer of 1946 to convince the Premier of Egypt, Isma'il Sidqi Pasha, to recommend both to the British and to his Arab League colleagues that partition ought to be the preferred solution to the growing Arab-Zionist impasse over Palestine. Other leading Egyptians, including the Arab League Secretary General, Abd al-Rahman Azzam Pasha, were reported willing to hear out this Zionist proposal, and Sidqi did send the appropriate first signals to the British in Cairo. In the end, however, the British were reluctant to encourage Sidqi and this Zionist diplomatic initiative came to naught.[4]

My third example is a meeting in London in September 1947 during which a private exchange of views marked by "candor and vigor" demonstrated the depth and width of the gap which separated Zionists and Arabs. While Aubrey Eban and David Horowitz sought to convince Azzam Pasha of the wisdom and realism of accepting the inevitability of a Jewish state, the latter predicted the inevitability of all-out war if the Jews insisted on having their state.[5]

I highlight these three episodes not in order to analyze them in any detail nor to examine the particular reasons for their failure to lead to an agreement. Rather, I want them to serve as a starting point for a review of the cumulative experience of Zionist leaders over the course of the Mandate period. This cumulative experience did not become obsolete or suddenly irrelevant after 14 May 1948, merely because the new Israeli state acquired international legitimacy and sovereignty. First of all, the Arabic section of the Jewish Agency's political department was transformed into the relevant bodies within the new Foreign and Interior Ministries. More importantly, the whole legacy of Zionist-Arab diplomatic maneuvering during the Mandate years became part of the baggage carried forward by the appointed administrators and elected officials of the new government of Israel.

Wealth of Experience

What were some of the main features of that legacy? First, let us focus on the quantity and the futility of Arab-Zionist political encounters. Even if they had been initiated largely for "tactical" reasons and even if they all ultimately proved futile, we must nevertheless recognize that there was a surprisingly large number of maneuvers and attempts at high-level and mid-level negotiation. For example, beyond his well-known meetings and agreement (1918–19) with the Amir Faisal ibn Husain (later King of Iraq, 1921–33), Dr. Chaim Weizmann met with more than a dozen leading Arabs in Cairo and in Palestine in 1918 alone.[6] Between the Faisal episode and the meetings with Abdullah mentioned previously, one can list some forty negotiation episodes which one could call serious.

Gap between the Terms of Agreement

At the same time, however, a survey of the various terms of agreement that were discussed reveals that by the late 1940s a deepening gap and the hardening of positions had occurred. Back in the early 1930s, Arab-Zionist negotiations had begun to explore a variety of formulas which, their proposers had felt, held some hope of leading to a mutual accord: the non-domination principle, parity, Zionist offers of support for pan-Arab unity or federation, Zionist guarantees against non-eviction of Palestinian Arabs, restrictions on Jewish immigration, a ceiling on the Jewish proportion of the population, and the cantonization or partition of Palestine. Largely because one party or the other felt it had the strength to hold out for a fuller satisfaction of its claims, no agreements were reached on the basis of any of these formulas.[7]

The Peel Commission's partition recommendation in 1937 provided a brief but intense interlude of negotiations centered around this idea of radical surgery. After the British withdrew the proposal, the gap which separated the Arab and Zionist positions at the close of the St. James's Conference in March 1939 was clearly defined for all to see. The Zionists clung to the status quo, that is, the terms of the Mandate, and asked for more generous opportunities for immigration and land purchase. They did not abandon their hopes of one day becoming a majority in Palestine and responded to Arab objections to such a scenario by the "economic blessings" argument, a commitment not to "dominate" them, and the prospect of a wider political arrangement with some of the neighboring Arab countries.

For their part, the Arabs, in 1939, maintained their claim that the Palestinians should be permitted to exercise their natural right to independence, which included the right of the majority to prevent the Jews from becoming more numerous through further immigration. There were, the Arabs argued, already enough Jews in Palestine, and these should be offered no more than constitutionally guaranteed minority rights.

The impact of the war did result in some changes in the parties' proposed terms of agreement. However, these shifts were almost all in the direction of intensifying rather than reducing the bitterness and mistrust between the two sides. The Zionist position during the war years hardened noticeably, reflecting the deteriorating plight of the Jews in Europe. From 1939 onwards, Zionist leaders looked to an imposed post-war settlement to bring them better terms than the 1939 (MacDonald) White Paper, which had been totally rejected for its drastic restrictions on Jewish immigration and land purchase. Well before the war's end—notably at the Emergency Zionist Conference held in New York's Biltmore Hotel in May 1942—they pressed for mass immigration to help rescue the victims of Nazism. Also during this historic conference, the official Zionist political goal was defined as making Palestine into a sovereign Jewish "commonwealth" (i.e., a Jewish state in all of Palestine), with no mention of either partition or a federal subdivision.[8] For their part, Arab spokesmen continued to argue that the European Jewish problem could not be solved by Palestine alone, and that *other* countries should share in a humanitarian solution.[9] But this argument had little impact in Western countries, where selfish interests, combined with feelings of guilt about the Holocaust, resulted in greater sympathy for the Zionist claim to Palestine.

Inspired by the model of the 1919 Weizmann-Faisal agreement, some Jewish leaders (but *not* Ben Gurion or Moshe Shertok) believed that an offer by the future Jewish state to enter into, and contribute its resources to, a regional federation would help to bring about Arab acceptance of the Zionist goal in Palestine. In trying to mobilize international backing for a partition solution in the face of strenuous

Arab objections, Zionist spokesmen once more invoked the "fait accompli" argument which they had been repeating to themselves and to the British since the late 1930s. "Once a Jewish state is established in an adequate area of Palestine," Dr. Weizmann wrote in September 1946, he was

> deeply convinced that . . . a new relationship will be created between us and our neighbours. We shall in all likelihood become an integral part of a Middle Eastern Federation—both they and we will realize this. There will be treaty relations, commercial relations, cultural relations, and beyond and above all this, there will be the guarantee of Great Britain and the United States (or, if you will, the United Nations), all of which will work towards collaboration and concord, perhaps more strongly than other influences have in the past worked for the contrary. I am convinced, too, that once we have a State in an adequate area of the country, and with it a real opportunity of constructive work, we shall find ourselves drawn more and more closely together with our Arab neighbours: our very separation, and our equal status with members of the Arab League, will greatly influence us all in that direction. That has been my own belief for many years past, and it remains my belief, despite all the rancour and bitterness lately engendered.[10]

As we all know, with the benefit of hindsight, this did not turn out to be an accurate prediction of the way Arabs reacted to the imposition of the U.N. partition plan a year later. Pan-Arabists made it clear that they were interested in the inclusion of Palestine *as it was* (i.e., a predominantly Arab country) and not of a "Jewish Palestine" in any proposed federation of Middle Eastern states. Some politicians in the neighboring countries were prepared to see a ratio of two Arabs to one Jew maintained under new arrangements, while the Green and White Books of Nuri as-Sa'id and the Amir Abdullah, respectively, offered the Jews a vaguely defined autonomous or semi-autonomous status within a future Middle Eastern federation. All these formulations fell far short of allowing the Jews a majority or sovereignty in any part of Palestine. For many Arab leaders, the terms of the MacDonald White Paper of May 1939, which had attempted to freeze the existing population ration of two Arabs to one Jew by sharply limiting Jewish immigration and which had promised an evolution to representative, constitutional government, were the most to which they would agree during the forties in response to Jewish claims.

In the aftermath of World War II, the options for a Palestine solution thus boiled down to the following four:

(1) an Arab state in an undivided Palestine, with minority guarantees and local autonomy for Jews—a slight revision of the original maximalist Palestinian-Arab stand of earlier decades;

(2) a Jewish commonwealth in all of Palestine, with constitutional guarantees for the (future) Arab minority—the original maximalist Zionist stand, pleaded with greater urgency in the shadow of the Holocaust;

(3) a federal Palestinian state with Arab and Jewish cantons or provinces—the British idea of the only solution which had a chance of being implemented without violence; and

(4) the partition of the country into sovereign Arab and Jewish states.

The chances of a *voluntary* agreement being built on any of these formulas were remote indeed. Given the sense of desperation and determination which animated leaders and their followers, both sides were preparing to exercise their military option in the approaching "winner-takes-all" confrontation.

During the final years of the Mandate, the Zionists showed some tactical flexibility by abandoning their insistence on the Jewish Commonwealth in all of Palestine, and there were, as previously mentioned, several eleventh-hour negotiation episodes which brought high-ranking Arab and Zionist leaders together between 1946 and 1948. But the most urgent Zionist diplomatic activity (Eban, Epstein, Shertok, and Weizmann in Washington and New York; Goldmann in London and Paris) was directed not towards the Arabs, but towards the Great Powers, pleading for the imposition of a partition solution, even in the face of Arab objections.

What did Israeli decision makers of the early 1950s consciously or unconsciously deduce from the fact that many meetings *had* taken place—without results—before 1948? Certainly, some of them must have concluded that negotiations on this front were not a fruitful avenue to pursue; given the previous record, there was little to expect from Arab-Zionist diplomatic activity. If military security and international political legitimacy could be achieved by other means and on other fronts, then there was little need to expend significant effort on this obvious "weak link" in the chain of Israel's foreign policy.

If the avenue of *direct* Arab-Zionist diplomacy was not a fruitful one, neither, one should add, was the early experience of multilateral negotiations. The London "Round-Table" conferences of early 1939 were one of the crucial turning points of the Mandate period. Born out of deadlock and mediated by the British through parallel consultations with official Arab and Jewish delegations, the conferences also ended in deadlock, and were followed, not unexpectedly, by the issuance of a decreed policy embodied in the MacDonald White Paper. Sobered by the 1939 experience, Zionists boycotted another British-inspired conference in September 1946. The resumption of the London conference in January–February 1947 turned out to be the last chance for Arab and/or Zionist acquiescence in British policy. When this conference also reached an impasse, the British handed the problem over to the United Nations.

Practical Experience: Political Maneuvering

Still, the pre-1948 legacy was not completely negative or useless. If the many meetings between Arabs and Zionists during the Mandate period had failed to produce any lasting mutual accord, they had, nevertheless, provided negotiators and would-be negotiators with much practical experience. These had ample opportunities to appreciate and develop the fine art of diplomatic maneuvering. Zionist leaders, like their counterparts on the Arab side, developed a keen sense of timing: when to initiate contacts and when to abstain, and finding the "psychological moment." In addition, they learned how to avoid negotiation when they felt themselves to be in a position of relative weakness. They also learned the importance of posturing so as to create the proper appearance of being reasonable and conciliatory even when they were not, in fact, interested in holding meetings with the other side.

During the Mandate period, another necessary learning process had taken place through which certain ambiguities were clarified within Zionist and *yishuv* leadership circles. In their recurring attempts to maintain or regain the initiative in Arab-Jewish contacts, official Jewish Agency spokesmen frequently found themselves locked in internal battles with their dissenters. Particularly during the 1930s, much frustration and confusion had developed as a result of splits between unofficial and official spokesmen over how to approach a solution to the conflict, and whether negotiations with Arabs were to be pursued or avoided at given moments. The most controversial episodes of the Mandate period were:

(1) H. M. Kalvaryski's maverick activity in promoting his own peace plan among Faisal's Damascus entourage in mid-1919 and his semi-

official activities in promoting would-be "moderate" Arab clubs and political parties in the early 1920s;[11]

(2) Dr. Judah L. Magnes' independent attempt to reach an agreement with the Mufti of Jerusalem in 1929, using British Arabist H. St. John Philby as intermediary;[12]

(3) political discussions with Jerusalem lawyer Musa Alami and Judge Mustafa al-Khalidi aimed at finding a way out of the Arab General Strike of 1936, undertaken (with the knowledge of the Jewish Agency Executive) by an ad hoc group of five prominent *yishuv* personalities: Judah Magnes, Pinhas Rutenberg, Gad Frumkin, Moshe Novomeysky, and Moshe Smilansky;[13] and

(4) Dr. Magnes' persistent involvement during 1937–38 in discussing drafts of the "Hyamson-Newcombe" proposals (which seemed destined to safeguard a perpetual Arab majority in Palestine) with Palestinian Dr. Izzat Tannous and Iraqi leader Nuri as-Sa'id.[14]

Likewise, the activities of liberal-minded Diaspora Jews such as Albert Hyamson and Lord Samuel in the late 1930s caused a measure of anxiety and embarrassment to men like Ben Gurion, Moshe Shertok, and Bernard (Dov) Joseph, who directed the Jewish Agency's political policy.

Periodically they reminded dissenters and Arab leaders alike that only *they*, the elected leaders, had the power to "deliver the goods" in any arrangement. Ben Gurion's and Shertok's activism on the Arab front during the thirties was predicated on this very assumption, coupled with their insistence on talking only with Arab counterparts who were, like themselves, capable of putting into effect any deal that might be struck. As promising or generous as the terms worked out among "moderate" Arabs and "moderate" Jews might have appeared, these dealings usually proved irrelevant whenever the authoritative spokesmen, who were probably more representative of the consensus within their respective national communities, chose to reject various compromises and held out for more. In the course of many secret meetings, Zionist leaders came to learn who, among their various adversaries, really had the ability to "deliver the goods" should an agreement ever appear likely.

Low Priority of Direct Talks

For almost all Zionist leaders, direct negotiation with the Arabs was often the least preferred option, since Zionist goals usually appeared to be more readily achievable either through outside decisions (whether imposed by the British or the League of Nations), or else through the force of the "fait accompli"—the building of a strong and vibrant *yishuv* which could stand its ground both economically and militarily. The attitudes of both Jewish and Arab community leaders reflected the low priority of direct negotiations. In 1919, for example, David Ben Gurion saw the conflict as having

> no solution . . . No solution! There is a gulf, and nothing can fill that gulf. It is possible to resolve the conflict between Jewish and Arab interests [only] by sophistry. I do not know what Arab will agree that Palestine should belong to the Jews—even if the Jews learn Arabic. And we must recognize this situation. If we don't acknowledge it, and try to come up with "remedies," then we risk demoralization. . . . We, as a nation, want this country to be *ours*; the Arabs, as a nation, want this country to be *theirs*.[15]

He had hoped, at that time, that the appropriate decision would be rendered by the Paris Peace Conference.

The Palestinian lawyer and politician, Awni Abd al-Hadi, also saw the conflict in similar terms. According to Haim Arlosoroff's record of a conversation between Moshe Shertok and the nationalist leader in 1932, Awni felt that

> there was no point whatever in negotiations or attempts to reach a mutual understanding. The goal of the Jews was to rule the country, and the aim of the Arabs was to fight against this rule. He [Awni] understood the Zionists quite well and respected them, but their interests were fundamentally opposed to Arab interests, and he saw no possibility of an agreement.[16]

These two statements give us a good indication of the tendency on both sides to downplay direct negotiations as a possible avenue of reconciling Arab and Jewish national claims. Ben Gurion and others were looking to European powers first, to grant international legitimacy to the Jewish national home and, thereafter, to reaffirm that legitimacy. Zionists were also hoping that the British Mandate authorities would sympathetically guarantee the future of the *yishuv* and would deal firmly with expressions of Arab objections. Palestinian Arab leaders like Awni Abd al-Hadi, on the other hand, were hoping that pan-Arab support, the sheer force of numbers, and ultimately military superiority would keep the Jews in their place, while allowing the Palestinian Arabs one day to rule the country.

Indeed, for most of the Mandate period, each party was able to entertain the conviction that it would be triumphant in the end without having to make serious concessions to its adversary. Hence, it should not be surprising that the Mandate period saw both sides developing a "holding pattern," with each party becoming adept at the tactical usage of the negotiation process, in effect inverting the dictum of von Clausewitz: for them, diplomacy and negotiation were an extension of their basic ongoing "war" by other (non-violent) means.

Mixed Motives

The conclusion of a full-fledged peace settlement was seldom the end goal of Arab-Zionist negotiating activity during the Mandate period.[17] What we find—in place of the search for a comprehensive peace plan—is an interesting variety of motives for initiating or pursuing contacts. Sometimes, leaders were merely interested in giving the appearance of serious talks, so as to create a favorable impression on some outside party (e.g., one of the Powers, world public opinion, the United Nations). Sometimes physical security was the motivating factor for Jewish leaders: to defuse tensions and forestall anticipated danger (often accompanied by public appeals or proclamations). Informal talks with Arabs also formed part of a systematic intelligence-gathering effort, so as to be better prepared for political maneuvers or for *hagana* (defense) activity.

Many Zionist negotiation overtures were aimed at forming tactical alliances with "opposition" politicians or with dissenters in the Arab camp—particularly since the Zionists found themselves in a deadlock with the recognized Arab leadership in Palestine (the Arab Executive Committee, the Supreme Muslim Council, and the Arab Higher Committee). The continual effort to encourage so-called "moderates" against the so-called "extremists" was based on the dictum: "My enemy's enemy is my friend." Members of the Nashashibi family, the "Muslim National Associations" formed in the early 1920s by Haim Kalvaryski, and Fakhri an-Nashashibi's "Peace Bands" during the 1936–39 revolt were all a part of this Zionist activity. In the process, a number of individual Arabs benefitted from Jewish support in the form of press subsidies, expenses for propaganda or speaking tours, the underwriting of personal loans, or recommendations for government favors.

But this stimulation of the so-called moderates brought much frustration and little satisfaction to those *yishuv* figures who worked at the task of trying to win Arab acquiescence in the advance of Zionism in Palestine. Many of the future shapers of Israel's Arab policies were no doubt left pessimistic and cynical from their experience during the Mandate years—pessimistic about the chances of ever genuinely "winning over" significant segments of Arab opinion to accept the desirability or the inevitability of Jewish predominance. They were also cynical about the venality and lack of genuine patriotism displayed by a number of figures within the Palestinian Arab political elite.

Palestinians versus Non-Palestinian Arabs

Perhaps one of the clearest patterns which emerges from the cumulative negotiation experience of the Mandate period is the Zionist attempt to exploit the problematic relationship between Palestinians and non-Palestinians. Indeed, the distinction between the two groups' interests, motives, and attitudes had become clear to the earliest Zionist representatives even before the First World War.

The Zionists' preference to negotiate with Arabs from the surrounding lands was, in many ways, a natural consequence of their frustrations at their limited success in obtaining sympathy or success with most residents of Palestine.[18] Those Palestinians who, for whatever reasons, were willing to come to terms with the Zionists were invariably among the least powerful. And, once word got out that they were "in the pay of the Jews," these would-be "moderates" lost whatever local prestige they possessed.

Political discussions with non-Palestinian spokesmen, like the Amirs Faisal or Abdullah, usually proved more favorable. Accordingly, Zionist leaders soon adopted a line of action which was to become a basic ingredient of Zionist and Israeli diplomacy to this very day. It was considered desirable and sufficient to develop healthy, "normal," economic and social relations with the Palestinians, while reserving political relations for leaders of the wider Arab world outside Palestine. Given the seriousness of the local contradictions, it seemed to many observers that any entente over Palestine would have to be in the form of an "exchange of services" between Zionists and a prestigious *non*-Palestinian pan-Arab leader. It was essential, most Zionists felt, to have someone who would not view the conflict strictly from a local point of view but consider it in a wider frame of reference.

This led the Zionists to favor a "Hashimite connection" for most of the Mandate period. After the First World War, Amir Faisal as the head of a proposed Greater Arab Kingdom—outside of Palestine—was asked to recognize Jewish claims to Palestine and influence the Palestinians to moderate their demands. In exchange, the Arab kingdom headed by Faisal could have expected to benefit from Jewish capital, technical skills, and international political support.

Zionist relations with Amir (later King) Abdullah of Transjordan were built on similar hopes and premises. During the Second World War, King Abd al-Aziz as-Sa'ud ("Ibn Sa'ud") was also indirectly approached through Harry St. John Philby with the same proposal for an exchange of services. Numerous suggestions along these lines were made to various Arab personalities by Weizmann, Ben Gurion, and others.[19] But the difficult question remained: Was there a non-Palestinian Arab leader who would be willing to agree in principle to an exchange of services with the Zionists and who would also be capable of influencing the Palestinians to go along with such a settlement?

The Zionist preference for negotiations with non-Palestinians was, of course, matched by the Palestinians' suspicions of the latter. These conflicting sets of expectations have become an enduring pattern in Zionist-Arab and Israeli-Arab diplomacy, from Faisal and Abdullah in those days to the late Anwar Sadat and King Hussein in our own.

There was, however, an interesting exception to this non-Palestinian preference which occurred during the transition years of statehood. As recent scholarship has revealed, some Zionist and Israeli policy makers examined the possibility of disengaging themselves from their tacit understanding with Abdullah for sharing the territories of Mandatory Palestine. Some were willing to consider jettisoning their Hashimite option in preference for a Palestinian option—that is, a final arrangement based on the original intent of the November 1947 United Nations resolution which recommended the creation of both a Jewish and an Arab state in a partitioned Palestine. But many regional as well as British policy makers feared that a separate Palestinian state, despite its small size, would nonetheless become a dangerous power base controlled by the ex-Mufti, al-Hajj Amin al-Husayni. For this and other reasons, any Zionist or Israeli interest in a "Palestinian option" was tactical and short-lived. In the early years of Israeli statehood, Arab policy was geared almost exclusively to the Abdullah "connection," warts and all.[20]

Role of Outside Powers

Finally, I want to mention one dominant pattern of the Mandate period which became even more complicated after 14 May 1948. This was the distinct pre-1948 preference of both Jews and Arabs in Palestine to go over each other's heads and appeal directly for intervention to influential outsiders—usually the British. From the first days of the Mandate period, Zionist leaders had recognized that, in the pursuit of their national goals, they had more to gain by turning to these outside powers than to representatives of the Arab community. This further reinforced the low priority assigned to direct Zionist-Arab contacts and attempts at a bilateral solution. It appeared that so much of what the Jews and Arabs wanted was achievable not through direct talks, but rather through effective lobbying and other pressures on the British or American officials, or on European and American public opinion.

Even when direct negotiations did occur, such as those between Weizmann and Faisal, each party's professed friendliness to the other was not usually motivated by spontaneous affection or anticipation of the benefits to be had from a direct alliance. Rather, both sides realized that their principal goals, which depended so much on favorable Great Power decisions, might be more easily won by cooperating with the British promoters of such talks. This tendency was evident throughout the Mandate period: Zionists and Arabs looked first to the British for what they wanted most and turned to each other only when it appeared that such a move would be useful or necessary in furthering their respective positions vis-à-vis the all-powerful British.

Behind frequent Zionist and Arab complaints that the British attitude was biased in favor of their opponents lay an implicit request for what was, in effect, an imposed solution to the conflict. To both parties, such a solution was preferable to one directly negotiated between them. The United Nations partition resolution of November 1947 was the last of a series of solutions "imposed" or strongly recommended from the outside. For the Zionist leadership, it was, despite its shortcomings, a favorable "imposed" settlement which they hoped would be enforced. Zionist diplomatic activity on the eve of statehood was thus mobilized with this end in view. But battlefield successes were required to ensure the physical security of the new state.

With the end of the Mandate and the advent of Israeli sovereignty, fewer "cards" remained in the hands of powerful outsiders. The British could no longer serve either as enforcers of the Balfour Declaration or of the White Paper, or even as "impartial arbiters" between the rival claims of Jews and Arabs for Palestine. Israeli policy makers now had more autonomy and direct responsibility both in their dealings with the Palestinian Arabs on both sides of their new frontiers and in their relations with the neighboring states. In the early years of statehood, they would attempt, in vain, to induce Transjordan, Egypt, and Syria into direct negotiations towards a full and final peace.

Among the complications to beset Israeli-Arab diplomacy and the Israeli quest for direct talks during this period was an ever more complex pattern of outside involvement: (a) a United Nations mediator; (b) a United Nations Conciliation Commission; (c) a number of ad hoc U.N., American, and British efforts aimed at reducing tension and stabilizing the shaky status quo created after the 1948–49 fighting and armistice agreements; and (d) several concerted Anglo-American initiatives aimed at a comprehensive settlement. These episodes must await further research and analysis.

Yet, it is clear that the heavy involvement of outside powers was a continuing pattern affecting Arab-Israeli diplomatic activity in the early years of statehood. Given the persisting gap between the positions of the Palestinian Arabs and the new Israelis, and given their determination to persevere in irreconcilable aims, it might be argued that the only real hope for a breakthrough continued to lie with those third parties.

NOTES

1. Zeev Sharef, *Three Days* (London: W. H. Allen, 1962), 72–76; Marie Syrkin, *Golda Meir: Woman with a Cause* (London: V. Gollancz, 1964), 195–202; Dan Kurzman, *Genesis 1948: The First Arab-Israeli War* (New York: World Publishing Co., 1970), 42–44, 246–47; and Golda Meir, *My Life* (New York: G. Putnam's Sons, 1975), 176–80.
2. Avi Shlaim, *Collusion across the Jordan: King Abdullah, the Zionist Movement, and the Partition of Palestine* (New York: Columbia University Press, 1988); Uri Bar-Joseph, *The Best of Enemies: Israel and Jordan in the War of 1948* (London: Frank Cass, 1987). For earlier analyses, see: J. Nevo, *Abdullah and the Palestinian Arabs* (Hebrew) (Tel Aviv: Shiloah Institute, 1975) and "Abdallah and the Arabs of Palestine," *Wiener Library Bulletin* 31 (1978): 51–62; Anita Shapira, "The Option on Ghaur al-Kibd: Contacts between Emir Abdullah and the Zionist Executive, 1932–1935," *Studies in Zionism* 2 (1980): 239–83; Avraham Sela, "Political Contacts between Jewish Representatives and the Governments of Transjordan and Egypt" (Hebrew), *ha-Tziyonnut* X (1985), and idem, *From Contacts to Negotiations* (Hebrew) (Tel Aviv: Shiloah Institute, 1985); Neil Caplan, *Futile Diplomacy* (London: Frank Cass, 2 vols., 1983, 1986) I:51–54 and II:11–14, 40–42, 65–67, 92–95, 145–47, 157–64, 188–89, 203–6, 216–17, 238–39, 268–71, 277–79.
3. Sela, *From Contacts to Negotiations*; Itamar Rabinovich, *The Road Not Taken* (New York: Oxford University Press, 1991).
4. See Neil Caplan and Avraham Sela, "Zionist-Egyptian Negotiations and the Partition of Palestine, 1946," *Jerusalem Quarterly* 41 (Winter 1987): 19–30.
5. Note of conversation of 15 September 1947, Central Zionist Archives (hereafter referred to as CZA), S25/9020; reproduced in Caplan, *Futile Diplomacy* II:274–76.
6. Including: Dr. Faris Nimr, Rafiq al-Azm, Dr. Abd ar-Rahman ash-Shahbandar, Sa'id Shuqair, Kamil al-Qassab, Sulaiman Nasif, Kamil al-Husaini, Musa Kazim al-Husaini, Isma'il al-Husaini, Abd ar-Ra'uf Bitar, Amin Tamimi, Hajj Tawfiq Hammad, and Ibrahim Shammas.
7. See Caplan, *Futile Diplomacy* II, ch. 1.
8. Walter Laqueur, ed., *The Israel-Arab Reader* (London: Pelican Books, 1969), doc. 19.
9. D. Auster, note of talks with Dr. H. F. al-Khalidi (Hebrew), June 1935, CZA, S25/3051; Rendel, note of talk with Dr. Naji al-Asil, 18 February 1937, Public Record Office, Colonial Office (hereafter referred to as PRO, CO) 733/341, file 75528/44; Ben Gurion Report (talk with F. Kattani) (Hebrew), Jewish Agency Executive meeting, 6 October 1942, CZA; Vilenski, note of talk with Awni Abd al-Hadi (Hebrew), 20 December 1943, CZA, S25/3115; Abdullah to Creech-Jones, 4 September 1946, PRO, CO

537/1776; Ireland, note of talk with Abd ar-Rahman Azzam, 2 November 1946, National Archives, 867N.01/11-546.
10. Letter to J. M. Martin, 16 September 1946, *The Letters and Papers of Chaim Weizmann* (series A: Letters), vol. XXII, ed. Joseph Heller (New Brunswick: Rutgers University/Transaction Books, 1979), no. 214.
11. Discussed in Neil Caplan, *Palestine Jewry and the Arab Question, 1917-1925* (London: Frank Cass, 1978), 40-45, 127-33.
12. See Caplan, *Futile Diplomacy* I:87-93.
13. See Caplan, *Futile Diplomacy* II:35-40.
14. Ibid., 78-84.
15. Speech to the *Va'ad Zmani* (Provisional Council of Palestinian Jews) (Hebrew), 10 June 1919, CZA, J1/8777.
16. 12 February 1932, CZA, S25/3051 (Hebrew); translated and reproduced in Caplan, *Futile Diplomacy* II:186.
17. It must be said, of course, that on a number of occasions individual Jews did present full-blown peace plans directly or indirectly for Arab representatives to consider (e.g., H. M. Kalvaryski in 1919-20 and in 1930; Dr. Judah Magnes, president of the Hebrew University, in 1929 and again in 1937-38). It is also true that David Ben Gurion, in his first years on the Jewish Agency Executive, talked to Arab leaders about long-term solutions to the Zionist-Arab problem. But even Ben Gurion's discussions were in the nature of trial balloons—intended mainly as feelers to sound out the other side. For a personal account of these latter meetings, see David Ben Gurion, *My Talks with Arab Leaders* (Jerusalem: Keter, 1972); cf. Caplan, *Futile Diplomacy* II:5-8.
18. See Caplan, *Palestine Jewry*, ch. 9.
19. In this category, one can also cite the Arab Decentralist Party in 1913; Iraq's Nuri as-Sa'id; Syria's Jamil Mardam, Abd ar-Rahman ash-Shahbandar and others; Riad as-Sulh, Emile Edde and other Lebanese politicians; and Isma'il Sidqi and other Egyptians.
20. See for example summary (26 March 1948) of discussions on political matters, in *Political and Diplomatic Documents, December 1947 - May 1948* (Jerusalem: Israel State Archives, 1979), doc. 319; M. Shertok to E. Sasson, 5 August 1948, in *Documents on the Foreign Policy of Israel*, vol. I (14 May - 30 September 1948), (Jerusalem: Israel State Archives, 1981), doc. 428; Ilan Pappe, "Moshe Sharett, David Ben Gurion and the 'Palestinian Option,' 1948-1956," *Studies in Zionism* 13 (Spring 1986): 77-96.

CHAPTER 14

Israel-Diaspora Relations in the Early Years of the State

RONALD W. ZWEIG

New historiography is fueled as often by the shifting perspectives of succeeding generations of historians looking at old issues with new insights as it is driven by the sudden availability of new archival material. The analysis of Israel-Diaspora relations is ripe for new approaches. This is particularly true for our own post-ideological decade, when the issue of principle that once caused such impassioned debate within the Zionist movement in the 1950s—*shlilat hagola* (the negation of the Diaspora)—sounds as dated and irrelevant to us today as the previous debates over *gegenwartsarbeit* (the importance of organizational and cultural activity in the Diaspora as opposed to Palestine-directed activity) must have sounded to the generation of 1948.

The term *shlilat hagola* encapsulates a number of assessments of the interaction of Israel and the Diaspora. The common denominator to all of them is a negative or pessimistic view of Jewish life outside of Eretz Yisrael (the Land of Israel). In one form, the concept refers to the inevitable withering away of Jewish communal existence in the Diaspora in the wake of the dual impact of anti-Semitism and assimilation. It is similar to the Marxist concept of the withering away of the state and has proven itself to be of equal predictive value. Alternatively, *shlilat hagola* has referred to the need to remove the influence of exile on current Jewish thought and life. The renewal of an independent Jewish national existence in Eretz Yisrael would allow a renaissance of Jewish awareness and creativity, purged of the negative influences caused by the struggle for survival amidst hostile, non-Jewish cultures over two thousand years of exile. Even Ahad Ha'am, who rejected the inevitability or even the desirability of the withering away of the Diaspora, argued for the preeminence of Eretz Yisrael in Jewish life because it would be liberated from the mindset of the Diaspora.[1]

This debate over *shlilat hagola* is a hundred years old; and well into the 1950s, it still determined the rhetorical parameters of discourse at Zionist congresses, conferences, and wherever else Israelis and Jewish leaders from the Diaspora attempted to define the ties that bound them.[2] At that time, the debate acquired many new subtle ideological nuances. Thus, at the 23rd Zionist Congress in 1951, held in Jerusalem (the first to be held in Israel), there was serious discussion about whether America was *gola* or *tfutza*, exile or merely dispersion. As a result of American Jewish pressure, the program adopted at the Congress talked of *Kibbutz Galuyot*—the ingathering of exiles—as opposed to *Kibbutz Hagaluyot*—ingathering of *the* exiles.[3]

These debates were as distant from reality then as they are far from current realities. Few Israelis today would share Ahad Ha'am's description of Jewish existence in the Diaspora, taken from the title of his famous 1891 essay, as "slavery in the midst of freedom." Since 1948, the real determinants of Israel-Diaspora relations have been hardheaded concerns for the mobilization of political influence, for fundraising, and the *aliyah* (immigration) of communities in distress. Philosophical and ideological issues played such a little role in the web of ties that linked the state of Israel to the organized Jewish world that a quote from Ahad Ha'am's same essay (taken only a little out of context) will be my last word on them:

> We are forced, despite ourselves, to smile . . . when we see distinguished men, who might have shown their sorely tried people real light on its hard and thorny path, wasting their time with such sophistries as these; . . .[4]

Aside from the ideological issues implicit in Israel-Diaspora relations, there were a number of concrete institutional questions that came to the fore following the creation of the state in 1948. The role of the Jewish Agency and the World Zionist Organization had to be redefined following the creation of a sovereign government and civil service in Israel. The specific problem was what role, if any, would these two organizations afford to Diaspora communities and Zionist leaders in the state's political life. The redefining of institutions required by the Zionist movement was only completed six years later, after the passage in 1952 of the Law on the Status of the World Zionist Organization-Jewish Agency, and the "Covenant" between the Israeli government and the Executive of the World Zionist Organization signed in 1954.[5]

In his own idiosyncratic manner, David Ben Gurion, as prime minister, preempted the ongoing debate in the Knesset and the World Zionist Organization on the proper relations between Israel and American Jewry. In 1950 he came to terms through direct negotiations with Jacob Blaustein, then the past chairman and most prominent member of the American Jewish Committee.[6]

The terms of the Ben Gurion–Blaustein agreement have been considered in detail elsewhere.[7] Briefly, Ben Gurion foreswore any Israeli claim to speak on behalf of world Jewry and undertook to recognize Diaspora communities as independent, organic communities whose ties to the new state were those of sympathy and support, but no more than that.[8] The agreement was informal and it was also incomplete. It only defined the boundaries of the issues at stake: Israel was a Jewish state but would not claim by right the loyalty of Jews outside of Israel.

The agreement was more important to Blaustein than it was to Ben Gurion. For the next fifteen years of his activity in Jewish public affairs, Blaustein was always vigilant that Israel should never step beyond the borders of principle that had been established in 1950.[9] On Ben Gurion's part, it signaled the prime minister's clear intention to regulate the relations between Israel and the Diaspora through the mediation of the established Diaspora Jewish organizations and not through the World Zionist Organization or direct contact with Jewish communities overseas.

In the remainder of this chapter, I will contend that precisely these links between Israel and the leading Jewish organizations were the primary means of interaction between Israel and world Jewry; that these links were functional rather than ideological; and that they evolved in the course of the 1940s and 1950s as the Jewish world in Palestine/Israel, in America, and elsewhere responded to the challenges facing Jews after World War II.[10]

In 1939, the leading American Jewish fundraising organizations, the Joint Distribution Committee and the United Palestine Appeal, combined forces (together with the National Refugee Service) to create the United Jewish Appeal (UJA). This was a landmark event for American Jewish history. Under the leadership of Henry Montor, the UJA increasingly acquired a Palestinian orientation and a Zionist hue.

As a recent historian of the UJA points out, Montor removed the negative motif of traditional Jewish fundraising (the devastation caused by war and Nazi persecution, American anti-Semitism, defense of Jewish civil rights) and replaced them with the positive, heroic themes of Jewish achievement in Palestine (pioneering, resettlement, survival, and renaissance of Jewish life).[11]

I mention these events because they have an indirect bearing on the subject at hand. Clearly, the combined effort invested in fundraising helped establish traditions of cooperation between organizations with a Palestine focus and those whose concerns were only local. However, the 1939 agreement primarily affected relations between Zionist and non-Zionist groups in America. In the international arena, war-related activities such as relief, rescue, and postwar planning forged effective ties between the Jewish Agency, the World Jewish Congress, and the Joint Distribution Committee and brought about a degree of contact that did not exist before.

Toward the end of World War II, both the Allied governments and the leading Jewish groups began to examine the question of the restitution of Jewish assets stolen by the Nazis. These funds were seen as a means of financing the tasks of rehabilitating the survivors after the war. The Jewish Agency, in fact, had first raised this possibility in 1939 immediately following the outbreak of war.[12] But at that time, such notions were simply expressions of faith. Only when victory was assured could the subject be discussed seriously.

During 1944, both the Jewish Agency for Palestine and the American Jewish Committee published studies on the fate of Jewish assets and their impact on postwar Jewish reconstruction.[13] In November 1944, the World Jewish Congress convened a War Emergency Conference at which the major Jewish organizations called for the restitution of individual assets as well as the payment of compensatory indemnification and collective reparations to the Jewish people.[14] The deliberations were supported by a detailed study of the extent of Nazi spoliation and looting of Jewish assets (estimated at $8 billion, excluding occupied Soviet territory) and by concrete proposals on how these assets could be restored.[15]

In September 1945, Nahum Goldmann led a Jewish delegation in talks with the American under secretary of state Dean Acheson to discuss the Jewish interest in reparations. Goldmann argued that any reparations received for the rehabilitation of Jewish victims should be sent to Palestine and that the Jewish Agency should be officially entrusted with the task of supervising their resettlement. In order to underline the unanimity among Jewish groups on the reparations question, Goldmann was accompanied by representatives of the World Jewish Congress and the American Jewish Conference.[16]

In the course of the complex negotiations on the general reparations question in 1945, the Allies accepted at least part of the Jewish claim.[17] All nonmonetary gold found in Germany (estimated to be worth $5 million) and $25 million derived from German assets in neutral countries were to be spent on behalf of the victims of Nazi persecution.[18] The monies were to be spent under the supervision of the Intergovernmental Committee for Refugees. These provisions were embodied in Article 8 of the Final Act of the Paris Conference on Reparations.

In a letter to the State Department shortly after the Final Act of the Paris Conference had been published, the American Jewish Conference called the reparations allocated to the nonrepatriable victims "pitiably small," given the extent of the material losses suffered by the Jews. The letter also pointed out that the vast bulk of the $25 million and the nonmonetary gold had been looted from Jews and therefore Jewish DPs (displaced persons) should be the prime benefactors. It called for the immediate release of $25 million by the Allies, secured by the funds allocated under the agreement, and the appointment of a recognized Jewish welfare agency to implement the rehabilitation and resettlement schemes the funds would make possible.[19]

The State Department was sympathetic to these demands in general,[20] but no action could be taken until a follow-up conference was held to conclude the details of implementing Article 8 of the Final Act on Reparations.[21] This second conference, called the Five Power Conference on Reparations for Non-Repatriable Victims of Nazism, was held in Paris in June 1946. The results were a diplomatic landmark for the Jewish world. The American delegation, led by Dr. Eli Ginzberg, succeeded in convincing the participants that the funds concerned should not only be allocated for the benefit of Jewish DPs, but that the "allocating agencies" that would handle the money should be the Jewish Agency and the Joint Distribution Committee. Needless to say, the British delegation opposed this conclusion strongly, as it believed (correctly) that any international funds paid to the Jewish organizations would only release other, private funds to finance illegal immigration to Palestine. But the Americans prevailed, and the two agencies were appointed.[22]

The Paris talks established a precedent by giving both the Joint Distribution Committee and the Jewish Agency a *locus standi* in reparations matters. They thus became the legal recipients of the reparations funds. Further, it established them as "successor organizations"—agencies entitled to receive funds derived from the heirless assets of victims of the Holocaust; and it bound the leading American Jewish welfare agency to the most prominent Zionist agency of all in a *formal*, internationally supervised program to jointly aid the Jewish DPs.

The Paris Agreement addressed the practical details of implementing Article 8 of the Final Act on Reparations. The $25 million was to come from German external assets deposited mainly in Switzerland, Sweden, Spain, and Portugal. Yugoslav opposition to any of these funds benefiting anti-Tito DPs resulted in 90 percent of these funds being set aside solely for Jews.[23] The neutral governments were also called upon to make available heirless funds (essentially bank deposits) whose owners had fallen victim to the Nazis. These were to be allocated between Jews and non-Jews in a 95 to 5 percent division. Finally, the Allies were called upon to make available all the nonmonetary gold found in Germany, to be divided on a 90 to 10 percent basis.

The implications of the new status accorded to the Joint Distribution Committee and the Jewish Agency were soon felt in other developments related to the restitution of Jewish assets. Within Germany, the American military government (OMGUS) had made serious progress toward creating legislation to facilitate the restitution of heirless Jewish property. The War Department in Washington and OMGUS in Berlin both looked on internal restitution funds as a potential source of funding for the rehabilitation and resettlement of the Jewish DPs.[24] OMGUS accepted the idea that heirless assets be restituted to "international Jewish organizations,"[25] and in June 1948 it authorized the Jewish Restitution Successor Organization (JRSO) to take action to recover any unclaimed and presumably heirless property.[26]

As a result of the unique standing the Jewish Agency and the Joint Distribution Committee had acquired in the Five Power Agreement, these two organizations were eventually appointed as the main operating agencies of the Jewish Restitution Successor Organization as well.[27] During the years of its operations, the JRSO and the related organizations in the British and French zones of occupation in Germany (the Jewish Trust Corporation) returned to Jewish public funds more than $100 million. The collaboration between the Joint Distribution Committee and the Jewish Agency in acquiring and allocating these funds, as well as the funds derived from the Paris Conference in 1946, was the foundation of a fruitful cooperation on the many issues concerning the fate of the Holocaust survivors, their well-being in the DP camps, and their resettlement in Palestine and elsewhere. Furthermore, this cooperation prepared the ground for a much larger resolution of the reparations question.

The restitution and reparation funds returned to the Jewish world in the immediate postwar years were only a very small part of the Jewish assets that had been lost. The problems relating to payment of real reparations, the full restitution of property, and appropriate indemnification to individual Holocaust survivors still remained unresolved. In order to handle these matters, the Jewish world was forced to deal directly with the Federal Republic of Germany.

After 1948, the Israeli government joined the Jewish Agency in its demand for a full reparations settlement from Germany. However, in the course of the preparation of the Jewish case against Germany, a conflict of interest quickly became apparent between the claims of Israel and the claims of the Diaspora. In 1951, when the German chancellor Konrad Adenauer made a public statement committing Germany to meet Jewish material claims, he specifically stated that the negotiations would involve not only Israel and Germany, but also a representative of the Diaspora Jewish organizations.[28]

At first, the Israeli Foreign Ministry believed that the organizations would limit themselves to negotiating on behalf of individual claimants of indemnification, and that they would leave the large global claim to be presented by Israel. After all, the mass immigration to Israel was at its height and Israel had done the most to resolve the Jewish refugee problem. However, the American Jewish Committee, particularly Jacob Blaustein, thought otherwise. While recognizing Israel's contribution to solving the refugee question, the Committee refused to allow Israel to present the general claim on behalf of all the Jewish people.

One month after Adenauer's statement, Nahum Goldmann, in his dual capacity as co-chairman of the Jewish Agency and president of the World Jewish Congress, invited twenty-three Jewish organizations from around the world to meet in New York and discuss the German proposal. Goldmann and the Israeli government expected that the meeting would reaffirm the principle of negotiating with the Germans over material claims and would also recognize Israel's right to receive reparations in the name of the whole Jewish world.[29]

At the meeting, this principle of negotiation received almost unanimous support, but Israel's right to present the sole global claim was challenged. While the organizations were prepared to accord priority to Israel's claim, they would not agree to it being the sole Jewish claim. The organizations decided that they would also present a global claim on behalf of the Jews in the Diaspora. As a result, Israel was forced to change the basis of its claim for reparations. Instead of reparations for the six million dead, Israel now based its claim on the costs of absorbing the five hundred thousand refugees from Nazism that had settled in Israel since 1933.[30]

In the course of the meeting in New York, the Jewish organizations decided to create a permanent umbrella body called the Conference on Jewish Material Claims against Germany. The conference appointed Moses Leavitt, the executive director of the Joint Distribution Committee, to lead its delegation in the negotiations with Germany. Leavitt was already experienced in cooperating with the Jewish Agency on the questions of reparations and restitution. He was concerned with practical solutions to the problems of the negotiations, and not with the ideological battles of the American Jewish Committee.

Blaustein and other Jewish leaders who supported his stand were distanced from the negotiating table. Under Leavitt's control, the Claims Conference and the Israeli delegation to the negotiations with the Germans coordinated their positions closely. Ultimately, the conference agreed to reduce its own global claim from $500 million to DM450 million—22 percent of the sum demanded—in order to facilitate the much larger settlement between Israel and Germany.

Blaustein and the American Jewish Committee were not the only ones opposed to Israel's global claim. The Anglo-Jewish Association, the Alliance Israelite Universelle, the Bundist Jewish Labor Committee, and the B'nai Brith were also opposed. When Leavitt returned to New York after the successful conclusion of the very difficult reparations negotiations, he was severely criticized for having made concessions on the Diaspora global claim.[31]

However, the stand of Blaustein and his supporters was rendered ineffective by a new situation that the negotiations with Germany had created in the Jewish world. The Federal Republic had made it clear that it was unable to pay a large reparations settlement in foreign currency. Instead, they offered to supply German manufactured goods.

Israel could agree to this arrangement because it suited her development needs, but the Jewish organizations could not accept German exports in lieu of cash payments. So it was decided that Israel would receive the German goods paid on account of the Claims Conference's global settlement (circa $10 million per year for twelve years) and would then make the equivalent foreign currency available to the Diaspora organizations. But Israel had fewer dollars than Germany in the early 1950s, and creative accounting was necessary.

The solution arrived at was simple and it served to stress the centrality of the Jewish Agency and the Joint Distribution Committee in the Jewish world. In 1949 the Joint had initiated a large welfare program in Israel, called MALBEN, designed to provide welfare services to the needy among the new immigrants to Israel. The program was funded from the dollars which the Joint received in New York from the United Jewish Appeal. Now, however, instead of sending these dollars to Israel, the Joint paid them directly to the Claims Conference (also headquartered in New York) and received in return Israeli lirot to finance the operations of MALBEN.[32] The agreement between the government of Israel, the Jewish Agency, and the Joint was signed in New York on the same day that the reparations agreements were signed with Germany in Luxembourg (25 August 1952).

This arrangement represented a form of bartering in which the Jewish Agency and the Joint Distribution Committee had both acquired a lot of experience during the war years. The agreement had two objectives: to cooperate in the resettlement and rehabilitation of Jews in Israel and elsewhere, and to overcome all barriers created by the legal restrictions imposed by governments on the transfer of currencies from country to country. Ironically, the arrangement brings to mind the "Transfer" agreement signed in 1933 between the Jewish Agency and the German government and the nonimplemented Rublee-Schacht proposal of 1939.

The entire reparations process, which began eight years earlier with the first serious postwar planning, helped shape the network of ties between Israel and the Jewish communities beyond its borders. The Claims Conference played a unique role in Jewish organizational and communal life in the years 1954 to 1966, thanks to the reparations agreements. For reasons that are too complex to explain here, Israel actually supplemented the conference's budget, adding an additional 13 percent to the sum received from Germany. In all, the conference was able to allocate $125 million to Diaspora communities and to finance much of the institutional and communal development in the Jewish world during its twelve years of operation.

These funds were important beyond the simple amounts involved. The conference was able to allocate a fixed income, independent of the United Jewish Appeal or the vagaries of individual philanthropy. Further, as the sums were to be paid over a twelve-year period, long-term planning for community reconstruction became possible. Legally, the reparations funds were paid for the benefit of the survivors of the Holocaust. In practice, the Jewish organizations used the funds according to the overall needs of the Jewish world, and most of the money was spent behind the Iron Curtain and in North Africa.

An ideological argument over the centrality of Israel in Jewish life informed the debates on the allocation of Jewish public funds. Were these funds to be spent on rehabilitating surviving Jewish communities in Europe, or were all funds to be directed to Israel to strengthen the new state and help in the absorption of the mass immigration? After 1948, a popular trend emerged in Diaspora Jewish communities in favor of supporting Israel's needs rather than diverting American Jewish money to Europe and elsewhere. Had decisions been made according to this popular opinion, little would have been spent in the 1950s outside of Israel. To a large degree, the availability of reparations funds precluded the necessity of making painful and difficult choices within the Jewish world.

The effectiveness of the cooperation between Israel and Diaspora Jewish organizations on the reparations problem was a decisive factor in shaping the ties between Israel and the Diaspora. The realities of Jewish life proved to be stronger than the ideological preoccupations of both the Zionists (*shlilat hagola*) and the non-Zionists like Blaustein. Years of cooperation and interaction forged ties at an organizational level and an individual level among Jewish leaders and officials in Israel and abroad. The cessation of organizational reparations payments in 1966 brought to an end the role of cooperative reparations activities in forging strong ties between Israel and the Diaspora. However, one year later, in 1967, the outbreak of the Six Day War provided a new force that contributed significantly to strengthening the relations between Israel and the Diaspora in the 1970s and 1980s.

NOTES

1. For a discussion of the various interpretations of the concept *shlilat hagola*, cf. Eliezer Schweid, "The Rejection of the Diaspora in Zionist Thought: Two Approaches," *Studies in Zionism* 5, no. 1 (1984): 43–70.
2. For a discussion of the ideological component of the early debates on Israel-Diaspora relations after statehood, cf. Reinhard Wiemer, "The Theories of Nationalism and of Zionism on the First Decade of the State of Israel," *Middle Eastern Studies* 23, no. 2 (1987): 172–87.
3. Cf. Proceedings of the 23rd Zionist Congress (Hebrew) (Jerusalem, 1951).
4. Ahad Ha'am, "Slavery in Freedom," in Leon Simon, ed., *Selected Essays of Ahad Ha'am* (New York, 1970), 189.
5. *Sefer Hahokim* 112 (2 December 1952): 2.
6. Cf. *American Jewish Yearbook* (1952), 564–68.
7. Melvin Urofsky, "The Vision Disrupted," *Forum* 28–29 (1978): 57–79; Charles S. Liebman, "In Search of Status: The Israel Government and the Zionist Movement," *Forum* 28–29 (1978): 40–56; Charles S. Liebman, "Diaspora Influence on Israel: The Ben Gurion/Blaustein 'Exchange' and Its Aftermath," *Jewish Social Studies* 36 (1974): 271–80.
8. One of the foremost scholars of Israel-Diaspora relations, Daniel Elazar, makes the following comment on the agreement: "the first generation of leaders to face these problems was a product of the last generation of the nineteenth century when the struggle between the Zionists and the *shtadlanim* was at its height. . . . The Ben Gurion/Blaustein agreement reflects the efforts of two men of good will trying to come to grips with a new situation, but bound by their experience and even the phraseology of an earlier age." *People and Polity: The Organizational Dynamics of World Jewry* (Detroit, 1989), 115.
9. Cf., for example, Blaustein's telegraphic response to Ben Gurion's speech at the 23rd Zionist Congress, Jerusalem, August 1951: "Extremely serious repercussions . . . [resulting from] tenor your and some other leaders amazing unrealistic statements and programs on relationship Jews in other countries to Israel. All these most embarrassing and detrimental to interest of Jews here as well as to Israel." Nahum Goldmann Papers, 23 August 1951, Central Zionist Archives (hereafter CZA), Z6-206.
10. In his recently published *People and Polity: The Organizational Dynamics of World Jewry*, Daniel Elazar provides an alternative, or at least a different perspective. Elazar provides a broad conceptual framework for studying Israel-Diaspora relations. He does not, however, examine in any detail the day-to-day practical issues that brought Jewish organizations in Israel and elsewhere together. The impact of German reparations payment on Jewish life after the war is not discussed at all.

11. Marc Lee Raphael, *A History of the United Jewish Appeal, 1939–1982* (Chico, Ca., 1982), 18–19. Cf. also Abraham J. Karp, *To Give Life* (New York, 1981), 77–85.
12. On 18 December 1939, Chaim Weizmann wrote to Leonard Stein, Jewish Agency, London: "It seems to me reasonable that some sort of provision should be made in any peace settlement for the restoration to the Jewish people of some part of the property stolen and confiscated from them by the Nazis in the years since 1933." CZA, Z4-15320.
13. In the fall of 1943, George Landauer prepared a memorandum for the Jewish Agency calling for that organization's active interest in presenting a restitution claim on behalf of the Jewish people. In 1944 Siegfried Moses, also employed by the Jewish Agency in Jerusalem, published a detailed study, *Die jüdischen Nachskriegsforderungen* (Tel Aviv, 1944), calling for Jewish collective as well as individual claims against Germany. In the same year, the Jewish Agency for Palestine put forward its defense of the Jewish right to reparations, accompanied with the slogan: "The Claim for Reparation is the Jewish People's Claim. The Jewish Agency is the Competent Representative of the Jewish People" (F. Gillis and H. Knopf, *The Reparation Claim of the Jewish People* [Tel Aviv, 1944]). The American Jewish Committee sponsored the writing of a legal study of reparations questions (Siegfried Goldschmidt, *Legal Claims against Germany: Compensation for Losses Resulting from Anti-Racial Measures* [New York, 1945]).
14. World Jewish Congress, War Emergency Conference, Summary of Proceedings, Atlantic City, 26–30 November 1944. See also account of conference by the Foreign Nationalities Branch of the Office of Strategic Services, Report No. 229, 18 January 1945, Abraham Duker Papers, Weiner Library, Tel Aviv University.
15. Nehemiah Robinson, *Indemnification and Reparations* (New York, 1944).
16. Memorandum of Conversation, National Archives (hereafter NA), RG 59, 740.00119 EW/9-2045.
17. For a discussion of Allied policy on the use of reparations and restitution funds for the benefit of Jewish displaced persons, cf. Ronald W. Zweig, "Restitution and the Problem of Jewish Displaced Persons in Anglo-American Relations, 1944–1948," *American Jewish History* LXXVIII, no. 1, (September 1988): 54–78.
18. This latter sum was just under 6 percent of the estimated German assets in Switzerland, Sweden, Spain, and Portugal. German assets in the neutral countries were, in toto, over $472 million (Seymour J. Rubin, *Allied-Swedish Accord on German External Assets, Looted Gold and Related Matters*, Department of State Bulletin, no. 17, 27 July 1948, 155, n. 2. Rubin was the State Department official who negotiated the agreement with the Swedes).
19. Louis Lipsky to James Byrnes, 7 February 1946, NA, RG 59, 740.00119 EW/2-746.

20. J. Kenneth Galbraith to Louis Lipsky, 2 April 1946, NA, RG 59, 740.00119 EW/2-746.
21. James Byrnes to American Embassy, Paris, No. 873, 25 February 1946, NA, RG 59, 740.00119 EW/1-2646.
22. Eli Ginzberg, *Final Report on the Five Power Conference*, 12. The author is indebted to Professor Ginzberg for providing a copy of this report, which could not be traced in the State Department records.
23. Ibid., 25.
24. AGWAR (Adjutant-General's office, War Department) to OMGUS for Clay, No. W-85545, 24 April 1946, and AGWAR to OMGUS, No. WX-94867, 18 July 1946, NA, RG 260, OMGUS, Civil Affairs Division, POW and DP Branch, Box 121. Throughout 1946 the American authorities in Germany pressured the state governments in its zone to adopt appropriate legislation. Ultimately, however, it recognized that no reasonable legislation could be expected, and in October 1946 OMGUS put forward its own draft legislation for internal restitution. The draft went through many revisions as the differing interests of OMGUS, the State Department, the major American Jewish organizations, and Jewish groups in Germany debated its final form. (Cf. correspondence relating to draft legislation on NA, RG 260, Civil Affairs Division, POW and DP Branch, Box 162.) In November 1947, Military Government Law No. 59 on the Restitution of Identifiable Property became law.
25. USPOLAD (United States Political Advisor) Murphy to State, No. 1193, 6 May 1946, NA, RG 59, 740.00119 EW/5-646.
26. Cf. S. Kagan and E. Weismann, *Report on the Operations of the Jewish Successor Organization, 1947–1972* (New York, n.d.) (pamphlet).
27. AGWAR to OMGUS, No. WX-94867, 18 July 1946, NA, RG 260, OMGUS, Civil Affairs Division, POW and DP Branch, Box 121. Between 1947 and 1972, JRSO restituted over DM 222 million; 57 percent was allocated to the Jewish Agency, 28 percent to the Joint Distribution Committee, 11 percent to the Council of Jews from Germany, and 4 percent for religious projects in Israel (S. Kagan and E. Weismann, *Report*, 37).
28. Adenauer's address to the Bundestag, 27 September 1951, is reprinted in Rolf Vogel, ed., *The German Path to Israel* (Stuttgart, 1969), 32–33.
29. Halperin to Nahum Goldmann, 17 October 1951, CZA, Z6-195.
30. Document dated 26 June 1952, Central Archives of the History of the Jewish People (hereafter CAHJP), CC 7016.
31. Minutes of the Claims Conference Presidium meeting, 11 August 1952, CAHJP, CC 16601.
32. On the Joint Distribution Committee's expenditures in Israel for MALBEN, and on the relationship between the Joint and the Jewish Agency, cf. File "MALBEN-Jewish Agency, 1953–1956," CZA, S42-235.

About the Editor

LAURENCE J. SILBERSTEIN is Philip and Muriel Berman Professor of Jewish Studies in the Department of Religion Studies, Lehigh University, and Director of the Philip and Muriel Berman Center for Jewish Studies. He received his Ph.D. from Brandeis University and was the recipient of a Fellowship for Independent Research from the National Endowment for the Humanities. He is author of *Martin Buber's Social and Religious Thought: Alienation and the Quest for Meaning*. His articles on modern Jewish thought have appeared in *Soundings*, *The Encyclopedia of Religion*, *Journal of the American Academy of Religion*, and *Journal of the Middle East Studies Association*. His current research involves the application of contemporary theories of discourse and ideology to to modern interpretation of Judaism and Jewish history.

About the Contributors

MYRON J. ARONOFF is Professor of Anthropology and Political Science and Chair of the Department of Political Science at Rutgers University. Founding president of the Association for Israel Studies, he is the editor of *Political and Legal Anthropology* and associate editor of *Transaction/SOCIETY*. His publications include *Frontiertown: The Politics of Community Building in Israel, Power and Ritual in the Israel Labor Party*, and *Israeli Visions and Divisions*.

URI BIALER is Associate Professor and Chair of the Department of International Relations at the Hebrew University of Jerusalem and a former Visiting Fellow at St. Antony's College, Oxford. His writings include *The Shadow of the Bomber: The Fear of Air Attack and British Politics, 1932–1939*, and *Between East and West: Israel's Foreign Policy Orientation, 1948–1956*.

NEIL CAPLAN teaches in the Humanities Department and the Jewish Studies Program at Vanier College, Montreal. Among his publications is *Futile Diplomacy*, a two-volume study of Arab-Zionist negotiations from 1913 through the end of the Mandate. His current research deals with the Arab-Israeli conflict during 1948–56.

BENNY MORRIS, Research Fellow at the Truman Research Institute for the Advancement of Peace at the Hebrew University of Jerusalem, is the author of *The Birth of the Palestinian Refugee Problem, 1947–1949*, and co-author of *Israel's Secret Wars*, a history of Israel's intelligence services. In 1989–90, he was a visiting fellow at the Brookings Institution, Washington, D.C.

DON PERETZ is Professor of Political Science at the State University of New York in Binghamton. His books include *Intifada, the Palestinian Uprising*; *The West Bank: History, Politics, Society, and Economy*; *The Government and Politics of Israel*; and *Israel and the Palestine Arabs*. He has worked in the Middle East with NBC, the American Friends Service Committee, and the American Jewish Committee.

ABOUT THE CONTRIBUTORS

DINA PORAT is Senior Lecturer in the Department of Jewish History at Tel Aviv University. Among her recent publications are *The Blue and Yellow Stars of David: The Zionist Leadership in Palestine and the Holocaust, 1939–1945*, and she has written the textual and historical notes for *Surviving the Holocaust, The Kovno Ghetto Diary*.

JEHUDA REINHARZ is Director of the Tauber Institute for the Study of European Jewry and Richard Koret Professor of Modern Jewish History at Brandeis University. He is the author of *Fatherland or Promised Land: The Dilemma of the German Jew, 1893–1914*, and *Chaim Weizmann, The Making of a Zionist Leader*. He was the recipient of the President of Israel Prize for 1990.

ELIE REKHESS is Senior Research Fellow, the Moshe Dayan Center for Near Eastern and African Studies, and Lecturer, Department of Near Eastern and African History, Tel Aviv University. From 1988 to 1990, he served as the Philip and Muriel Berman Visiting Scholar at Lehigh University. He has written extensively on Israel's Arab populations and Palestinian society. His book *Between Communism and Arab Nationalism* discusses the political orientation of the Arabs in Israel.

AVRAHAM SELA is Lecturer, Department of International Relations, the Hebrew University of Jerusalem, and Research Fellow, the Truman Institute for the Advancement of Peace, the Hebrew University of Jerusalem. His recent publications are *Unity within Conflict in the Inter-Arab Relations*, *The Palestinian Ba'th*, and *From Contacts to Negotiations*. He is currently completing a book on the Arab states and the question of Palestine during the British Mandate.

ANTON SHAMMAS, writer and translator, is an Adjunct Professor of Literature at the Department of Near Eastern Studies, University of Michigan. His novel *Arabesques* was chosen by the editors of the *New York Times Book Review* as one of the seven best fiction books of 1988. His fiction, book reviews, and articles on the current political and cultural scene in the Middle East have appeared in *Tikkun*, *Harper's*, *Granta*, and the *New York Review of Books*.

KENNETH W. STEIN is Associate Professor of Near Eastern History and Political Science and Director of Middle Eastern Programs at the Carter Center, Emory University. He is the author of *The Land in*

Question in Palestine, 1917–1939, and collaborated with President Jimmy Carter in writing *The Blood of Abraham: Insights into the Middle East*. His scholarly publications focus on the origins of modern Israel, Palestine's social history in the twentieth century, American foreign policy toward the Middle East, and the Arab-Israel peace process.

YAEL ZERUBAVEL is Assistant Professor of Modern Hebrew Literature and Culture in the Department of Oriental Studies and is a member of the graduate faculty of the Folklore and Folklife Department, University of Pennsylvania. She is the former Associate Director of the Center for Jewish Studies at the City University of New York, Graduate Center. She is currently completing a manuscript entitled *Constructing the Past: National Myths and Collective Memory in Israel*.

RONALD W. ZWEIG is Senior Lecturer, Department of Jewish History, and Director of the Institute for Research in the History of Zionism, Tel Aviv University. He is the author of *Britain and Palestine during the Second World War* and *German Reparations and the Jewish World*, and the editor of *David Ben-Gurion: Politics and Leadership in Israel*. He is also the editor of *Studies in Zionism*.

Index

Abdullah, King of Jordan
  criticism of Mufti al-Haj Amin
    al-Husseini, 133
  criticized for role in 1948 War,
    134–35
  memoirs on 1948 War, 132–34
  role in 1948 War, 132–36
  secret talks with Golda Meyerson,
    242–43
Absentee Property Law
  criticized by Israeli judiciary, 94–95
  opposition of Israeli political parties
    to, 93–94
  and Palestinian Arab minority in
    Israel, 95
Alterman, Nathan
  on behavior of European Jewry dur-
    ing Holocaust, 157, 170
  on Holocaust survivors, 166
  on world Jewry and Holocaust sur-
    vivors, 165
Arab Legion and 1948 War, 133–35,
  136–37
Arab-Jewish conflict, possible solutions
  to following WW II, 246–47
Arab-Zionist pre-state negotiations,
  10–11, 242–248
  goals of, 251
  growing hardening of positions in
    1940s, 244–45
  impact of, on Israeli leaders, 247–48
  legacy of, 243–44
  role of outside powers in, 254–55
  unofficial Zionist efforts at, 248–49
  Zionist position in 1940s, 245–46
Arabs, Palestinian
  acquisition of their lands by State of
    Israel, 92–93
  dispossession of land, 65–67, 74–75
  flight from Haifa, 52–53
  in Ottoman period, 60–62
  refugees, increase of, 57

refugees, international concern
  over, 54
refugees, Israel's position on, 49–
  50, 54–55
role in 1948 War, 143
Zionist perspectives on, 83
Arabs, Palestinian, as citizens of Israel
  civil rights of, 89, 105–106
  conflicting perspectives of govern-
    ment ministries on, 99
  conflicting policies toward, of inte-
    gration vs. separation, 100
  economic efforts in behalf of, 106–
    107
  educational system, 107
  and emergency regulations, 89,
    91–92
  and equal rights, 103–104
  factors shaping early state policy
    toward, 84
  geographical distribution, 85
  government control of affairs,
    97–99
  and government ministries, 110–
    117
  and government-sponsored educa-
    tion, 99, 107–108
  and Hebrew language, 216–17
  internal political debates over, 96
  and Israeli Arbor Day (Tu be-
    Shevat), 222–23
  and Israeli Independence Day,
    220–21
  and Israeli judiciary, 89–91
  and Israeli national symbols, 219–
    20, 223–24
  legislation on, 91–93
  liberal approach to, 104–106
  local services to, 98–99
  and military government, 85, 89–92
  and Ministry of Defense, 91–92
  and new Israeli immigrants, 221–22

Arabs, Palestinian, as citizens of Israel (*continued*)
  policies toward, criticized by Israeli press, 99–100
  political conflicts concerning, 89, 92
  and Prime Minister's Office, 110
  removed from village of Iqrit, 90
  security-oriented approach to, 108–109
  social conditions of, in 1949, 84
Arabs, Palestinian, exodus of
  and Arab historiography, 144
  attitude of Israeli military to, 50–52
  Ben Gurion's views on, 51
  first stage in, 43–44
  fourth stage in, 50–52
  impact of Arab leadership on, 45, 47–48
  impact of "atrocity factor" on, 46
  impact of Israeli military actions on, 44–47
  impact on Israeli society, 37–39
  multi-causal explanation for, 52–53
  prevailing explanations for, 43
  relationship of Haganah's Plan D to, 46
  and reports of broadcasts by Arab leaders, 48
  second stage in, 44–49
  stages in, 43
  third stage in, 50–51
Arabs, Palestinian, peasants
  conflict with Arab landowners, 67
  dispossessed of land, British response, 68–71
Arabs, Palestinian, role in Arab-Zionist negotiations
  Zionist attitude toward, 252–53
Army of Deliverance and 1948 War, 137–39

Ben Gurion, David
  agreement with Jacob Blaustein on Israel-Diaspora relations, 260
  on Holocaust survivors, 162–64
  on Holocaust victims, 159
  on Palestinian Arab exodus, 51
  on Palestinian Arab minority in Israel, 86-88, 91, 110
  on Palestinian Arab refugees, 49
Ben Zvi, Yitzhak, on Palestinian Arab minority population, 104–106
Bove, Paul, on discourse and knowledge, 17

Compensation Law
  opposition to, 95
  for siezed Arab lands in Israel, 95
Czechoslovakia, and arms sales to Israel, 232–33

Diaspora, Zionist negation of, 258–59
Disciplines, academic, 13
Discourse
  Arab and Israeli contrasted, 17–18
  historical, 12
  historical and social scientific compared, 13
  and ideology, 16–18
  and knowledge, 17
  and power, 16–18

Foreign Ministry, Israeli, and Palestinian Arab minority, 110–12

Haikal, Muhamad Hussein (Egyptian official), memoirs on 1948 War, 127–28
Hebrew language, as symbol of Jewish cultural hegemony, 216–18
Historiography, Arab, on 1948 War, 8
  Egyptian sources, 126–29
  Iraqi sources, 129–31
  Jordanian sources, 132–37
  major motifs in, 126
  and Palestinian nationalism, 143–45
  on Palestinian refugees, 144–45
  Palestinian sources, 140–45
  Syrian sources, 137–40
Historiography, Israeli
  established, 4
  new, 3–4
Holocaust
  memories of, and Israeli foreign policy, 234

INDEX

Holocaust (*continued*)
  official Israeli pronouncements on, 168–69
  reactions of *yishuv* leaders to, 159–61
  reparations for victims of, debate over in Israel, 169
  reparations for victims of, Israel-Diaspora conflict over, 264–67
  reparations for victims of, negotiations for, 261–67
  silence over, in post-war years, 166–68
  survivors, attitude toward in *yishuv*, 162–66
  survivors, silence in post-war years, 167–68
  and Zionist ideology, 159–62

Husseini, Mufti al-Haj Amin al-
  criticized for role in 1948 War, 133, 140, 142
  memoirs on 1948 War, 142

Ideological criticism and Israeli society, 16
Ideology, 16
  and discourse, 16–17
  and power, 16
Iqrit, Arab village in Israel, removal of population from, 90
Israel
  adjustment of new immigrants to, 29–30
  economic impact of British departure on, 35–36
  immigration policy, 29
  impact of exodus of Palestinian Arabs on, 37–39
  and institutionalization of Zionist ideology, 28–31
  military dangers to new state, 34–35
  policy on Arab property, 92–96
  and problem of mass immigration, 29–31
  problems deriving from pre-state pluralistic organization of, 33–34
  problems of conversion to sovereignty, 32–35
  as solution to Jewish problem of exile, 28, 31
Israel, foreign policy, 234
  and concern for immigration, 230–32, 234–36
  and debates within Mapai, 228–30
  and defense issues, 232–33, 238–39
  and Eastern bloc nations, 231–37
  and economic issues, 237
  and energy needs, 233–34
  and Mapai-Mapam conflict, 229–30
  and memories of the Holocaust, 234
  and Western bloc nations, 237–39
Israel, Independence Day, impact of, on Palestinian Arab minority, 220–21
Israel, Jewish immigrants in, and Palestinian Arab minority, 221–22
Israel, national holidays of, and Palestinian Arab minority, 220–24
Israel, national symbols of, and impact on Palestinian Arab minority, 219–20, 223–24
Israel, state of
  compared with new Asian and African nations, 27–30
  early social structure, 27–31
Israel-Soviet relations, and Korean War, 233
Israeli political culture
  impact of intifada on, 187
  and memorialization of the dead, 181–83
  and reinterment of remains of heroes, 182–85

Jewish Agency, and German reparations, 262–64

Khalidi, Walid, on Palestinian refugees, 145

Law of Return, and Palestinian Arab minority in Israel, 96–97
Liebman, C., and Don-Yehiya, E., on Israeli civil religion, 176–77
Lustick, Ian, on state policy toward Palestinian Arab minority, 116–17

Majali, Hazza' al-, Jordanian Prime Minister, defends King Abdullah's role in 1948 War, 135–36
Mapai, conflict with Mapam, and Israeli foreign policy, 229–30
Mapai, debates within, and Israeli foreign policy, 228–30
Minorities Ministry, Israeli
  closing of, 115–16
  closing of, criticized by left-wing circles, 116
  limited powers of, 114
  and Palestinian Arab minority, 106, 112–15
Morris, Benny, and new Israeli historiography, 3–4
Mussa, Sulaiman, on King Abdullah's role in 1948 War, 136–37

Nasser, Jamal Abd al-, on 1948 War, 128–29
Nationality Law, and Palestinian Arab minority in Israel, 96–97

Palestine
  land ownership in, during British Mandate, 63–64; in Ottoman period, 61–62
  Jewish land acquisition in, 64–67, 72–73
  Jewish land acquisition in, Palestinian Arab response to, 73
Palestinian nationalism and Arab historiography, 143–45
Palestinians, *see* Arabs, Palestinian

Qawaqji, Fauzi al-, Commander of Army of Deliverance, 138–40

Refugees, Palestinian, *see* Arabs, Palestinian, refugees

Shammas, Anton, as cultural critic, 15–16
Sharett, Moshe, and Palestinian Arab minority population, 111–12, 117
Shitrit, Bekhor Shalom, Director of Minorities Ministry, 112–115, 118
Smooha, Sammy, on policy toward Palestinian Arab minority, 117

Tal, Abdullah al-, memoirs on 1948 War, 134–35
Tel Hai, myth of
  ambiguity of, in Israeli political culture, 194–95
  in contemporary Israeli culture, 207–209
  decline of popular appeal, 202–207
  in Israeli educational texts, 197, 200–202
  and Israeli political culture, 179–81
  as myth of new beginning, 195–99
  as object of popular humor, 202–208, 209–210
  as symbol of harmonious relation to nature, 199
  as symbol of heroism, 200
  as symbol of struggle for national independence, 200
Teveth, Shabtai, on new Israeli historiography, 4
Trumpeldor, Yoseph
  as counter-model to Diaspora Jew, 195–99
  myth surrounding his last words, 198
  as object of popular humor, 203–210
  as role model for Israeli soldiers, 201–202

United Nations, plan for partition of Palestine, Arab reactions to, 246

Weizmann, Haim, on Middle-Eastern federation, 246

INDEX

Zionism
    and aspiration to national normality, 178, 186
    and aspiration to national uniqueness, 178, 186
    conflicting aspirations of, 177–78, 186
    institutionalized in State of Israel, 28–30
    and Israeli political culture, 177–78, 185–86
    and negation of Diaspora (shlilat hagola), 258–59
Zionist movement, objectives of, 28
Zionist-Arab negotiations, unofficial Zionist efforts at, in pre-state period, 248–249. *See also* Arab-Zionist pre-state negotiations

www.ingramcontent.com/pod-product-compliance
Lightning Source LLC
Chambersburg PA
CBHW022039290426
44109CB00014B/917